Nursing Home Renovation Designed for Reform

Nursing Home Renovation Designed for Reform

Lorraine G. Hiatt, Ph.D.

Butterworth Architecture
Boston London Singapore Sydney Toronto Wellington

Library of Congress Cataloging-in-Publication Data
Hiatt, Lorraine G.
    Nursing home renovation designed for reform / Lorraine G.
        Hiatt.
            p.   cm.
    Includes bibliographical references and index.
    ISBN 0-7506-9126-3 (casebound)
    1. Nursing homes—Design and construction.   2. Nursing homes—
Remodeling.   I. Title.
RA998.5.H53   1991
725'.5—dc20   90-28849
                                                                                                CIP

British Library Cataloguing in Publication Data
Hiatt, Lorraine G.
    Nursing home renovation designed for reform
    1. United States. Nursing homes
    I. Title.
    725.560973

    ISBN 0-7506-9126-3

Butterworth–Heinemann
80 Montvale Avenue
Stoneham, MA 02180

10   9   8   7   6   5   4   3   2   1

Printed in the United States of America

Most of what I have learned has been from people like you: administrators and staff members who are eager for self-assessment and willing to consider change; designers who listen, improvise, and work with their clientele to discover appropriate design; regulators and state agencies who facilitate better functioning environments and willingly agree to reconsider their policies, codes, and practices; and older people who struggle for their personal best. By sharing your visions you have provided insights for us all.

Contents

Foreword

This book comes at a turning point in our understanding of the issues in properly housing and caring for America's elderly. Architecture and environmental design for the elderly are beginning to receive the attention they need and deserve.

Prepared primarily for architects and design specialists, this book fills a void in the literature. It challenges the practitioner and planner to critically examine our existing facilities and identify ways to improve them. It can also serve as a text for students and staff members and as an evaluative tool for boards and administrators.

This book has many unusual, beneficial features and much sound advice. More than a how-to manual, it attempts to analyze and understand the major factors for successful planning and satisfying, supportive living. The material is carefully organized and draws upon Dr. Hiatt's many years as a consultant. She is in a position to be an advocate for the environment she recommends and to understand the ways in which the environment affects the functioning of the nursing home, the lives of residents, the tasks of caregivers, and the concerns of sponsors. With *Nursing Home Renovation,* Dr. Lorraine Hiatt continues to make a significant contribution to the field of long-term care.

Herbert Shore, Ed.D.
Past President
American Association of Homes for the Aging
Executive Vice President
Dallas Home for Jewish Aged

Preface

Over the past twenty years, I have visited more than three hundred licensed nursing homes, five hundred retirement services, and facilities of all types across the United States and Canada for research or consultation. These have included diverse sponsors and involved contact with various architects, designers, and health departments. Travelling often offers useful insights; what is problematic for one area, sponsor, or design firm has sometimes been effectively resolved elsewhere. Similarly, what is unacceptable in one state may be approved in another.

When I started to assemble materials for this book, I thought the information had two natural audiences: architects and administrators. Now, I believe it has one audience that draws from several professions: architecture, design, regulators, and long-term care. This book was written for architects, designers, nursing home or health care staff, policy makers, and those who inspect nursing homes. Rather than try to explain each group to the others, this book offers a meeting place and an invitation to collaborate. That collaboration will be fruitful to the extent that each partner understands the others' missions. Although many professions are involved in nursing home renovation, there must be just one ultimate client: older people.

Nursing home care is usually supervised by licensed nurses, although the most prevalent caregivers are nursing assistants, housekeepers, and members of the food service staff. Each state differs with respect to the regulations it imposes on nursing homes, because Medicaid/Medi-Cal, the primary source of payment for about 75% of all nursing home clients, is administered at the state level. States vary with respect to staffing requirements, review procedures, requirements regarding compliance, and available options for new construction or renovation. It is essential, therefore, for architects and designers to cultivate a formal and informal understanding of the requirements. Formal understanding is obtained through reading the regulations. Informal understanding may involve meeting with officials prior to drawing, working with consultants who fully understand the regulations involved, and personal experience.

According to the National Center for Health Statistics, most of the 19,000 nursing homes and related facilities in the United States were built before 1969.* The population of these nursing homes has changed, and our concept of

---

*National Center for Health Statistics, 1985.

service has expanded. Even the equipment we use is different than in the early days. It is not surprising, then, that so many sponsors are interested in assessing their services and facilities. This concern is underscored by the Omnibus Budget Reconciliation Act of 1987 (OBRA), also referred to as the Nursing Home Reform Act. One result of this legislation is to focus on-site reviews on the humanistic qualities of nursing homes and related facilities.

When approaching renovation and refurbishment projects, sponsors should tap the solid body of knowledge available from residents and staff. This book suggests ways to use their information while incorporating it with new options. Experienced sponsors will learn how to work within the fixed parameters, including legislation where appropriate, funding, and site; start with an accurate understanding of the nursing home's needs and clients, now and in the future; and respond to the need to increase staff effectiveness.

Different groups of people will approach this book in different ways. Sponsors may use the material provided here to conduct a self-analysis to determine what they need to do. Sponsors and architects may find the readings helpful before launching a project. Architecture or design firms may use this book when approaching a particular problem, project, or area; a new state; or a client that is unfamiliar with the process of participatory planning. Interior designers may use this book as a source for ideas, background orientation to the expectations of sophisticated clients, or subjects requiring creative energies and insights. Equipment manufacturers and designers may discover by reading this book areas where equipment availability or design hinders innovative nursing home services, product information that nursing home sponsors find useful, and insights on the products they need and the products that require particular care and handling within some state agencies.

Even with limited funds, you can benefit from the suggestions in this book. Whether your resources are substantial or limited, it pays to think in terms of life-cycle costs. *Life cycle* refers to the useful life of a building in terms of materials, systems, and spaces. How long is a life cycle? In practice, nonprofit homes often deal in computations of 30 to 60 years. Developers may look at very short periods or, like the nonprofit sponsors, at longer building life cycles to obtain greater value from subsequent sales. Life-cycle costs include capital expenditures (one-time design, construction, and site costs, which usually amount to 8% of life-cycle costs), consumables (energy, food, products, and other billable items that are consumed), and labor (the greatest investment, typically 60% to 75% of life-cycle costs). Consider each design option in terms of its impact on life-cycle costs. Will the overall savings be worth the investment? How can you influence the greatest number of residents and the greatest number of staff members?

Many changes discussed in this book require no investment in capital costs. These include refurbishment, rearrangement, and organizational alterations. Some refurbishment changes, like repainting, can be done during conventional maintenance cycles. Rearrangement changes sometimes involve analyzing storage facilities or furnishings and finding ways to better utilize existing resources. Some of the organizational changes require altering staffing and scheduling to improve services. Other suggestions concern the use of personal items: furnishings or gifts to personalize rooms, supportive furnishings, memorabilia to extend a memory development program. Other changes involve the reallocation of existing funds.

The lack of funds is a false barrier in self-evaluation and planning more effective environments for older people. Sponsors sometimes pay dearly for design that does not work, in terms of nonproductive labor, wasted time, turnover, and increased resident dependence. Much can often be done to refurbish a facility without raising rates, increasing reimbursement, or reducing profits.

Acknowledgments

Many individuals and organizations contributed to the development of this book. It was conceived of by professionals dedicated to quality care and design. Specific impetus for this book came from Ed "Buz" Dowling, Associate Director, Office of Health Systems Management, Division of Health Facility Planning, New York State Department of Health; Mary Jane Koren, M.D., Director of Long-Term Care for the State of New York; and their dedicated staff of experts in management, nursing, and programming. Their question? With all that appears to be changing, how can we give the sponsors of today's 19,000 nursing homes and hospitals guidance that will enable them to keep abreast of changing populations, services, and equipment as they examine their facilities? Their interest led to the support of the Commonwealth Fund, a nonprofit foundation based in New York.

Funding for the research and writing of this book was provided by a generous grant from the Commonwealth Fund. The grant was administered through the Health Facilities Research Program (HFRP), a consultant program of the Joint Council on Architectural Research of the American Institute of Architects and the Association of Collegiate Schools of Architecture. Special thanks are due to the HFRP Board of Trustees for their aid in the review process.

I am also grateful to the American Association of Homes for the Aging for assistance during the book content review process, and specifically to Ira Robbins, Cynthia Wallace, and especially Dr. Herbert Shore for his gracious foreword. This book would not have been possible without the many older people, professionals, architects, and facilities who contributed examples and ideas.

The following abbreviated list represents those who made particular personal contributions:

Keith Anderson, Engberg Anderson, Milwaukee, Wisconsin
Alexander Barker, Barker Associates, Palo Alto, California
Ronald B. Blitch, Blitch Architects, Inc., New Orleans, Louisiana
Timothy C. Boers, Boulder Associates Architects, Boulder, Colorado
Jack Bowersox, Ray Scott Associates, Tampa, Florida
Martin Cohen, FAIA, Armonk, New York
Rosemarie Courriere, Interior Design, Chicago, Illinois
Ronald O. Crawford and Rudy Jennings, SFCS, Roanoke, Virginia

Barbara Eden, Eden Design Associates, Inc., Carmel, Indiana

Deane Evans, HFPR, American Institute of Architects, Washington, D.C.

David Frank and Gaius Nelson, Korsunsky Krank Erikson Architects, Inc., Minneapolis, Minnesota

Scott L. Parkin, American Association of Homes for the Aging, Washington, D.C.

Diane Renberg, Diane Renberg Design, Boulder, Colorado

Ken Ricci, Ricci Associates, New York, New York

Philip Rogers, Lewis and Rogers, Fort Washington, Pennsylvania

Zachary Rosenfield, NBBJ-Rosenfield, New York, New York

Dale Tremain, Ellerbe Beckett, Minneapolis, Minnesota

Many facilities have worked with the processes described in this book. Their work has been instructive, and we all profit from their willingness to improve existing institutions. The following facilities shared ideas for this book:

Arizona
Handmaker's Jewish Geriatric Center, Tucson
California
Pacific Presbyterian Medical Center, San Francisco
Connecticut
Masonic Home and Hospital, Wallingford
Delaware
Cokesbury Village, Wilmington
Delaware Long-Term Care System, Smyrna and elsewhere
Florida
Florida Christian, Jacksonville
Illinois
Duffy Hall/Sisters of St. Joseph, La Grange
Indiana
Hooverwood Indianapolis Jewish Home, Indianapolis
Iowa
Ramsey Memorial, Des Moines
Maryland
Asbury Methodist Retirement Center, Gaithersburg
Michigan
Glacier Hills, Ann Arbor
Jewish Home for the Aged (Borman and Prentis Halls), Detroit
Minnesota
Charter House, Rochester
Ebenezer (Luther Hall, Field Hall, and Ridges), Minneapolis
Sholom East, St. Paul
Missouri
Center for Jewish Aged, St. Louis

New York
 Central Islip State Hospital, Central Islip
 Isabella Geriatric Center, New York
 Jewish Home and Hospital, New York and Kingsbridge, Bronx
 Metropolitan Jewish Geriatric Care Center, Brooklyn
 Morningside House, Bronx
 New York State Veterans Home, Oxford
 Parker Jewish Geriatric Center, New Hyde Park
 Parkshore Manor Health Center, Brooklyn
 Presbyterian Home of Central New York, New Hartford
 Rosa Coplon Home, Buffalo
 Veterans Administration Hospital, Albany
North Carolina
 Blumenthal Jewish Geriatric Center, Clemmons
 Southeastern Hospital, Lumberton
North Dakota
 Lutheran Home and Hospital Society: Villa Maria, Fargo; Fargo NH,
 Fargo; Sheyenne NH, Valley City
Ohio
 Heritage House, Columbus
Pennsylvania
 Chandler Hall, Newtown
 Presbyterian Home, Allentown
 Simpson House, Philadelphia
Tennessee
 B'nai B'rith Home, Memphis
 Erlanger Medical Center, Chattanooga
Texas
 Golden Acres, Dallas
Virginia
 Beth Sholom Home of Central Virginia, Richmond
 Commonwealth of Virginia, State Hospital System
 Westminster Canterbury, Richmond
Wisconsin
 Evergreen Manor, Oshkosh
Canada
 Bolton Nursing Home, Ontario
 Sheridan Place, Municipality of Peel, Ontario

An additional 48 facilities were visited as part of a random selection of nursing homes for a 1978 study (Berkowitz, M., Hiatt, L., deTolèdo, P., et al. 1979).

Finally, thanks are due to Richard Rush, Evelyn Laiacona, Judith Mara Riotto, Russ Till, Mary Jo Orzech, Ph.D., and Jud Mead for assistance with the editorial review and production.

Nursing Home Renovation Designed for Reform

1
Introduction to Environmental Design for Older People

Sponsors renovate their facilities for many reasons. Some need to bring the building into compliance with state regulations. Others strive to make the facility run more efficiently by improving the organization of staff work areas, for example, or by replacing unacceptable furnishings in dining rooms or social areas. Other sponsors seek to improve the quality of life for residents. They increase privacy in multiple-occupancy rooms, provide more opportunities for residents to get outside, or create special programs, like one for people with dementia. Others want to organize the appearance of the environment or in some other way make the facility more marketable. Many changes are made to increase the opportunities and comfort of residents, staff members, and other users, like families. These are all significant reasons for renovating existing facilities, but perhaps the major reason is that the primary population has changed dramatically since the building was constructed, and the facility is no longer capable of effectively serving it.

The first step in renovating an existing nursing home is to get to know the people who live there from a designer's and caregiver's point of view. Without a good understanding of the resident populations's functional characteristics, environmental design cannot meet its needs. This chapter, therefore, provides a general overview of the significant characteristics of older people, and it discusses the impact of the environment on their lives. Common misconceptions are replaced with data-based descriptions, and insights regarding older people are discussed. Because individual facility planning best begins with an accurate description of those who live in the facility, this chapter provides directions for creating a systematic profile of a specific resident population.

OVERVIEW OF THE POPULATION

To ensure success in remedying existing problems and to avoid creating new ones, design planning should start with a clear understanding of the population. Data may be precise or more general, depending on the time available or cost implications of inaccurate estimates. You might use the average age of residents on admission to give you a general indication of the population's health, demand for services, and shared interests, and it may even indicate the length of stay. You must also know the average (median) age of people in the facility. For example, the average age might be 86—a time of life when most individuals experience minor to moderate impairments in daily activities. The average age of the population often suggests that the visitors and "adult" children of residents may themselves be retired.

A full understanding of the population for design purposes must include the mobility and abilities of residents. In the average nursing home, for example, most residents are out of bed for a large part of the day. Many can walk or stand, but 75% use wheelchairs. Almost half are incontinent, but many of these could be helped to use toilets with dignity and greater independence if the toilet room were appropriately designed. More than half have impaired memories, but many are amenable to some cuing or compensation for memory loss. Many residents could dress themselves if bedroom design did not hinder them from reaching and using closets independently, and many could do more to feed themselves if they were not encumbered by cartons, utensils, table placement, chair design, and the presentation of food. In fact, you may find a substantial difference between what residents are currently doing and what they would be doing if they were aided by good programming and effective design. With the right environment, opportunities, equipment, and training, many more residents would be less dependent on staff members.

THE IMPACT OF ENVIRONMENTAL DESIGN

Without seeing a specific facility, it is difficult to name its particular strengths, weaknesses, and priorities. It is possible, however, to identify common sources of frustration typical of many nursing homes. These are examples of how today's nursing home residents are challenged by yesterday's facility design.

Wheelchair Use

Nursing home planners of the past did not anticipate the number of people who would use wheelchairs or walking aids today (Figures 1–1 and 1–2). Consequently, the design of many older facilities hinders some residents. The lack of adequate space in bedrooms makes self-wheeling nearly impossible and forces residents to rely on staff assistance for maneuvering, obtaining clothing, and using their bedrooms as living and conversational areas (Figure 1–3).

The design of wheelchairs is another, related issue. Today, many inappropriately large and bulky chairs are used that further complicate space allocation. Nursing literature contains frequent reference to the need to improve positioning (how people sit), seating (support), and the variety of seat styles to improve posture and weight distribution. Many of the chairs used today are not consistent with what is known about seating, however.

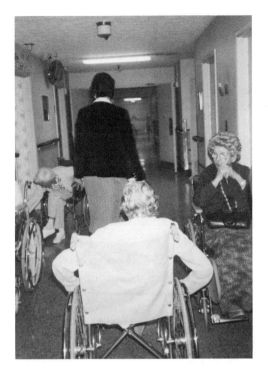

Fig. 1–1 Characteristics of wheelchair users. You must allow adequate space for the wheelchairs themselves and the elbow room users require when designing facilities for older people.

Fig. 1–2 Walking devices. In addition to wheelchairs, walkers and canes are still commonly used.

Incontinence

Incontinence among older people is more prevalent now than in the past, yet many institutions commonly ignore the problem. Too often, the management of incontinence involves simply mopping up or absorbing the fluid in a pad or diaper afterward. This practice adds unnecessarily to staff time and costs. In many nursing homes, incontinent people are confined to wheelchairs for staff convenience. This confines the liquid to the seat area and minimizes soiling and tracking, but it also produces horrendous odor problems. Confinement to a wheelchair immobilizes the resident, limits participation, and compromises dignity. All of this contributes to a negative image of the institution and its people. In addition, devices used allegedly to improve safety, such as restraints, may increase incontinence and risk of injury, especially in nighttime toileting. Confinement to a wheelchair further exacerbates problems of balance and coordination, which impede toileting.

Many staff members, institutions, and even product manufacturers appear unaware of the literature suggesting that there are more satisfactory, dignified, and healthful ways of dealing with incontinence. The focus must be shifted to anticipating bathrooming needs and working to maintain toileting skills.

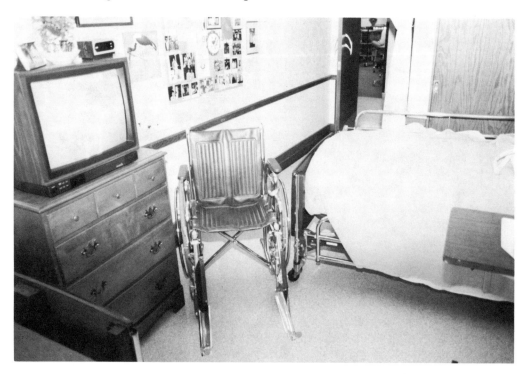

Fig. 1–3 Recognizing common bedroom problems. Bedroom configuration and inadequate space are usually to blame when there is no elbow room for wheelchairs, when bedside areas and closets are not accessible, and when staff must maneuver residents through their rooms. These problems can be resolved by reducing bedroom population, decreasing the size or number of furnishings (within legal requirements), and adding space to the room through exterior additions.

Unfortunately, older facilities were not designed to meet the needs of an aggressive, preventive program of incontinence management. Not only do these institutions have too few bathrooms—the typical facility requires four residents to share one bathroom—but they are poorly located. Often the toilets are grouped near the bedrooms, when residents need them near dining rooms, program facilities, and outside areas, as well.

In a typical health care facility offering an active program of toileting, nearly half of all older people need help in the bathroom, and perhaps one quarter require the assistance of two people. Bathroom configuration, hardware, and door design might be improved to enable more people to use toilet rooms independently and spend less time negotiating the space. Better design, hardware, lifts, and training also might reduce the number of staff members required to assist one individual.

Cognitive Impairment
Cognitive impairment, such as Alzheimer's disease or other forms of dementia, is more common today. Mental impairment may characterize 60% of present day nursing home clients. Additional impairment in response time sometimes results from other physical and mental conditions (for example, stroke, di-

abetes, malnutrition, and depression) and from medications. As a result, many residents experience diminished capacity for one or more of the following:

- Memory for fact: names, numbers, and sequences
- Action and motion: ability to balance, coordinate, swallow, and maneuver utensils
- Emotion: capacity to match emotions with situations (for example, a person may have "flat" affect—that is, be expressionless—or be easily piqued or agitated)
- Social behavior: ability to relate to people in conventional ways; need for smaller groups
- Judgment: ability to plan, anticipate, change behavior midcourse, override situations, and anticipate danger

Although we are beginning to recognize that cognitive impairment has management implications, most buildings are not designed with an understanding of these phenomena.

Wandering
Fewer than 11%–15% of the residents of a typical nursing home wander, yet the control of wandering requires a disproportionate amount of staff time. Facilities of the past were not designed to tolerate exploration, movement, pacing, or wheeling about in safe and interesting areas. The management approach of the past was to stop wanderers from moving at all by tying or otherwise confining them in chairs, with belts, chair trays, or a combination of these. Confinement sometimes causes additional problems, including the increased risk of certain injuries, atrophy, and reduced muscle tone, which make individuals more dependent. Confinement does not necessarily stop the will to move. For many individuals, motion may be preferable to the alternatives: inactivity and atrophy.

Features of the environment often contribute to unsatisfactory responses or behavior in mentally impaired people. The older people of today need variation in design to help reinforce cognitive skills like wayfinding. Most buildings are monolithic and repetitious, and they have few nameable landmarks that reinforce locational skills. Most hallways are long and littered with carts, providing few residential landmarks and little stimulation for conversation. Buildings lack texture, touchable surfaces, and manipulable objects, yet many cognitively impaired people demonstrate an interest in handling materials. As a result, the cognitively impaired person explores inappropriate places like a neighboring room or controlled access utility closet or manipulates unacceptable objects, like staff members' desks, or is denied access by restraint or confinement.

Dining
Dining room equipment, furnishings, spaces, and systems shape dining services. Older people can be unnecessarily hindered by dining areas that fail to accommodate their unique needs. Consider the following, for example:

- Self-feeding is encumbered by chair to table distances that frustrate the reach of residents. Some people may appear to spill when, in fact, the chair to table relationship adversely influences their capacities.
- The majority of people in dining rooms are usually in wheelchairs. When the space is not adequate to accommodate everyone properly, residents sit too far from the table, along walls eating on a tray by themselves, or in hallways or other nondining areas. With mobility problems, small elevators, and the need for frequent toileting, many older people are gathered in hallways near the nursing station rather than in central dining rooms.
- Food temperature and quality are not good. This often results from a food delivery system that does not match the time and distance that food must be kept hot or fresh. More people than before eat on the unit or floor where they sleep. Food gets cold or overcooked in systems designed for the central dining rooms previously used.
- The practice of affording choice (of food or activity, for example) is not particularly well managed. With mental impairment, it is difficult to make a selection today for a meal that will appear tomorrow. Choice is made easier when only two options are presented at the meal, but this is seldom done because of the operational implications and lack of understanding of the older person's capacities.
- The majority of older people in nursing homes are sensitive to glare, which causes discomfort and breaks their attention span. The majority are also hearing impaired and find it difficult to understand conversation in the presence of background noise. Yet, dining areas are often filled with glare and noise, making them feel crowded and nonresidential. This is often because hard surfaces have been used on the assumption that they are safer or easier to clean, which is not always true.

Socializing

Although many older people benefit from socializing, few facilities provide appropriate opportunities for small groups to gather. In many cases, the most interesting seating in the facility is in front of the nursing station, forcing residents to focus on the institution. Evidence suggests that television does not promote social behavior, yet television sets dominate most of the available social spaces. Research suggests that conversation can be stimulated by activity and changing sites. Residents should sit at tables in appropriately designed chairs that focus their attention on other people and do not recline backward.

In a typical facility, older people receive visitors. However, there are often no easy diversions available for amusement, and family visits take place in multiple-occupancy bedrooms, in uncomfortable seating, and without the types of normal activities that spark conversation, such as gardens, ice cream, pets, or changing elements or surroundings.

With more than half of residents having memory impairments, today's facility should be designed with different places for people of varying abilities to gather. Older facilities may have a lobby lounge or one or two social areas, but these are often "off limits" to frail or mentally impaired people.

Motoric Behavior (Motion and Dexterity)

The average older person is capable of gross motor function (standing and walking, for example) and many fine motor skills (using hands, coordinating fine muscles to grip and smile).

Regrettably, the average facility and common management practice conspire to reinforce dependency and immobilize residents. Medical research suggests that lack of motion causes other difficulties, which could be prevented or delayed if the individual engaged in movements within his or her capacity. The person who cannot stand might be able to rock, for example; the person who cannot manage a fork might be able to handle finger foods. The objective is to retain as much gross and fine motor function as possible.

The fear of falling may result in other debilitation. If floors were softer and clothing padded, the risk of injury from falls might be diminished. Better yet, if objects that lead to imbalance were better designed or more secure, residents might be able to move more safely.

People do not make sufficient use of their hands and upper body. Manipulating fingers, using tools, and exercising the upper torso are all significant motions. Because it is difficult to manipulate eating utensils, clothing, and grooming aids, people are often encouraged to simply stop doing so for themselves. Strictures against residents touching things and extensive use of hand restraints are among the more frustrating aspects of institutional living. Very few families restrict older people the way some institutions do. Institutions routinely fail to respond to the need to touch, hold, grasp, exercise fingers, and coordinate hand and eye movements. The challenge for the future is to offer the right tools—items that can be safely handled—and to train staff in encouraging older people to continue to exercise manual, dexterity, and coordination skills. In many states, occupational therapy is not fully recognized and is not part of the services offered by nursing homes. Occupational therapists, to be distinguished from recreation and activity staff people, are trained to teach older people and other staff members in self-care techniques and to help older people to use the tools that match their capacity levels. Ideally, these tools look conventional and do not draw attention to the frailties of the individual.

Frailty

It is commonly observed that older people in nursing homes are getting more frail. What does this mean? Frailty refers to vulnerability and multiple diagnoses. Frailty by itself does not require bed care, however. It has been estimated that fewer than 12% of today's nursing home clients are in bed. This is a challenge for most of today's nursing homes. These facilities (with their small bedrooms, insufficient toilet areas, and distant social facilities) would be more suitable for the ambulatory older people such as those requiring only "assisted living" or personal care adult homes. The building does work well for bedridden older clients unless they require equipment or have visitations at bedside. The irony is that most clients are up and could be moving about.

NINE COMMON MISCONCEPTIONS (AND ONE IMPORTANT INSIGHT)

Twenty years of experience working with nursing home administrators, staff members, and older people have revealed a number of misconceptions about environmental design for long-term care facilities. Many of these are based on fallacies about older people that were once believed to be true. The following are common misconceptions held by sponsors and designers alike:

1. *There is a perfect facility.* Sponsors often request a list of "perfect" facilities that are worthy of touring. In fact, there are no perfect facilities, although there are workable solutions to different types of problems. Efforts to develop plans tailored to your particular needs are more likely to prove valuable than emulating neighboring facilities.

2. *New buildings are better buildings.* In fact, newness does not guarantee anything. All new homes are not necessarily responsive to the needs of older people; all vintage facilities are not necessarily poorly designed. It is possible to find features in new buildings that do not work well. New facilities sometimes lack texture, are noisy, and provide less space than older ones. Older facilities may have excellent features that are worth maintaining, such as spaces, grounds, or materials.

3. *Good staff people can overcome poor design.* This is one of the more troubling misconceptions of management. A good staff may be able to take the extra steps required to overcome a building's weaknesses, but why deploy their energies compensating for poor design when they are desperately needed to provide human services? Good design attracts staff members and supports their efforts.

4. *Design efforts should focus on improving the image of lobbies, dining areas, and the impact of curbside appeal.* As our understanding of environmental design's impact on the lives of older people has broadened, so has our vision of its role. We were once content to focus on improving the appearance of nursing homes, but now we realize that design for older people must transcend appearances and curbside appeal. It must work. Exteriors are lost on a population that struggles for independence and a staff that struggles to please. Sponsors and designers now pay greater attention to how individual living spaces function in order to improve their usefulness to older people. We no longer overlook the environmental attributes of lighting, acoustics, seating selection, and furniture placement to the detriment of older people's independence. Now

that we understand the impact on the facility's effectiveness and image, we devote more effort to improving halls and nursing stations. We used to believe that mentally impaired people could not benefit from environmental design; now we have begun to recognize that they may be aided by design more than any other group and that our responsibilities to them do not end with "special" or secure units. We no longer focus on first impressions to the exclusion of other important issues like the significance of motion, socialization, and flow of activity. Now we want it all, and we have been working to improve our capacity to deal with paradoxes in design: safe but not stifling; efficient without appearing institutional; stimulating but not overly arousing.

5. *People in nursing homes are sick.* Although nursing home residents are frailer today than in the past, most are not bedridden. They are capable of doing partial sequences of activities with appropriate human and environmental design assistance.

6. *Hospitals make good models for long-term care facilities.* We used to incorporate ideas from hospitals into nursing home design, based on the assumption that construction standards from medical settings were most appropriate for older people. We are now beginning to see that long-term care has its own special features, and much of what is acceptable in short-stay hospitals is not acceptable in long-stay nursing homes.

7. *Financial considerations end with the renovation.* We are beginning to recognize that certain one-time, capital investments offer operational savings, such as increased labor efficiency or reduced labor costs. It is essential to design with a good understanding of what staff actually do. Such knowledge comes from experience with several different facilities.

8. *There are colors for older people.* This is one of yesterday's many truisms that have no place in today's facilities. We now recognize that color is only one part of a system of environmental considerations (including lighting, acoustics, texture, landmarks, objects, and variations) and that no single color can guarantee a beneficial environment or particular human response.

9. *Interior design need not be given much thought.* The truth is that many refurbishments require interior space planning, design of the building's interior, selection of appropriate materials and furnishings, and careful placement of these with respect to how the building is used, not how it should look. This has resulted in a need for design professionals who understand safety standards, are knowledgeable about new materials, respond to the clients (staff people, residents, and families), and appreciate how sponsors must be introduced to new options through reading, testing, and touring. This is a wonderful area for newcomers who are willing to devote time to learning about the issues involved and how to implement more innovative options.

Not to be overlooked is one important insight: *Participatory planning works*. Effective design teams involve sponsors, staff members, residents, and families in the planning process. Staff members, in particular, have important contributions to make to nursing home renovation. Project leaders must know, however, how to get at the underlying issues and how to use participant recommendations. Participatory planning works best when sponsors, staff people, designers, and older people understand the basic management goals. The planning that goes into renovation projects is a good way to become acquainted with an operation from the point of view of those who know it most intimately: those who live and work in the building. Evaluation sometimes suggests that the building would be fine for a different segment of the existing population or an entirely different population. Evaluation may also suggest ways of using staff, resources, and services more effectively.

THE RESIDENT POPULATION PROFILE

Before beginning any design work, especially the interior design of spaces like dayrooms and dining rooms, create a functional profile of the residents that reflects present and future considerations. Appendix A contains a worksheet that will help you to obtain information on the existing population of the facility or unit of interest. It can be adapted to suit the particular needs of your institution. Through the population profile, you will try to identify the following:

1. Expected capacity for each unit or area involved
   a. How many people presently use this space?
   b. What is its estimated or licensed capacity (assume no architectural change)?
   c. How might this be changed in the future?
2. Mobility, assistance in transfers, and devices used
3. Assistance needed
   a. For unit redesign, information on the assistance needed can be obtained from an occupational therapy evaluation or other method that considers the assistance required for toileting, dressing, eating, and communicating, and the abilities related to the use of this space.
4. Mental function
   a. What are the real functional characteristics of the people here? It is important to work with actual data rather than stereotypes of what people can and cannot do.
   b. What is the range of abilities and disabilities that people demonstrate? This information is best obtained through the direct observation of people rather than through estimation; it will be used throughout the planning process to estimate room sizes and plan multiuse spaces.

Suggestions for Creating a
Population Profile

- Choose an arbitrary date and collect all the information for that date.
- Record all data and tabulate frequencies and percentages. A spreadsheet computer program makes this work relatively easy.
- Organize or analyze your responses by unit, area, or room and by the different levels of care within the building.
- Subtotal your responses by building, floor, and unit. Units refer to special areas, like a section of a building devoted to Alzheimer's care or to bedrooms for people receiving rehabilitation, or to the older people assigned to a particular nursing station.
- If you plan to create a special unit, try to identify potential residents in advance, using profiles or charts, so that you can consider their characteristics as though the unit were already operating.

ADDITIONAL READING

For further background information, consult the Annotated Bibliography. It contains sources on older people, nursing home staffing and personnel, labor costs versus capital costs, design basics for new and existing facilities, and terminology.

2
Approaching the Renovation— The Environmental Design Inventory

Chapter 1 provided an introduction to the characteristics of older people and the design issues affecting them, and it offered guidelines for developing a profile of your resident population. You are now ready to determine how successfully a specific facility meets its population's demands. With the help of the Environmental Design Inventory in this chapter,* you can evaluate individual facilities, identify their weaknesses, and prioritize needs.

The inventory consists of groups of statements describing common problems in these areas: image and interior appearance; the resident population; resident-use areas and features; services, staffing, and related spaces; gerontologically meaningful programs; and furnishings and equipment. It concludes with questions to help guide your planning. Appendix B will help you to interpret the results of your self-assessment before you begin planning the actual renovation. This facility-wide inventory was designed to stimulate discussion. If it precedes a full-scale building analysis, it will place facility personnel in a better position to discuss their needs with design or engineering professionals.

DIRECTIONS

1. Read over the questions. Add or adapt items appropriate to your design.
2. Form a group that represents different departments and includes staff members from all shifts and all levels of responsibility. Determine how best to include family members and residents. Be sure to

---

*This material has been updated from: Hiatt, L. G. 1981. Renovation for innovation. *Nursing Homes* 30(1), 33–39.

obtain a good representation of people familiar with different units or sections of the building.

3. Determine who is best qualified to answer each group of questions. Some items are best answered by those in direct contact with the particular area. Receptionists may have been insights on lobbies, for example. Several different people may work on one section.
4. If the statement is true of your facility, indicate this by marking "Yes" in the blank space. Mark "No" if the statement is not a problem or issue for your building, and mark "N/A" (not applicable) if it does not apply to your program or facility.
5. Meet to discuss the responses. Appendix B, "Key to Interpreting the Environmental Design Inventory," may be helpful in evaluating the results. You may wish to circulate the key and use it to stimulate discussion.
6. After you have conducted the inventory and discussed the results, begin to identify priorities. Go back to each item marked "Yes," and assign it a priority. The following categories may be helpful:

1a Immediate priority to meet compliance or safety needs for building upkeep

1b Immediate priority for program objectives

2 Highly important, near-term priority

3 Medium attention, near-term priority

4 No design action, but may have management implications; worth sharing with others

5 Important, long-range priority

6 Medium attention required, long-range priority

7 To be dealt with in ongoing capital improvements or building maintenance

Ideally, priorities will relate to the schedule for implementation. However, items of mid-range priority sometimes are implemented before more important items because of outside forces.

7. Meet with participants to discuss these priorities and rank them again, taking into consideration such factors as available funds, the season, and vacancy.
8. Using published literature, consultants, peers, and tours, obtain additional information about each weakness the Environmental Design Inventory uncovers. Chapter 3 will guide you in developing "to . . . by" statements to convert these weaknesses into plans of action.

IMAGE AND INTERIOR APPEARANCE

_____ 1. The building looks nice, makes a good impression, and is the source of many compliments by residents and staff.

_____ 2. We painted, but it doesn't seem to be enough.

_____ 3. Our place looks like a hospital.

_____ 4. We had a designer or a committee of people who helped us obtain art or who gave us some ideas, but it isn't enough yet.

_____ 5. The building is old.

_____ 6. While our programs and activities are fairly varied, the place looks the same throughout.

_____ 7. The floors bring down the appearance of the building.

_____ 8. The handrails do not seem to work; no one uses them.

_____ 9. Wheelchairs, carts, and other vehicles clutter the hall.

_____ 10. Visitors only come to visit the people, never to admire the building.

_____ 11. People don't visit often, and they don't stay long when they come.

_____ 12. We have a hard time balancing energy and cost savings with the lighting we'd like to provide.

_____ 13. The air seems stuffy or stale; bad aromas greet visitors as they enter certain areas of this home.

RESIDENT POPULATION

Characteristics and Changes

_____ 1. The building is flexible in the sense that we can respond to changing needs and shifts in market demand. We are usually comfortably full with the type of residents we are licensed to serve and can respond to shifts in population profile.

_____ 2. The resident population has changed over the past few years, and we have been unable to adapt to their needs and develop new programs.

_____ 3. Our ideas seem superior to the building's capacity to support them.

_____ 4. We have a system of grouping people by abilities, but they keep spilling over into other areas.

_____ 5. We have trouble getting people of different abilities to mingle.

_____ 6. We have a problem discharging people to their own homes or to a lesser level of care.

_____ 7. People under our care could look better.

Quality of Life

_____ 1. Next to their own homes, people tell us that this is one of the best places they have lived or that it's the place they would choose if they needed long-term care.

_____ 2. People have choices, territory, access to privacy, control over their own belongings, freedom of schedule, or a sense of self-determination.

_____ 3. There are many ways of spending time; there are places and features to visit.

_____ 4. Residents' rooms have a certain dignity and comfort; they match the cultures, backgrounds, or local customs of their occupants.

_____ 5. We have a formal program of providing art or sculpture, designed gardens, or other visual amenities.

_____ 6. There are touchable features available to 90% or more of the residents.

_____ 7. Residents are roused quite early and go to bed quite early.

_____ 8. Residents spend a lot of their time waiting.

_____ 9. Residents do not seem to know each other and often bicker.

_____ 10. The environment is noisy; even the public address system seems penetrating.

_____ 11. There's no place for a person really to be alone—except maybe in the bathrooms, chapel, or outside.

_____ 12. We tried personalization, but someone put paper cutouts and decals on the walls and now they look shoddy.

_____ 13. We have difficulty handling people's private possessions, including furniture and knickknacks.

_____ 14. People complain of being lost or they ask for directions.

_____ 15. People seldom get outside.

RESIDENT-USE AREAS AND FEATURES

Bedrooms

_____ 1. The bedrooms are well designed with good provision for privacy, territory, and personal possessions.

_____ 2. The bedrooms are functional for wheelchair users; they can easily wheel up alongside the bed, get to and use the closets, and have space for visits in the room.

_____ 3. Bedroom windows are well designed for viewing, and residents have equal access to window space.

_____ 4. Bedroom lighting is related to the activities that might occur there, including reading, visiting, and recognizing faces at the door.

_____ 5. Within the room, it is relatively quiet; one does not hear noises from people, the hall, or other sources.

_____ 6. Each person has places for his or her own possessions, for securing valuables, and for displaying personal items.

_____ 7. Each person has ready access to a mirror at the proper height for grooming.

_____ 8. The bedrooms have little variety; they all look the same.

_____ 9. Each person's room is clearly labeled within eye level; and names appear on a legible, professional-looking identifying label or plaque next to the door.

_____ 10. There are some three-bed rooms or wards here.

_____ 11. We have quite a problem with residents wandering into other people's rooms and handling their things.

_____ 12. Some rooms seem to get less attention or feel more remote than others.

_____ 13. There isn't enough room for residents to move easily around their beds.

Bathrooms

_____ 1. Bathrooms are efficient for older people to use with or without wheelchairs and with or without assistance.

_____ 2. Residents sometimes fall next to the bed or in the bathroom.

_____ 3. The bathroom is not as accessible as it could be; the door is difficult to use and people cannot use the available assistive devices.

_____ 4. It takes staff members a long time to bathroom older people.

_____ 5. Use of commode chairs is widespread.

_____ 6. Privacy seems compromised in the bathrooms.

SERVICES, STAFFING, AND RELATED SPACES

Nursing and Health Care

_____ 1. There never seems to be enough staff, where and when we want them.

_____ 2. It takes the staff a long time to answer calls for assistance; residents or families complain that staff do not respond quickly enough.

_____ 3. Morning care is very chaotic here.

_____ 4. It is difficult to handle two-person transfers.

_____ 5. Nursing and activities staff have some difficulty deciding who's responsible for the activities, transportation, and grooming of some residents.

_____   6. Staff members complain that there's no space for this or that activity; yet, there seem to be unoccupied rooms or areas within rooms.

_____   7. There is much confusion around shift changes and dinner, bathing, and visiting times.

_____   8. Some parts of the facility get very dark at night, which causes concern for the staff.

_____   9. Many of the staff complain of headaches, which might be related to resident calling out.

_____ 10. Staff members balk at giving frequent showers or baths.

_____ 11. We do not have work space for physicians that comfortably accommodates charting, treatment, and communications.

_____ 12. The staff station is not designed for efficient use by those who must do paperwork.

_____ 13. Residents feel that too much time is spent waiting (for elevators, food trays, and staff to return from transport errands, for example).

Dining

_____   1. Mealtime is not a highlight for residents or staff members.

_____   2. Too few people feed themselves.

_____   3. The dining areas are not comfortable; there is too much noise and glare.

_____   4. The dining area lacks adequate space at the tables and in the aisles.

_____   5. There are no convenient toilets near the dining area; residents must be taken all the way back to their rooms during meals.

_____   6. The chairs do not fit well under the tables, preventing residents from getting tucked closely under the table.

_____   7. People are lined up along long tables for meals.

_____   8. Tables have sharp edges.

_____   9. The dining room is not set up for efficient staff assistance; serving beverages and feeding are difficult.

_____ 10. Some residents prefer to eat alone in their room rather than with others in the dining area.

_____ 11. We use feeding tables in our facility.

_____ 12. Many people here are fed using feeding tubes or nasogastric feeding techniques.

Activities

_____   1. Nearly everyone in our facility is involved in some aspect of the activities program.

_____ 2. There is great variety in the type of activities offered here, including space to accommodate nearly all of our residents.

_____ 3. Activities staff have moved many of their programs to where residents are: onto the unit and to the bedrooms, and are offering them in smaller groups.

_____ 4. We have nighttime activities and can offer them without disturbing those who prefer not to attend.

_____ 5. It is difficult to get people to go to activities.

_____ 6. Activities focus on programs, entertainment, games, and crafts in the hobby shop or activities room.

_____ 7. Activities focus on games, holidays and birthdays, large group events, and making items for sale.

_____ 8. Fewer people get to programs or participate in crafts than once did.

_____ 9. Fewer people participate in crafts or activities than once did.

_____ 10. The activities room looks cluttered.

_____ 11. The activities room lacks storage.

Socializing and Lounges

_____ 1. Lounges work really well; residents and families alike seem to get a great deal of enjoyment out of these spaces.

_____ 2. Social areas work well for our alerter and more ambulatory older people, but they seem less successful for our frailer, more confused, and multiple-impaired residents.

_____ 3. There doesn't seem to be sufficient space in our social area for residents, especially those in wheelchairs.

_____ 4. Residents line up around the walls.

_____ 5. The lounges go unused; people gather in the halls or in front of the nursing station.

_____ 6. It's difficult to run programs and serve meals in the same room.

_____ 7. Residents here do not join in social activities.

_____ 8. Lounges or dayrooms look _cluttered, barren, or unused._ If lounges vary, describe each:

                                                    Description

a. Location _____ 1. _____

b. Location _____ 2. _____

c. Location _____ 3. _____

_____ 9. Our residents sit around a lot, and they don't seem to do much; the television is on, but they don't seem to be watching.

Lobbies

_____ 1. The first things people see when they enter our facility are _____ _____. These give the impression that we are _____ _____ (homelike? comfortable? security conscious? financially oriented? focused on rules and regulations? a grand hotel?).

_____ 2. The lobby is a popular gathering place for residents; staff or visitors object to this.

_____ 3. If someone is hurt, dies, or is newly admitted, he or she is taken through a well used and occupied area.

GERONTOLOGICALLY MEANINGFUL PROGRAMS

Care of Mentally Impaired People

_____ 1. The facility's location, equipment, furnishings, and design pose no evident hazards, risks, or problems for mentally impaired people.

_____ 2. We do not offer enough services for people who are mentally impaired.

_____ 3. We have a unit for mentally impaired people.

_____ 4. We are uncertain how to respond to mentally impaired people.

_____ 5. Mentally impaired people do not look well cared for or carefully groomed; they do not have healthy-looking skin.

_____ 6. Mentally impaired people rarely get outside or have access to fresh air.

_____ 7. We have problems with people who seem to lack judgment and who elope from the facility.

_____ 8. We have a wandering garden.

_____ 9. We have a wandering loop or protected area inside the building for people who wish to explore.

Allied Health and Education

_____ 1. Residents get training in gait, balance, manual dexterity, and coordination skills, both in appropriate therapy spaces and on their living units.

_____ 2. The therapy rooms seem to be a jungle of equipment.

_____ 3. There are good facilities and spaces for podiatry and dental care and the staging or waiting involved.

_____ 4. The admissions area has no space for effective family meetings.

_____ 5. We have no facilities and little equipment for the ongoing education of the staff.

_____ 6. There is a hair care salon with good facilities.

FURNISHINGS AND EQUIPMENT

_____ 1. Our chairs were selected haphazardly, with no regard for personal preferences, bodily needs, or seating comfort.

_____ 2. Chairs are not uniform or standardized.

_____ 3. There are some chairs that are gliders or that swivel, providing exercise.

_____ 4. Some people's feet do not touch the floor. Five percent or more of the residents slump in their chairs (that is, they lean to one side or lean forward, sliding out of the chair).

_____ 5. Most chairs lack armrests or have loose or spindly ones.

_____ 6. Chairs are low and soft.

_____ 7. Many chairs go unused.

_____ 8. Chairs tip easily.

_____ 9. Pressure sores are a problem.

_____ 10. Odor is a problem.

_____ 11. There are people who do not have a chair.

_____ 12. We use geriatric wheelchairs or tray/table chairs in our facility.

_____ 13. We use recliners in some areas.

_____ 14. More than 5% of the older people are in bed at 11 A.M., and more than 20% spend over 20 hours per day in bed.

QUESTIONS TO HELP
GUIDE PLANNING

_____ 1. Staff members seem eager to see some changes and have started a core group to discuss quality of life, staffing, and environmental implications.

_____ 2. Everyone complains that "things aren't like they were."

_____ 3. We would like to have a more functional environment, but we have so many other priorities.

_____ 4. There's not much we can do with what we have.

_____ 5. The staff is exhausted from, bored by, or embittered about more changes.

_____ 6. Our management, staff, and families establish most of the patterns for activity, which then dictate design. If they would do more _____ and less _____, our environment would not be so problematic.

_____ 7. We have communications problems.

_____ 8. We don't spend money on the facility environment because we can't obtain the funds.

_____ 9. We know what we want to do, but the regulations are too stiff to allow for any innovation.

_____ 10. After we make changes, we never evaluate what we have done from the point of view of all those affected.

3
Planning

So here you are. You have completed the Environmental Design Inventory, carefully examined your facility, identified its weaknesses, and prioritized its needs. You now have some general ideas about what you would like to change. Why not just jump right into your first project? Why spend time planning when you could be acting?

Making changes in an operating facility is a serious business. It is perhaps more difficult to improve an existing building—with its residents, daily routines, and ongoing operations—than it is to start from scratch and design a new one. Whether your intended project is large or small, you must think it through carefully. Planning helps you clarify what you need to do and how you will do it. It will save you time and money over the long term, and it will help your project run smoothly. Whether a simple rearrangement of furniture or a major renovation of a facility, quality planning distinguishes the outstanding projects from the less successful ones.

Consider the following examples:

- Facility A receives a donation of several thousand dollars for upgrading the lobby. The sponsors immediately contract directly with an interior designer. Not until the job is finished does anyone suggest that the designer could have improved lighting and signs or created a kiosk for posting information about the diverse services of the home. The designer did not know these were issues for the client because staff members were not invited to offer suggestions. Poor planning often leads to unsatisfactory results.
- Facility B's budgetary process involves staff members working on the yearly budget for their departments. Capital improvements are discussed by department heads, and suggestions from one department are integrated with those of the others. Using this method, the following improvements are accomplished over a three-year period: (1) The facility is repainted with nonglare paints. (2) More functional seating is selected, and it is placed in more accessible locations. This helps the posture or "positioning" of older people. (3) Initial plans for adding a greenhouse and improving the beauty parlor are altered to benefit more residents; for the same cost, four projects are completed instead of two.

Facility A took a specific job out of context and lost some opportunity to maximize the results. Facility B is an example of using planning to provide a roadmap. Facility B may get more mileage out of each improvement and may find the journey through changes far more comfortable.

What happens when planning is inadequate or nonexistent? Here are eight probable results:

1. Without a cohesive structure, only fragments of ideas are implemented, and opportunities for resolving other related problems are lost.
2. Alternatives, including cost-saving changes, are not addressed.
3. Different points of view emerge too late in the process, resulting in delays and dilemmas that add to costs.
4. If one consumer group has the opportunity to offer suggestions and others do not, emotional strain and unanticipated operational problems, including additional costs, may result.
5. Changes benefit fewer people than they might.
6. There is no documentation, no record of information, and no paper trail that would allow people to trace decisions, join the process late, miss meetings, or understand the thinking of others.
7. Decisions lag, increasing the financial and emotional cost of the project.
8. Fund-raising efforts suffer from the lack of justification and a careful, thoughtful description of intended design features.

Suppose a well-meaning staff member, friend, benefactor, or family member makes this offer: "Let me redo that room for you. It's such a small project, we can get it done this week without a lot of fuss." Bear in mind that planning is not "fuss." Outsiders who attempt to redo someone else's home, work environment, or service system without adequate preparation may complicate matters. Even decorating the walls requires knowledge of fire safety and should involve those who live within the space. With a planning process in place, you are more likely to foster the largess and good will of the constituency. With an overall plan, little suggestions may contribute in unexpected ways to fulfilling facility improvements.

No matter what the size of the project or whom you are working with, it is advisable to articulate your objectives in clear language and to document them. Consider at least two levels of detail: (1) a broad statement that provides generalizations and overall objectives for the project and (2) a more detailed statement that includes specific features, areas, and even a space-by-space description.

Effective planning involves sharing ideas, gathering information through observation and other techniques, and making decisions. The remainder of this chapter discusses these elements of the planning process and offers practical suggestions for making the most of your project.

SHARING IDEAS

Perhaps you have known for a while that your facility requires some changes. Perhaps you have had a sudden inspiration. How do you go from a general sense that "something needs to be done" to a specific project plan? The first step, sharing ideas with others, is best accomplished by systematically obtaining and integrating input from several sources. This process is called *participatory design*. Your original project might not change as a result of the ideas you discuss with others, but it might have greater impact. Failing to include in the planning process the people who will live and work with the changes you make often diminishes the quality and increases the cost of renovations.

Participatory Design

Participatory design requires the involvement of many people and the synthesis of different input, levels of detail, and points of view. It is, however, more than asking "What do you want?" and acting on it. It is more than watching a designer draw. It involves carefully integrating information and opinions to craft a better building.

Technique   These steps increase the effectiveness of participatory design:

1. Select someone to coordinate the information you will obtain from staff members, residents and their families, research literature, and tours of other facilities. This person should understand how the institution operates and should know something about design possibilities. Useful skills include the ability to ask effective questions, keep project documents, and anticipate scheduling questions.
2. To facilitate information gathering, do the following before bringing everyone together to discuss changes:
   a. Choose a small group of staff members to describe the resident population. Appendix A contains the information needed to develop a resident population profile.
   b. List the ideas to date. What have you been thinking of doing? Describe the background or planning parameters (the "givens"). They may include schedule, financing, and features that must be assigned priority due to safety or similar considerations.
   c. Draft an introductory statement that clarifies the difference between sharing and implementing ideas. For example

   > We will discuss many topics today, and we will hear many good ideas. Some we will be able to implement, some we will not. We may discuss ideas that cannot be incorporated in design, and we may leave many issues unresolved. However, unless we hear your ideas, we may overlook some interesting and viable possibilities. We invite different points of view, as these help explain the paradoxical viewpoints that emerge from your individual responsibilities or schedules. Finally, there are many new products and materials available. If you have an idea about something, even if you've never seen it, we'd like to hear more about it.

3. Suggest that participants jot down their ideas. This helps stimulate conversation and ensures that information is not lost, should time pressures curtail the meeting.

4. Phrase your questions to elicit information about how space will be used, rather than just what features the participants want. Effective questions include these:

   - What would you like to have or see, and why?
   - What would you prefer not to have or see, and why?
   - How do you imagine the space would best be used?
   - Who has a different point of view on this topic?
   - Does anyone have a suggestion about what might be studied or an idea that needs further investigation before we decide on its practicality in this facility?

5. Keep preferences, such as color, in perspective. The process is designed to deal with individual differences and varying points of view. Expect people to have different preferences, and devise a method for accommodating the variations in imagery or points of view such as maintaining a running list of ideas or offering later chances to resolve differences using some of the information provided in this or other publications.

6. Keep a record of the information you obtain and make it accessible to everyone involved for further clarification.

7. Give participants several opportunities to see how decisions affect their choices. They must have the chance to reconsider requests that are no longer viable, given other decisions or changes. This is a variation of the Delphi techniques. These methods respect the impact one set of opinions or decisions has on others by cycling information through different groups of participants.

8. Make sure that participatory planning precedes full floor plan drawing or at least takes place when options are still open. Participation is frustrating when plans are so well developed that one group feels that its participation serves only to validate the work (or, worse yet, the egos) of others.

9. For each topic that requires additional follow-up, convene a focus group, that is, a group of people gathered to address a specific topic during a set time period (Figure 3–1). The focus group should include a cross section of people with insight on the subject matter. Focus groups can be useful in developing initial "to . . . by" statements (discussed below) on a particular topic, such as food service, bedroom design priorities, and caregiving specialization.

"To . . . By" Statements

When participants clearly articulate their objectives and how they might be accomplished, the planning process runs more smoothly. The "to . . . by" statement is one tool people can use to help clarify their thoughts. It also helps

Fig. 3–1 Participatory planning in a focus group. Focus groups comprise a cross section of people addressing a specific issue. Ideas are recorded here by the facilitators (an environmental psychologist and an architect) and by participants. (By Korsunsky Krank Erikson Architects, Inc., Minneapolis, for Sholom East, St. Paul, Minnesota.)

to stimulate the thinking of others and to facilitate the sharing of ideas. Once participants understand what others are trying to accomplish, they can offer options for implementing goals from their own areas of expertise. For example, housekeepers can support nursing staff, and designers can strengthen dementia program ideas.

A "to . . . by" statement consists of two parts: (1) an objective—what you want to do (To . . .) and (2) the means—how you plan to do it (by . . .). The first portion of the statement often expresses values, such as independence, comfort, and ease of movement. The second portion helps to achieve or operationalize the value by citing specific program and design features. "To . . . by" statements are used extensively in the following chapters.

Here is a sample "to . . . by" statement:

To increase the independence of residents in the dining room,

- *by* increasing aisle space so more people can wheel themselves
- *by* increasing the involvement of occupational therapists in selecting eating implements
- *by* selecting new furnishings so that chairs fit properly under the tables, thereby limiting spills
- *by* creating double doors at the entry so people can come and go more efficiently
- *by* adding an accessible toilet near the dining room to minimize the need to return to the unit for toileting

"To . . . by" statements are particularly useful when staff members from different departments try to accomplish something within a shared space. For example, many different people must operate in the bedroom. Multipurpose rooms, lobbies, and program rooms for Alzheimer's care also warrant interdisciplinary comments and advice from the residents and their families.

"To . . . by" statements are also useful when starting a new program or designing a new area. They help to clarify such issues as "What will we really offer in day care?" and "What is different about Alzheimer's care?" and "What do we want to accomplish with our meal service?"

Without "to . . . by" statements, participants in the planning process may describe in detail the features they want and yet fail to convey clearly to the designer what they are trying to accomplish. For example, a participant may say, "I want a tile floor," when what he or she means is, "I want a floor that is easy to clean." The stated desire may not, in fact, be the best or only way to accomplish the unstated objective. "To . . . by" statements help to separate what is wanted from how it might be accomplished.

GATHERING INFORMATION

The second component of the planning process is gathering action-oriented information. This may be accomplished through several methods: research, observation, behavior mapping, schedule analysis, tours, re-enactment demonstrations, mockups, questionnaires, and facility inventories. You may choose to use a variety of these techniques depending on the size and complexity of changes. You are unlikely to cull all the information you need from just one article, one observation session, one tour, or one questionnaire.

Assembling the Facts

Assembling the facts is an important part of the planning process. Through fact finding you obtain information on current regulations, sources of funding, and different design solutions. Through research or use of primary data sources you apply information from functional profiles of older people or post-occupancy evaluation of design effectiveness. Assembling facts includes strategic planning, incorporating patterns for scheduling, statistics on costs of similar projects, specific product and furnishing ideas, and names of people and agencies that might be of help.

As you assemble the facts from published literature, it is important to bear in mind the distinction between descriptive project articles written as public relations pieces and reliable empirical data that help evaluate the effectiveness of design under specified conditions. If you are unable to differentiate between the two, consider hiring a researcher to assist you. They can be found at graduate-level universities.

Technique The technique for assembling the facts varies by project and according to how many times the information will be needed for future reference. Some people start notebooks or files and keep logbooks and minutes of important questions, replies, and transactions. Others set up a shelf and even "library" or media room with regular bulletins for orientation and meetings held to alert colleagues to the "facts" assembled.

The assembly process itself involves reading; writing letters; clipping or photocopying; photography; collecting reports, interviews, and conversations. It should also involve conferences and tours.

Sources   Organizations of long-term care and other health professionals often sponsor conferences or exhibits and tours and may be good sources of information. The following organizations may be helpful:

- Activity Leaders of Therapeutic Activities Programs (ALTAP)
- Alzheimer's and Related Disorders Association (ARDA)
- American Association of Homes for the Aging (AAHA)
- American College of Health Care Administrators (ACHCA)
- American Health Care Association (AHCA)
- American Hospital Association, Committee on Aging (AHA)
- American Nurses Association
- American Society on Aging (ASA)
- Canadian Association on Gerontology (CAG)
- Gerontological Society of America (GSA)
- Human Factors Society
- International Gerontological Association
- National Association of Jewish Homes and Services for Aging
- National Council on the Aging (NCOA)
- Ontario Association of Homes for the Aging

Architecture and design professionals have their own associations. The following may be able to provide useful information:

- American Institute of Architects, Health Care and Aging Committee
- Environmental Design Research Association

There are state and regional affiliates for most of these national organizations, particularly those for long-term care, architecture, and interior design. The organization's national directory will have information on local affiliates.

Some of the organizations listed above also publish newsletters or journals, which frequently contain project summaries. Noteworthy examples are the AAHA's *Provider* and the AHCA's *Provider News.* The American Society on Aging publishes *Generations,* which features articles on long-term care, technology, and design; the National Council on Aging publishes *Perspectives on Aging* and *Abstracts on Aging,* which review developments and literature. Two nursing magazines, *Journal of Gerontological Nursing* and *Geriatric Nursing,* also highlight design issues. *Housing the Elderly* and *Untie the Elderly* are other newsletters worth investigating.

Other periodicals feature occasional articles on environmental design. Some devote special annual issues to design for older people. Explore the following sources:

- *Architectural Record*
- *Architecture* (formerly *AIA Journal*)
- *Construction Specifier*
- *Contemporary Administrators in Long-Term Care*
- *Generations*
- *Gerontologist*
- *Housing the Elderly Report* (for sponsors and managers of housing and long-term care facilities)
- *Interiors*
- *Journal of Alzheimer's Disease and Related Disorders*
- *Journal of Geriatric Nursing*
- *Journal of Health Care Finance Administration*
- *Pride Institute Journal of Long-Term Home Health Care*
- *Progressive Architecture*

Catalogs can be good sources of information about products and furnishings. Try the following: Comfortably Yours, Sears Health Catalog, Sharper Image, Sweet's Catalog, and Ways and Means.

Observing

Magazine articles on facility design can be misleading sources of information on how space is used. They show only still lifes of places devoid of people, and they often describe features without considering their users. One of the surest ways of understanding how a space is used is to observe it in use on several occasions. Note how residents, staff members, and visitors interact with the environment. Observation often suggests the questions that most need to be addressed before changes are made.

Observation is particularly appropriate for spaces that have multiple users, such as dayrooms, dining rooms, therapy areas, nursing stations, and lobbies. Time-interval observation refers to establishing a limited time period for observation. Fifteen-minute intervals are typical, but an hour is not unusual. Shorter intervals are good for simple questions (Are people using a particular area? What are they doing at a particular time of day?) and for semi-private areas. Longer intervals are appropriate for public areas.

In all cases, observation should occur only with the knowledge and consent of those involved. Residents and staff become accustomed to people sitting in their areas and writing. Observers are often more noticeable when they stand and do not try to fit in. Be candid about why you are there. The response, "To learn more about how the room works or is used," usually satisfies most queries. If "outsiders" do the observation, it is imperative that a notice be posted, that staff be apprised at shift changes, and that observers inform the supervisor of their presence before beginning. Such courtesies are in the best interest of residents.

Technique   Before you start, determine what you will be looking for. You might decide to look at the images or messages the facility conveys to staff, families, visitors, and residents. You might list the features you want it to convey and ask others to observe how well it succeeds. Or, you might assess your facility against the following criteria for humane long-term care. Read over the items listed, and add your own. Then develop examples for each one. The first four have one example each; you will want to add others. How well does your facility meet these criteria?

1. To provide access for people in wheelchairs
   Example: By offering bedrooms arranged for ease of self-dressing
2. To be aromatically pleasing
   Example: By providing aromas of freshly baked goods at mealtime
3. To facilitate attention span and concentration
   Example: By reducing background noise and traffic interruptions
4. To promote routine bathrooming
   Example: By providing bathrooms near dining areas
5. To promote choice and decision making
6. To evoke conversations
7. To offer cultural familiarity through recognizable imagery and sounds
8. To convey dignity as alternatives to nudity and ungainly self-presentation
9. To reinforce or invite community and intergenerational contact
10. To support consultation and staff meetings
11. To afford diversions for people of every ability
12. To encourage appropriate exercise
13. To provide flexibility and options for change
14. To stimulate grooming
15. To offer group activities
16. To provide landmarks for wayfinding
17. To stimulate memory development through cues
18. To afford surroundings for peace
19. To allow space for personalization
20. To offer options for privacy
21. To convey and provide safety
22. To provide textural variety
23. To afford views to the outside and of activity
24. To be visually and acoustically responsive to older people

Technique   Read these values as if they were a checklist. Circle or mark those that need work based on multiple observations or experience with the facility.

Behavior Mapping

Behavior mapping is a form of observation in which you record detailed information about the people who use a space at a particular time and about their activities. It is useful in obtaining information about areas that are not "ruled" by a single user and spaces with no clear-cut departmental responsibility.

Lobbies, dayrooms, dining rooms, therapy areas, and nursing stations are good candidates for this technique. It is most appropriate in larger rooms, in areas used by different residents, and in larger institutions. Information obtained through behavior mapping often helps diagnose problems, such as conflicting patterns of use, underutilization of a space, and dominance by one set of users.

Technique   Use a blank piece of paper or a prepared recording sheet. Record information through stream-of-consciousness writing for low-use spaces, and develop categories and short-term samples over several days for high-use spaces. Your behavior map might answer the following questions:

- Who? (Users, including staff, residents, and visitors, and their characteristics, including needs for furnishings or implements)
- Does what? (Specific activities or postures)
- With whom? (Roles of those involved)
- Where in the space? (Area or zone, if the room is thought of as being divided into a grid)
- When? For how long?
- What problems do they have?

Schedule Analysis

For some topics or areas of a building, the most appropriate method of understanding present concerns and future possibilities involves development of a "master schedule." It is useful when the objective is to make design changes that will affect congestion and crowding, morning care, multipurpose room use, dining, or care of the mentally impaired. Schedule analysis may be used, for example, to examine the impact the proposed relocation of a service or unit will have on congestion and transportation. It may also be helpful in predicting the impact on operations of an additional piece of equipment (anything from a housekeeper's cart to an elevator). Schedule analysis often reveals that staff members are competing for residents or elevators, and it may suggest a combination of management changes (such as schedule rearrangement) and design options to alleviate the problem.

Technique   Your objective is to record everything that happens in a particular area. You will therefore identify those who enter and leave the area by their job titles and duties, and you will record the time of day and the activities performed.

Find a large wall or series of table tops on which to spread shelf paper or some other large piece of paper. Across the top of the paper, label each department and all the roles within those departments. The nursing heading, for example, may have four subheads: nursing assistants, licensed staff, supervisors, and unit clerks. The activities heading may have different subheads according to where staff are assigned. Continue until all the major staff members are represented, including the housekeeping and clinic staffs. Down the left side, list time intervals (5 A.M. to 9 P.M., for example). Try using removable, adhesive-backed paper for the hours to allow for adjustments. Using larger pieces of adhesive-backed removable paper, record the activities that take place in that area during each time period.

Once the schedule is done, department heads and key staff members might meet to discuss any areas that need improvement. Improvements might involved changing the sequence of duties, bringing more programs to the floor to minimize transport or waiting time, or shifting the schedule to bring recreational staff in later in the day to provide evening programs. The removable paper helps everyone see the proposed schedule and make changes; it minimizes the need to recopy (see Table 3–1).

Making a schedule such as the one shown in Table 3-1 helps a facility to learn where time is spent, what services and spaces deserve priority attention, and helps those planning changes to understand the impact of locating certain facilities in different locations.

Tours

Tours can be useful for gathering information. By visiting other facilities, you can see alternative service concepts in action. Tours help you learn how new equipment works, envision the effects of various spaces or systems, and gather ideas. You must remember, however, that a concept or feature that works in one facility will not necessarily translate directly to another.

Technique   To determine whether an idea from another facility will work in yours, consider the following questions. Ask your tour guide the questions on the left as you tour, then ask yourself the questions on the right.

For whom is this feature intended?	Will it be used by the same type of older person or staff member in your facility?
Does it work for these people?	Do you expect it to work for your residents?
Does it require special staffing or duties?	Will you be able to staff it effectively?
How would you change it?	Can you make those changes?
Were there any difficulties obtaining approval?	Should you expect any approval problems?
Are there any problems obtaining or maintaining equipment and furnishings?	Are the equipment and furnishings still available?
What are the age, systems, and other background characteristics of the facility and management?	Will the concept work in your building given its similarities and differences?

If you are unable to take actual tours of other facilities, consider "arm chair tours." These are photographic or slide presentations that will acquaint you with available options. "How might this work here?" is a useful departure point for discussion.

Table 3-1 Sample Schedule of Morning Care

Time Morning	Residents Involved	Nursing Assistants	Nurses	Dietary	House-keeping	Activity	Social Work	MD	Physical Therapy	Hair Care
5:00	Any SNF resident	Wake 10 people and toilet; clean teeth and glasses.								
6:00	One-third are in the dining room. Two-thirds are in bed-rooms.	Transport to dining. Set up meals for 1/3 in dining room. Half stay in dining room to help feed and pass. Half return to feed the 2/3 in bed-rooms.	Nite staff finishes charting and de-briefs arriving day staff.	Take up food carts; place trays on table. Open cartons of milk.	Stock carts of linen and paper and bring and stock on each unit.					
7:30	One-third of resi-dents who were in dining room.	Transfer out of dining room and into halls or room.	In kitchen prepar-ing next meal.	Start room cleaning for empty rooms or especial-ly soiled ones.						

(continued)

Table 3-1 (Continued)

Time Morning	Residents Involved	Nursing Assistants	Nurses	Dietary	House-keeping	Activity	Social Work	MD	Physical Therapy	Hair Care
	Two-thirds of residents who are in or getting out of rooms.	Dressing, bathing, bed-baths and assisted toileting.								
8:00	Any	Continue dressing and grooming. Range of motion.	Pass medications and give treatments. Communicate with MD/specialists.	Remove food trays.	Clean dining room floors and tables.		Small group discussion with 8 residents.	Rounds		
8:30	One at a time w/ MD; 4 with activities.	Continue	Rounds with MD. Medication passing.	In kitchen, clean up and prepare for lunch.	Bedroom cleaning.	Discussion group with 4–6 people.	Telephone and arrange transfers.	Rounds	On-unit therapy.	In room therapy re: grooming.
9:00	Any	Continue and toileting; transport to off-unit programs.	Charting	Continue		Begin group programs; transport residents to music or other. Run program.	Staff meeting			

Re-Enactment Demonstrations

Designers and executives are infrequently present for actual caregiving procedures, yet this information is often critical for improving design. It is sometimes useful to demonstrate how things are done and to explain why. Some of the procedures that it is particularly important to re-enact are these:

Transfer. Many design books lead architects and sponsors to believe that older people always make a side transfer or that they must wheel their chairs in a 5-foot circle to transfer.

Transportation. It is often difficult to visualize the maneuvering, congestion, and waiting involved in moving people into and out of dining areas and programs.

Fitting people onto an elevator. Books seem to suggest different elevator capacities than people can actually negotiate.

Using outdoor areas. The public often cannot envision the challenges of doors, doorways, and uneven terrain.

Ramps. Ramps are often difficult for ambulatory older people and those with walkers to use. Many ramps hinder those who wish to propel their own wheelchairs, and some even challenge the staff members who try to assist residents safely.

Technique   Select your models carefully. Re-enactments must involve a representative sample of the population. Credibility is lost when staff members perform as clients (unless risks are involved) and when elderly demonstrators are considerably healthier than the average resident. Be willing to re-enact the procedure several times. Demonstrations often must be followed by a discussion or follow-up to generate solutions.

Mockups

When new construction is planned, models are sometimes built to give those involved a better sense of the project than they could get from blueprints or floor plans alone. Models are similarly useful when renovation or an addition is considered. While small-scale models help some people, a full-sized representation, or mockup, of the space may be more useful. Mockups assist the estimated one of every two who are unable to visualize space or floor plans well. Mockups may also be useful in fund raising, and, if a regulatory agency agrees to send an observer or watch a video, they will help you illustrate particular concepts or spatial concerns for official approval.

There are two common types of mockups. Two-dimensional mockups transform a proposed design into a full-scale floor plan. They can be used to determine room configuration and furniture placement (Figure 3–2). Three-dimensional mockups feature walls as well as floors, and they are useful when the space is small and the questions engage the walls, windows, built-ins or maneuverability.

Fig. 3–2 A two-dimensional mockup. A full-scale floor plan may facilitate decisions regarding room configuration and details of placement.

Technique   For a two-dimensional mockup, select a large, empty space. Use colored tape or masking tape to outline the proposed plan on the floor. If no appropriate space exists inside, use a large parking lot. Instead of tape, mark the area with the type of device used to mark lines on a football field (Figure 3–3). Place the actual furnishings in the space to try out different arrangement ideas and obtain reactions (Figure 3–4). For a three-dimensional mockup, use lightweight materials, such as Homosote ™, foam core, or plywood to simulate walls.

Mockups are for walking around in, not just for looking at. Have staff members engage in actual activities, preferably working with residents representing the different types of clients you serve. Use staff people or family members to represent those who are extremely frail.

Questionnaires
Of all the methods of gathering information, questionnaires are the trickiest and should rarely be used without advice from research methodologists. There are two common problems with questionnaires. The first is bias. Without proper training, it is easy to write questions that lead, skew, or anticipate answers. The questions and answers may misrepresent priorities or be incomplete, resulting in inappropriate conclusions. The second problem concerns imagery. Questions often relate to preferences, and preference data assume personal experience with the feature or concept. In design we often want new solutions. Since it is hard to form a preference for the unknown, these questions often lead to simple and known responses, rather than the best solution. If questionnaires are imperative for your planning process, try to obtain help in developing the questions. Psychologists, sociologists, and meth-

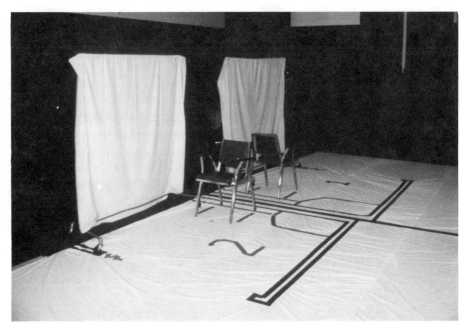

Fig. 3–3 Using mockups for comparison. Different bathroom configurations were studied by mocking up two bedrooms and two variations on the bathroom. Vintage portable privacy curtains give the impression of walls. Chairs or actual commodes can be used to model toilet placement.

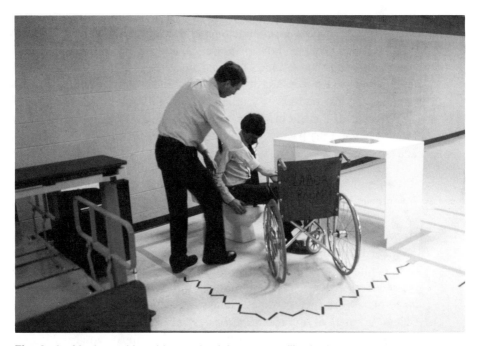

Fig. 3–4 Mockup with cabinetry. In tight spaces, like bathrooms, the placement of fixtures can be ascertained using mockups. Designers try out the mockup before asking older people to work with it. The experience of using a wheelchair often provides additional insight for those involved in design, facility management, and review.

odologists in various university departments are possible sources of such expertise.

Technique   List the topics you want the questionnaire to cover. These might include institutional versus "homelike" features; workable bedroom, bather, and toilet layouts; objects, furnishings, and landmarks. Make your list before worrying about the wording of questions. Then meet with a survey expert to learn how to draft the questions. If you must develop the questions on your own, consult question-writing references (see the Annotated Bibliography).

The following tips will help you make the most of your questionnaire:

- Questions that begin "Would you like . . ." and "How often would you personally use . . ." often elicit useful information.
- Use questions to obtain reactions to images or features observed on tours. This is often most successful when two or three different solutions can be contrasted.
- Instruct respondents to explain their choices. Be sure to ask "Why?" and "What would make you feel differently?"
- Include the staff people who are directly responsible for the area or task you are investigating as well as administrators or board members.
- Work with respondents while they answer the questionnaire so you can explain anything that is not clear.

Facility Inventory

Facility inventories are often conducted as a part of master planning when it is known that a number of changes must be made, but it is not clear how ideas relate to each other or how priorities should be established. They are useful when full-scale renovation is planned, when new management is interested in understanding how a facility operates, and when refurbishment is being weighed against more costly renovation or addition.

How does facility inventory compare with a state inspection? The inventory goes beyond the basics of the state audit and focuses on the facility's values and attributes.

Technique   Chapter 2 contains directions and starter questions for a facility inventory. You may want to add to the topics and questions provided. For example, you might choose to include questions on safety and accessibility from a state audit so that you can develop one consolidated set of priorities.

The inventory may be conducted by facility staff members, working alone or in conjunction with an outside consultant or design team, or it may be done by outsiders. Peers, such as administrators and nurse managers or therapists, sometimes work together to evaluate each others' facilities, for example, when several are part of a corporation or system or that share similar values.

You can analyze the inventory results yourself, or you can hire an outside team to do it. Self-analysis is appropriate when the issues relate to appearance, arrangement, ease of movement, program assignment, and response to special user groups. You may need to follow your self-analysis with more systematic evaluations by licensed professionals or people with training and credentials in the topics that interest you. Outsiders may have their own lists and assessment techniques, but you should share your findings and questions with them.

Outside experts are valuable if you have insufficient time to write and analyze. Professionals and administrators are not generally expert in all aspects of long-term care, and specialists may be needed to analyze the efficiency of staffing, dietary issues, and programs for greater habilitation or for people with cognitive impairments. Professionals are also usually necessary for comprehensive design planning, and they can help with issues involving electrical and mechanical systems, such as lighting, communications, ventilation, heating, cooling, and structural changes.

MAKING DECISIONS

Making decisions is the third component of planning. Its importance should not be underestimated. Successful projects are often distinguished by a meaningful decision-making process and a solid system for communicating information among those involved in implementing the changes, like designers, state officials, estimators, and contractors. An effective decision-making process has these qualities:

- It allows time for discussion.
- It incorporates notes, minutes, reports, or planning documents to ensure that information is not lost or repeated.
- It enables planners to obtain cost information early.
- It has a single project coordinator who is accessible and responsible for information.

When there is no decision-making process, meetings often lack purpose and a clear outcome, discussions go on too long, and people feel uncomfortable because issues have not been adequately introduced or addressed.

Two important decisions to make during the planning process are these:

- What levels of change are appropriate?
- Is this change worth the investment?

The remainder of this chapter addresses these issues.

What Levels of Change Are Appropriate?

Design improvements may require many different levels or degrees of physical change. The six that are introduced in this chapter are rearrangement, refurbishment, renovation, conversion, addition, and replacement.

Rearrangement   The least complicated and least expensive of the six, rearrangement involves moving furnishings or reassigning offices or rooms. Such changes often ease mobility-related difficulties. Rearrangement may also alleviate problems resulting from having too many furnishings or too little storage.

Tips

- Be sure to involve residents and staff in the rearrangement process. Changes sometimes work best if they are explained and those affected are consulted.
- Display a drawing of planned changes to allow people time to critique them prior to implementation.
- Notify everyone when implementing a change. Suppose, for example, that you rearrange the dining room furniture without informing the housekeeping staff. You might return to the area later to discover that the room has been "fixed" and the furniture shifted back to its original position.
- Furniture changes are sometimes more acceptable when made in conjunction with a special event, party, or holiday, when change is expected. You can then consult people about the change: "Was this a good idea? What if we left it this way?"

Refurbishment   Surface alterations, from paint to minor hardware changes, constitute refurbishment. These tend to brighten or alter the perception of a space, but they may not dramatically change the inherent space allocation or functioning. Refurbishment should be done regularly to keep the facility looking fresh, inviting, and clean. Refurbishment may be warranted to keep up the facility and maintain the population while plans are made for more extensive changes.

Tips

- Plan a refurbishment as carefully as you would new construction, developing concepts and obtaining estimates before starting.
- When adding equipment (such as computers, bathers, medication units, and chart racks) consider the product dimensions and required space, connections, and utilities before making the purchase. Many new products will not fit into old spaces.
- When refurbishing, consider how you can solve common problems like glare, noise, and lack of fresh air. Refurbishments obviously should not make these problems more severe, but without planning they often do.
- Do not expect refurbishments to solve space allocation problems or to perform miraculous transformations. For example, wall covering and a paint job will not change a custodial care facility into an Alzheimer's care unit.

Although some facilities have a good competitive position in the community, offer good service, and have an admirable reputation, consumers are becoming increasingly sophisticated and demanding more. They are beginning to expect nursing homes to have a new look every five to seven years, just as hotels do. Nursing homes must maintain their competitive edge by illustrating their sensitivity to consumers. New facilities often pressure other local institutions to upgrade their appearance and demonstrate their commitment to high standards of care.

Renovation   Renovation, the most general term used to describe building restoration, involves renewal through some combination of cleaning, repairing, and rebuilding. Nursing home renovation should contribute to the improved functioning of the facility. It is called for when a portion of the building is nonfunctional or at odds with population characteristics and marketing or program goals. Sponsors usually explore the options for rearrangement and refurbishment before considering renovation. Common renovations include adding windows, changing a lobby or kitchen (Figures 3–5 and 3–6), upgrading toilet rooms, and improving the front entry (Figure 3–7) or image (Figure 3–8). Renovations are sometimes accompanied by plans for additions.

Renovation, like new construction in many states, sometimes requires a two-part review process. You must establish need and submit to a facilities review of the planned features. This is also true of conversion, addition, and replacement.

Conversion   Conversion involves changing a building or part of a building from one function to another. For example, a nursing home might be converted to an assisted living residence for people who require little nursing care (Figures 3–9 and 3–10). A two-bed room might be converted to a one-bed room (Figure 3–11). Conversion is selected when the original structure is thought to be inadequate for present and future needs, and it is often accompanied by renovation or refurbishment (Figure 3–12).

Sponsors are usually reluctant to reduce the overall bed count without studying other alternatives, because revenue is based on the number of beds. The key to more effective units may be to swap space; that is, to maintain the same bed count, but to move the beds to an area of the building that can be effectively supervised with the existing staff. Some facilities have created new bedrooms from areas that are no longer used or have functions that could be moved off site. Such changes sometimes require the approval of the state health department. To gain approval, you may need to explain the advantages of the conversion in terms of space for effective caregiving, improved supervision, more effective use of labor, and marketability. It is sometimes useful to point out that when there is insufficient square footage, staff effort and time are compromised, and older people spend more time confined to bed or chair because it takes less space to care for a person who is confined and prone.

Addition   This change involves new construction. It is called for when there is not enough of the right kind of space in the appropriate location. Typical nursing home additions include bedrooms and social areas (Figures 3–13 to 3–

Fig. 3–5 Before renovation of lobby, social areas, and kitchen. The original entry offers little space for seating, social areas, multipurpose activities, or a covered entry. The kitchen needs additional refrigerator and freezer capacity in keeping with the expanding number of residents. Seating areas for dining and front door visiting are cramped, and the use of free-standing chairs in the corridors violates corridor requirements. The library is too narrow and rarely used. (By Timothy C. Boers, Boulder Associates Architects, Boulder, Colorado, for Hooverwood Jewish Home, Indianapolis, Indiana.)

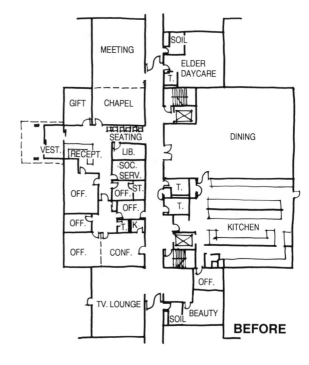

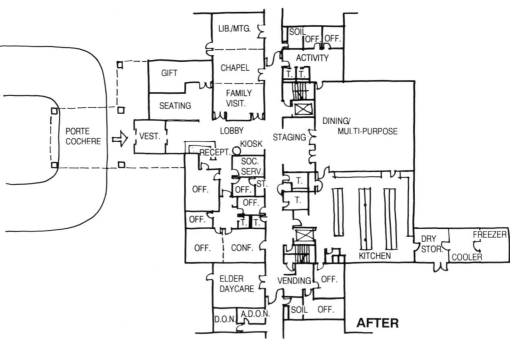

Fig. 3–6 After renovation of lobby, social areas, and kitchen. Adding on to the front of the building afforded larger social areas, better facilities for day care, and consolidation of staff offices. The kitchen addition involved the use of outside refrigeration and freezer units. The improved staging area for dining responds to the increased number of wheelchair users. (By Timothy C. Boers, Boulder Associates Architects, Boulder, Colorado, for Hooverwood Jewish Home, Indianapolis, Indiana.)

Fig. 3–7 Replacing the grand stairway. Formal stairways in vintage buildings sometimes pose hazards. To change the flow of people and goods to alternate second entries that are on grade entries may not always be possible nor as aesthetically appealing as in the original entry. Here, the stairs were removed, the roadway adjusted, and a new, lower entry created. At the same time, the lower level was transformed into a promenade—virtually a gerontological mini-mall. (By Lewis and Rogers, Philadelphia, for Simpson House, Philadelphia, Pennsylvania.)

Fig. 3–8 Impact of renovations on image. Renovations that attach to the exterior and fill in buildings may transform the overall image of buildings. The new exterior bathrooms and community areas shown here change the facade of the building and give separate structures visual and actual connections. (By SFCS, Inc., Roanoke, Virginia.)

Fig. 3–9 Before conversion of nursing home to assisted living facility. Some buildings lend themselves to transformation better than others. The two small, narrow toilet rooms and adjacent wardrobe closets shown here will be replaced with a larger, more accessible area. The adjacent rooms will then be transformed into a living room and bedroom that are suitable for assisted living. In some instances, small kitchen or bar sinks, microwave ovens, and full-sized refrigerators are added to provide a homelike appeal. In others, bay windows or window boxes are used to make the exterior character of the nursing home more marketable. Nearly all converted facilities require additional closet space and the refurbishment of walls and floors. (By SFCS, Inc., Roanoke, Virginia.)

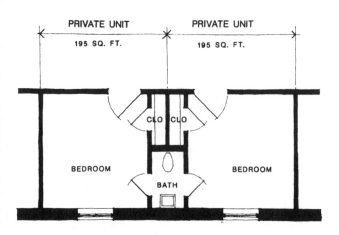

PLAN – BEFORE

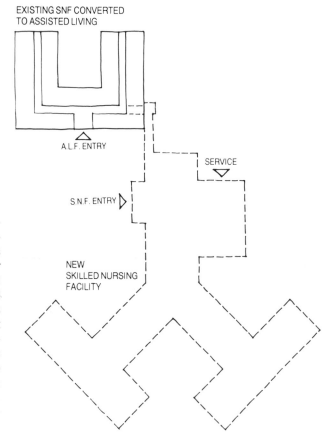

Fig. 3–10 Conversion of nursing home to assisted living facility. The original nursing home was converted to an assisted living or personal care facility. It required the refurbishment of rooms and the renovation of public areas and utility spaces. A replacement facility was built as new construction. Converted nursing homes are sometimes converted back to their original use for people with minor frailties. (By Timothy C. Boers, Boulder Associates Architects, Boulder, Colorado.)

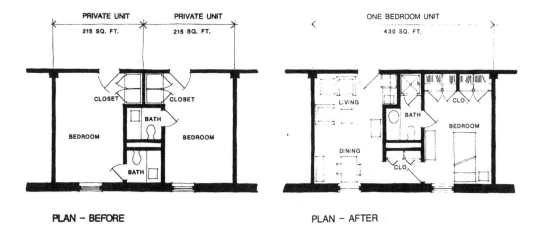

PLAN – BEFORE

PLAN – AFTER

Fig. 3–11 Conversion of adjacent two-bed rooms with one toilet. In this instance, two-bed rooms were converted to more functional one-bed rooms. Small toilet rooms (Figure 4–25) were made larger and more accessible to wheelchair users, and the closets were expanded.

Fig. 3–12 Finished conversion of the rooms shown in Figure 3–11.

17), although additions of toilet rooms, utility areas, kitchens, and administrative spaces are also common. Some buildings are easier to add to than others because of their configuration and the available land.

When planning an addition, investigate your state's stipulations regarding construction in existing nursing homes. Many states prohibit construction above rooms occupied by residents unless those rooms are vacated. Some sponsors anticipate these limitations when constructing new facilities and plan future expansions under their "first" floor, on a patio level that is above ground.

Stay alert to your state's policies regarding new construction. The eighties were marked by control over the growth of nursing homes. In many states, construction was all but halted. Statistical projections for increases in the geriatric population and the demand for nursing home beds suggest, however,

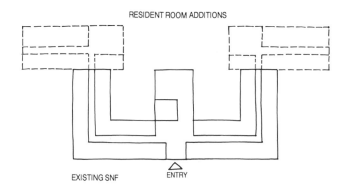

RESIDENT ROOM ADDITIONS

EXISTING SNF   ENTRY

Fig. 3–13 Bedroom addition. Bedrooms and some social areas were added to an existing facility. Options for further expansion were left open here. The older portions often must be refurbished to maintain their marketability. (By Timothy C. Boers, Boulder Associates Architects, Boulder, Colorado.)

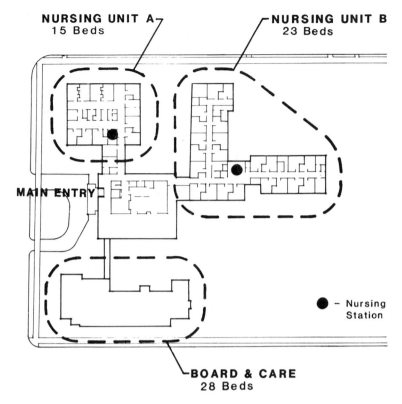

NURSING UNIT A
15 Beds

NURSING UNIT B
23 Beds

MAIN ENTRY

● – Nursing
Station

BOARD & CARE
28 Beds

Fig. 3–14 Before addition and conversion. As in many institutions, one or more portions of the building must be connected, and some areas have a higher proportion of small double rooms than desired. (By Korsunsky Krank Erikson Architects, Inc., Minneapolis, Minnesota.)

that we will see an increased willingness to accommodate new facilities in the future. In most states, free enterprise does not prevail; you cannot build a new facility without proving a need for it. A moratorium is in effect in some states that has stopped construction of nursing homes. In response, sponsors occasionally erect assisted living facilities that can be readily converted to nursing homes once the strictures are lifted.

Replacement Governments use this term, often as part of an effort to control the cost of care by controlling the number of beds, to refer to changes that do not alter bed count or licensure. A facility may replace bedrooms without increasing or decreasing the number of nursing home beds. This occurs, for example, when the population of multiple-occupancy rooms is reduced through the conversion of four-bed to two-bed rooms, and additional beds are added to maintain the original census. Some state governments are reluctant to support the addition of new beds, but are willing to entertain proposals for replacement. Figures 3–9 and 3–15 might involve replacement. Replacement may be considered in situations where the demand for services and beds is robust but regulatory or financial factors limit new construction.

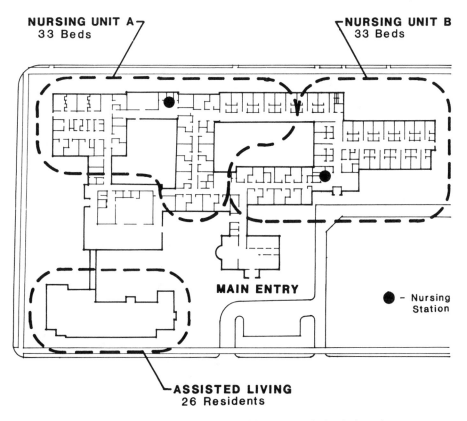

NURSING UNIT A
33 Beds

NURSING UNIT B
33 Beds

MAIN ENTRY

● - Nursing
  Station

ASSISTED LIVING
26 Residents

Fig. 3–15 After addition and conversion, with improved circulation. A common approach to renovation today is to add new beds, sometimes converting small doubles to larger single rooms. (By Korsunsky Krank Erikson Architects, Inc., Minneapolis, Minnesota.)

The six types of change described above all involve the reuse of some part of an original or parent structure, and all warrant planning. Some people presume that refurbishment, for example, can be done without careful consideration, or that it is solely the responsibility of the maintenance department. Even alterations in lighting and wall covering can have implications for caregiving or operational costs and may vary from unit to unit. All the changes described above would benefit from the wisdom of the staff.

Renovations, conversions, and additions pose some challenges. When planning a change of this type, you should consider the following:

- How does the addition fit on the site? What is its best location, and what is the most feasible location?
- How will existing mechanical, electrical, and other systems handle the demand of the new facilities?
- How will the circulation of people and services be affected? Will wayfinding be compromised?
- How will the floors line up? Ramps and grade changes are exceedingly difficult for older people. When connections result in ramps,

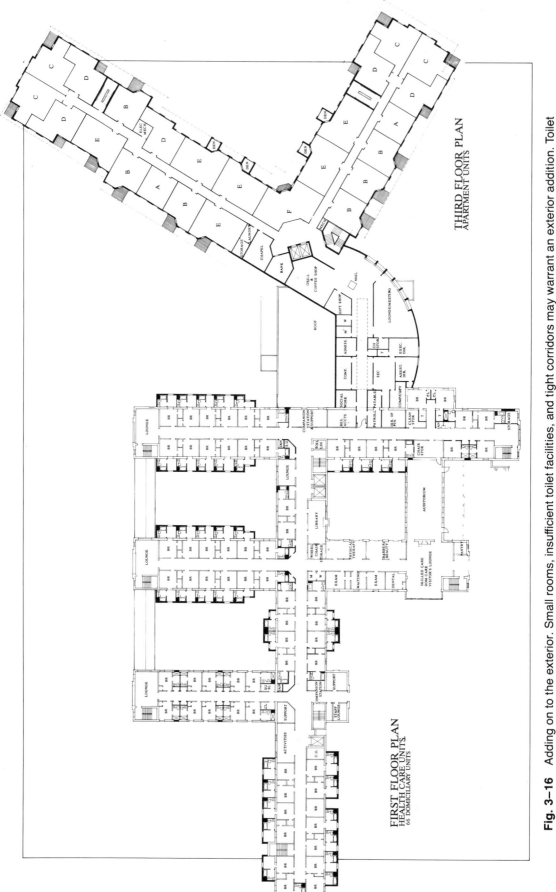

Fig. 3–16 Adding on to the exterior. Small rooms, insufficient toilet facilities, and tight corridors may warrant an exterior addition. Toilet rooms added to the exterior are shown here. Program spaces (dining or activity areas) can be attached to longer stretches of corridor. Exterior additions offer two additional advantages over other types of renovation. They do not disturb the interior, which is sometimes a

THIRD FLOOR PLAN
APARTMENT UNITS

FIRST FLOOR PLAN
HEALTH CARE UNITS
66 DOMICILIARY UNITS

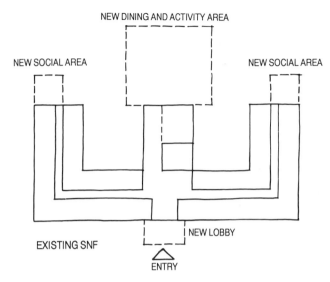

NEW DINING AND ACTIVITY AREA

NEW SOCIAL AREA

NEW SOCIAL AREA

NEW LOBBY

EXISTING SNF

ENTRY

Fig. 3–17 Addition of social areas. The social areas shown here have been expanded. Bedroom problems have been left unresolved or will be resolved through depopulating or refurbishment. This is common when extraneous factors affect the sponsor's ability or need to add bedrooms or to change the number of residents. (By Timothy C. Boers, Boulder Associates Architects, Boulder, Colorado.)

older people often require additional staff assistance. Ideally, original floor levels should be maintained, or a main circulation level should be established to minimize grade changes.

- How can changes be made with minimal disturbance to occupants and necessary services? Noise and vibration can be extremely disruptive.
- What season is best for the proposed changes, and can they be completed in a timely fashion?
- Will the addition fully satisfy your needs? Additions sometimes become another level of "make-do" that does not fully satisfy the needs of the organization. With careful planning, you may be able to create an addition that fulfills a broad set of needs.
- Will the addition satisfy the majority of resident needs? Money is sometimes spent on projects that benefit only a small proportion of the population. Gardens for wanderers are a good example of this.
- How will the added feature blend in with the existing facilities, materials, and circulation?
- How will the materials, chemicals, and procedures used affect the existing population? For example, the removal or enclosure of asbestos in an existing building or the use of particular sealants or chemical finishes may require protection for contractors, staff members, and residents. Leaching a urine-soaked floor may require evacuation to minimize the exposure to toxic substances or unpleasant odors. Temporary closures, acceptable in other circumstances, may be hazardous to older people who do see well or who lack judgment. Breezes from an open area may invite confused older people to explore; screens, doors, and windows must be secure.

Is This Change Worth the Investment?

One of the most difficult questions that a sponsor must think through is this: What is the life-cycle value of this change? It is sometimes necessary to call in professionals to look at the life span of mechanical systems, roofs, building structures, fire and life safety systems, asbestos removal, changing site conditions, parking additions, and the facilities themselves. Sponsors, board members, and owners sometimes raise another question: Will the facility be marketable as a nursing home in the next two or more decades? To answer that question, look at the facility itself and consider its location and competition.

Cost Comparison Techniques   A comparison of the costs of renovating an existing facility versus constructing a new one often proves helpful. The analyses must include capital or hard costs, operational impact such as new staff or lost days of resident/patient revenue, and any interim cost such as catered needs. Directions for making a simple set of calculations follow:

1. List the changes you are considering.
2. Calculate the square footage involved per room, and multiply by the number of rooms affected. Preliminary calculations usually involve inside room dimensions (net square footage). This is the usable space from the consumer's point of view.
3. Add a factor for grossing. Grossing accounts for the thickness of the walls, supporting mechanical spaces, and spaces like stairwells and hallways that are not listed as net areas. These computations vary according to such factors as whether the net areas include mechanical systems and whether the corridors have nooks, seating niches, or features like recessed doorways. Grossing may range from about 1.6 to 1.74 times the net square footage for resident-use areas along an 8-foot (2.5 meter) corridor, but it may be 1.54 to 1.6 for office areas. An additional three percent may be added where room changes involve expansion of mechanical space. Square foot analyses and costs are not complete without a thorough analysis of the net areas plus the gross areas affected.
4. Add together any special costs related to these changes, such as asbestos removal or bringing other systems into compliance, and any demolition costs.
5. Add to the subtotal a factor for all the fees involved (design, cost estimation, construction, legal, and filing). About 15% to 31% of the subtotal may be appropriate. This may not include planning costs for study of various alternatives.
6. Add any operational costs associated with lost beds, the purchase of temporary services, moving, filing, and so on.
7. Multiply the total square footage by current costs for nursing home renovations. These might range from $67 to over $140 per square foot ($622 to $1300 per square meter), depending on local

economy and labor situations, the amount of plumbing, and the complexity of the systems involved in the renovation. Some refurbishment projects cost less; they range from $35 to $90 per square foot (or $325 to $835 per square meter).

8. Add together the costs calculated in Steps 6 and 7. This is the cost for renovation. Set it aside.
9. Estimate new construction costs by calculating the total square footage from net and gross areas and multiplying it by the cost per square foot (which may be less than the renovation figure, depending on complexity).
10. Add costs for financing, moving, and lost revenue.
11. Also add land costs, fees, and professional charges for zoning. The result is the cost for new construction.
12. Add to the figure in Step 8 a contingency for unexpected discoveries during renovation, and to the figure in Step 11 add one for client changes during construction. These contingencies may be as low as 3% to 5%, especially when the client has worked with the design team on a specific design program document, or they may be as high as 10% when the client or board are known for indecisiveness, written documents and decisions are scarce, or work has begun without program consensus.
13. Compare the results.

Executives or management staff are sometimes asked to draft space programs for refurbishment or renovation projects for others to use in estimating costs before hiring a planner, architect, and cost estimator familiar with this form of architecture. It is tempting to arbitrarily choose dimensions, pick a square foot cost, and run with the numbers. Such projects invariably result in disappointment or changes, especially when cost or square footage expectations are established on the basis of net area without appropriate grossing factors.

New facilities that are functionally accessible to wheelchair users, have distinct spaces for dining and programs, and offer at least one bathroom for every two people average about 500 square feet (46.5 m²) per bed for the resident-use areas. This does not include public areas, clinics, laundry, pharmacy, religious areas, or multipurpose rooms. Figures as high as 700 to 750 square feet (65 to 70 m²) per bed are becoming more common in the state-of-the-art facilities. Many recently constructed facilities, however, offer less than 400 square feet (37 m²) per bed due to construction or cost ceilings or "caps" adopted by their states. These caps are not based on current operational data nor on space implications of meeting full accessibility criteria. In facilities of this size, it is difficult to offer efficient care to people who are in wheelchairs and participate in group dining or programs. These facilities might be more effective if they house a different population. For example, they might serve less frail older people. Many older nursing homes were designed for a population with only 25% in wheelchairs. These facilities may be remodeled to serve assisted living residents or populations that do not require as many prosthetic devices or utility areas or high levels of staffing.

A basic comparison can be made among facilities by calculating square footage per bed (or person). Although states often have minimums or even maximums for new facilities it is helpful to relate your facility's size to different comparison groups, to others in your state, to newer buildings, and to state-of-the-art facilities. In general, nursing units under 500 square feet (46.5 m^2) per bed have less architectural access, more people to a bathroom, fewer bathrooms, and share dining with activity space. Newer, state-of-the-art facilities with full access, better designed toilet rooms, more toilet rooms, better options for on-unit dining and activity space, and more functional bedrooms are running closer to 525 net square feet (49 m^2) per bed in the nursing unit, exclusive of chapels or auditoria and clinics and support space such as kitchens, laundries, and administrative suites.

Calculate the square footage associated with direct patient care by summarizing the area you have for bedrooms, bathrooms or toilets, nursing stations, and on-unit service or dining facilities. It is appropriate to use gross square footage for these areas in some states and net square footage in others. Include any spaces that are adjacent to bedrooms. Divide by the licensed capacity or the capacity used to determine the square footage per bed for resident-use areas. If your facility has resident areas on some floors and dining and program areas on other floors, these calculations may need further interpretation. A facility often looks as though it has generous amounts of space when you add in the total square footage for all program and resident-use areas, including those off the unit. Do all of the residents actually get off of their unit and use these areas? If so, the facility is probably in good shape. If, in fact, the residents are not using these facilities, you may need to develop programs, such as in-house day care for dementia clients or a transport corps, that move people to these areas, as appropriate.

4
Trouble-Shooting

Troubleshooting involves focusing planning and designing on select priorities. This chapter includes problems and solutions common to many nursing homes. When planning a renovation, it is valuable to work with a representative cross section of the nursing home's constituents (those who live, work, or visit there). Direct care workers have particularly valuable insights on operations. People often have special knowledge of areas that affect them the most. Residents and their families are often struck by bedrooms, entries, dining rooms, and social areas; they may miss the significance of support spaces. Staff members, on the other hand, sometimes focus on utility areas, staff stations, meeting rooms, and hallways; they overlook bedrooms and bathrooms—the basic building block of the nursing home—which are certainly as important to their ability to operate effectively as are other spaces. If you fail to obtain a good sampling of views, you might end up with a somewhat skewed image of the facility.

This chapter details some of the most common issues that arise in nursing home design related to eight areas that are usually the focus of many operational problems: bedrooms, toilet areas, bathrooms, nursing and staff work areas, utility spaces, social areas, dining rooms, and outdoor areas. Your facility may have other rooms, but they will share some of the features of the spaces discussed here. Each section begins with a list of problems that site visits have shown to be common to many facilities. Then a series of objectives is offered to help you plan your own. Finally, approaches are discussed for working with the social and physical environments to meet these objectives. These lists are not meant to be exhaustive; personalize them to suit your particular needs and add to the suggestions offered.

BEDROOMS

Bedrooms are where people live. They are a focus of morning care and important to marketability or image building. Bedroom changes may help realize many of the goals of The Nursing Home Reform Act in the United States or similar concerns over humanism and access heard worldwide.

After reading the objectives and approaches, you may want to convert the information to statements applicable to your own facility. That is, take those items from the approaches that apply to your objectives and create your own "to–by" statements.

Common Problems

- The bedrooms provide inadequate visual privacy for residents.
- The bedrooms and their resources are divided unequally among occupants, or there is inadequate identifiable territory.
- The space within bedrooms for maneuvering wheelchairs or using storage is insufficient for residents' needs.
- The bedrooms look shabby or disorganized.
- Individual bedrooms all appear similar; there is no personalization.

Special Problems

- Multibed rooms are common within the facility.
- Residents do not have a view to the outside from their bedrooms, or the view is inadequate.

Objectives

- To provide each resident with adequate visual privacy.
- To allocate bedroom space and resources equally among occupants, and to provide each person with identifiable territory.
- To provide sufficient space within bedrooms for maneuvering and storage.
- To give each bedroom a fresh and comfortable appearance.
- To personalize bedrooms for their occupants.
- To minimize multibed rooms or the problems associated with multibed rooms.
- To offer residents a view to the outside (preferably a view to the ground).

The approaches that follow offer possibilities for how to respond to these problems.

Approaches

Conduct an environmental inventory (see Chapter 2) or review previously collected data to determine which problems you will address. Identify the functional characteristics and needs of your resident population, the activities that can or must take place within the room, and the furnishings and equipment that must be located there, and review a schedule of room use. Then consider the social and physical solutions that follow and identify those that are most appropriate for your facility.

Social Solutions

- Occupants of multibed rooms may require actual privacy (solitude) and sensory privacy (acoustic and visual aloneness or control). To provide some semblance of visual privacy, consider ways to divide the room without compromising light, sprinklers, or access. For

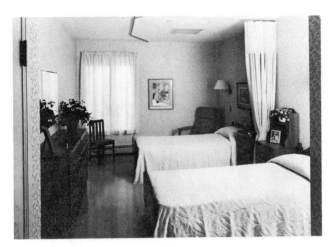

Fig. 4–1 Optimizing visual privacy. In two-bed rooms, where the beds are arranged side-by-side, you can improve visual privacy through the judicious placement of curtains (almost as a canopy bed) or hutch-style bedside stands (in this position or back-to-back). Do not allow the new arrangement to impede access to light or circulation paths. In this case, the curtains are near to the end of the bed. (By Hoffman Partnership, Inc., for The Argyle.)

example, use a 4-ft-tall (1.25m) hutch or bedside stand to separate the heads of two adjacent beds (Figure 4–1). If you cannot provide actual solitude in the bedroom, consider other places in the building where residents can experience solitude, enjoy a visitor or telephone call in privacy, or just escape from the stimulation of other people. Plan this solution on an individual basis and do not allow it to become a "sentence" to privacy. Toilet stalls sometimes provide some of this privacy—though you should be able to offer better options than that!

- If some bedrooms offer better resources than others (for example, greater access to windows, natural light, or seating), involve residents and their families in developing a new system for assigning these beds. You may find that lotteries and options for quarterly change are preferable to seniority.
- If floor space varies among residents, consider ways to compensate. For example, give greater storage space to the occupants of the less spacious sleeping areas.
- Use storage items to reinforce a sense of territory by clearly identifying closets or wardrobes.
- If bedrooms with inadequate space are a problem for some residents, determine whether it would help to reassign rooms on the basis of physical and equipment requirements. That is, give the largest rooms to the residents with the greatest need for space, regardless of whether they are Medicaid recipients. (Some sponsors allocate better bedroom space to "private-pay" clients or feel that shared occupancy rooms should only be for government supported care. Some governments allow sponsors to charge more to private-pay clients, and sponsors try to attract them to increase their revenue.) When the lack of adequate space hinders resident independence or the efficient delivery of services, it becomes an operational cost through increased

Fig. 4–2 Staggered bed arrangement. Where space is adequate and the state allows it, staggering the beds may afford each resident a greater semblance of privacy and improved window access. (By Eden Design Associates, Inc., for American Village Skilled Care, Indianapolis, Indiana.)

staff time. Therefore, inadequate room space should be equally important to government, voluntary, and proprietary nursing homes.

- Check with your state's department of health to explore alternate ways of arranging the bedroom furniture. They may allow you to position one or more beds against a wall, thus increasing the usable area within the room (Figure 4–2).
- Rooms that look shabby or disorganized must be dealt with through refurbishment or community effort. Whatever the situation, it is best to be forthright about room appearance. Why does the room look shabby? What's being done? What are a family's options in the meantime? (See Figure 4–3.) Encouraging residents to bring possessions from home sometimes solves minor appearance problems, such as repetition or lack of texture.
- When you personalize a resident's space, you give it an individual character and improve its identifiability. There are many options for personalizing bedrooms. Consider the following, for example. Allow residents to bring items from home, like a safe, personal chair, and to decorate their rooms with fire-rated chair cushions, bedspreads, pillow shams, or coverlets of their own choosing. Make sure that these items are compatible with the institution's laundry facilities (or that the family will launder them), and consider smoke and fire safety when approving all selections. Ask residents and their families to provide decorative items for a dresser, shelf, bedside stand, or bulletin board (Figures 4–4 and 4–5). When repainting, use nonglare paint or a border print selected by the resident to give the room a fresh look. Border prints are available with removable adhesive backings that permit quick changes. If someone will be available to tend them, hanging plants in individualized containers add a pleasant touch to a room. Distinctive lamps and shades can also help to

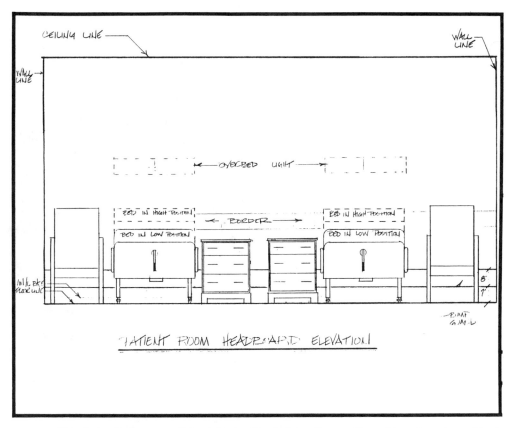

Fig. 4–3 Bedroom wall treatments. By studying the position of headboards and horizontal lines created by windows or other room elements, a good location for a decorative border print was selected. Such features protect walls and lend the appearance of organization to a room. (By Eden Design Associates, Inc., Carmel, Indiana.)

personalize bedrooms. Touch-operated lamps are available through popular consumer catalogs.

- Sponsors in some states commonly use multibed rooms for public assistance or Medicaid recipients or clients who pay less than others. In the spirit of turning lemons into lemonade, some sponsors have established programs to make the most of these spaces. One nursing home developed a "constant care" program for bedridden people who require constant attention. These residents are effectively served in multibed rooms, which can be gaily decorated to minimize a sense of second-class service. Another nursing home developed a cooperative care program for rehabilitation residents, who serve as role models for each other and become sources of information and inspiration. The length of stay is limited to three months to ensure the privacy needs of those who require long periods of care. Would any subset of this population benefit from the companionship of a multibed room?

Fig. 4-4 Bedroom storage and display. Built-in cabinets give bedrooms the look of apartment rooms and offer storage for heavy personal items.

- Fresh air and outside views are important for a resident's health and well-being. They often aid disposition and reduce the sense of confinement. When residents do not have a view to the outside from their bedrooms, encourage staff members to describe weather conditions and to bring individuals to an area where they can see outside for themselves.

Physical Solutions

- Try these techniques to improve visual privacy in bedrooms:

  1. Use a tall hutch, placed perpendicular to the wall, to block off a portion of the room (Figures 4-1 and 4-2). This arrangement must not block access to needed equipment, and the hutches should be readily moveable to respond to emergencies or the changing needs of residents that affect bedside caregiving or use of special equipment such as portable oxygen.
  2. If state codes and the available area permit, place two hutches in a row between beds, one facing each bed. Cover the back of each

Fig. 4–5 Room personalization. Tackable walls (or a maintenance staff willing to hang and repaint frequently) allow a room to be transformed by personal belongings. These should be hung in an eye-pleasing arrangement using the site line of features, such as mirrors or other strong horizontal elements.

hutch with a vertically fire-rated material and use it as a bulletin board. If you do not fully understand the fire ratings, consult an architect or interior designer who is familiar with your state's hospital or health facility specifications. A material may be safe for floor use (based on horizontal testing methods), but it may not be approved by the American Standard Testing Methods (ASTM) for vertical use. Do not be reluctant to ask for fire-safety and flammability information from designers, suppliers, or manufacturers. You must have such product information on file. The state of California has particularly stringent requirements and may serve as a standard for textiles and furnishings.

3. Install individual privacy curtains and tracks at the head of each bed to give individuals the option of controlling their own space without cutting off full use of the room. This technique may be more useful in some rooms than in others, and it assumes that the beds are maintained in one primary position (Figure 4–1).

- If there is insufficient space in bedrooms for maneuvering, consider working with smaller furnishings or equipment. For example, the average bed is between 78″ and 94″ long (198 and 239 cm) and requires 3″ (8 cm) from the head wall. (Some older models and some newer ones designed for clinical uses, such as reduction of decubiti ulcers, are longer.) Would smaller beds or a variety of sizes increase usable space within bedrooms? Beds in institutions usually have footboards that beds at home lack. The footboard sometimes can be removed without affecting the mechanical operation or sturdiness of the bed. (Contact the manufacturer and test the bed before adopting such changes.) Removing the footboard often increases elbow room for self-wheeling and may minimize wall damage.

- Where appropriate, consider switching residents to the new, streamlined wheelchairs. They turn more efficiently and have a smaller profile than older models. Remember, though, that wheelchairs must be fitted to individuals the way that glasses are prescribed. Not everyone can use the streamlined chairs. Those who can may be able to negotiate narrower passage ways and smaller toilet rooms. Explore also alternatives to the large, uncollapsable geriatric wheelchairs.

- Determine whether there are places other than the bedroom where wheelchairs can be stored. For example, try removing them at night for washing and returning them in the early morning. Consider using stackable chairs for visitors. These could be stored in a central place to leave more room in bedrooms for the occupants.

- Publicize areas for visiting outside the bedroom. Families often are unaware of acceptable places for visiting or are unsure whether they are available. Develop a simple handout to let visitors know about good places for visiting and how to deal with bedroom drawbacks, such as scheduled clinical care or cleaning. Create some comfortable places for families to gather or share a meal or beverage with residents.

- If there is insufficient space in bedrooms for storage, consult Table 4–1. It lists some methods of getting more storage space from existing facilities. Table 4–2 also addresses options for better storage. Residents find it difficult to manage without at least 18″ (46 cm) of linear hanging storage space (3′ or 91 cm would be preferred) and three 18″ by 18″ drawers, especially for a stay of one week or more.

- If the bedrooms look shabby or disorganized, consult Table 4–3. It lists ways to improve appearance through interior design. Some of the suggestions in Table 4–2 also may be helpful.

- There are no quick solutions for the problems associated with multibed rooms. Rooms with two, three, and four beds face different problems.

  1. Two-bed rooms. It is often difficult to provide equal territory in two-bed rooms when one bed is next to a wall, closet, or toilet room, and the other is next to a window (Figure 4–10). When adding or converting bedrooms, consider biaxial rather than asymmetric bed placement. Biaxial placement allows equal access to heat, light, seating, and circulation routes.

  2. Three-bed rooms. Options are usually the most limited when the room is deep and has a narrow wall of windows. The beds in the center and near the door are usually the least desirable. In this

Table 4–1 Approaches to Inadequate Personal Storage

1. Closets are inadequate or unreachable.
    a. Take a special look at wardrobe space. Consider alternatives to built-in storage for greater flexibility, alternative locations for hanging storage, and the use of taller dressers to expand storage (Figure 4–6).
    b. Consider popular closet-shop systems, such as pull-out hanger rods or double rows of closet rods with suspension hangers. (See Coen & Bryan, 1988, listed in Bibliography.)
    c. Upgrade closet doors for safety and appearance. Consider sturdy accordian doors for easier access. The hardware must be sturdy, and the door will probably need tracks at the top and bottom.
2. There is insufficient space for personal hygiene products.
    a. In bedrooms, consider a bedside table with hutch.
    b. Offer lockable storage areas for valuables, thus making more room available in drawers to store hygiene products.
    c. Obtain surface-mounted cupboards or corner cabinets to use in bedrooms or bathrooms.
    d. Add storage vanities in bathrooms.
    e. Shower room lockers might also provide protection for individual supplies.
3. There is no place to store soiled personal laundry.
    a. Consider creating individual receptacles for bedrooms or bathrooms.
    b. Receptacles may be net bags, bags on frames, cleanable hampers, or plastic bags that dissolve in water. Regulations may vary regarding devices, requirements for separation, and materials that can be used for receptacles.
    c. Some sponsors wash personal laundry on the unit in specially designed laundry facilities. This can minimize loss and offer an area with appropriate ventilation to store soiled items.
    d. Consult with laundry professionals. Lists are available in national association directories, and many display at conventions. Make sure you talk with more than one sales representative.
    e. Check with your state's regulatory agency before implementing a new plan.

situation, alternatives to the bedroom are important. Consider ways to compensate residents in center beds. Can they be accorded especially good seats at the dinner table? Are there any areas elsewhere in the facility where they can have a special space? Look for ways to clearly delineate territory within three-bed rooms, unless the occupants jointly request otherwise. For example, you might use individual bedspreads or pillow cases, or

Table 4–2 Bedroom Furnishings and Equipment

A. CHAIRS
  1. The bedroom is unsuitable for individual body mechanics or
     needs.
     Even people in wheelchairs need bedroom chairs to provide
     variety in seating surfaces and minimize pressure sores. (See
     "Chairs and Seating" in Chapter 6.)
     a. Involve family members and professionals who are
        knowledgeable about body positioning in the chair selection
        and acquisition process.
     b. When you have no other means of personalizing the fit of
        the chair, consider "chair inserts," back aids, or cushions.
B. BEDS
  1. The beds are unsafe. For example, they cannot be lowered far
     enough, or they have siderails that do not work.
     a. When ordering new beds, make sure they are the proper
        length, preferably less than 90″, and have appropriate design
        features.
     b. Consider the selective replacement of particularly
        problematic beds or rails. Consult with manufacturers
        regarding replacement parts.
  2. Beds cannot be raised or lowered. This often inconveniences
     staff members when providing bedside care or making beds.
     Many states require adjustable beds.
     a. Consider the selective use of "high-low beds" if costs are of
        concern. High-low beds vary height only, not the angle of
        head or foot placement.
     b. Some beds allow selective mechanization: They may mix
        mechanical and automatic operations for height or angles.
        Consider those options that respond to present population
        needs and revenue. Some special-feature beds are required
        for health care, and costs may be covered through various
        insurance or government programs.
C. BEDSIDE STANDS AND DRESSERS
  1. Bedside furniture rolls or shifts when residents lean on it.
     a. Use wheel locks on bedside furnishings, especially for
        residents who must lean on them for support.
     b. Replace wheels with gliders.
     c. Consider the stability of the item when making a purchase.
  2. Drawers are inappropriately used.
     a. Empty the bedside stand of unneeded items, and place them
        in a specially designed cabinet in the toilet room or within
        reach of staff members.
     b. Return bedside storage areas to residents by providing
        drawers they can operate and reach.

(continued)

Table 4–2 (*Continued*)

      c. Consider installing drawer dividers if staff people have trouble with drawer organization.

D. DESKS
    1. Desks are rarely used, and most bedrooms have insufficient clothing storage.
      a. Consider converting the desk to a dual-function unit with more drawers and an optional writing area (Figure 4–7).
      b. Remove the desk, and replace it with appropriate storage items.
      c. Remove the desk, rearrange the beds, and create drawers under the windows.
    2. Desks date the room.
      a. Refinish them, remove them, or replace them.

E. TELEVISIONS
    1. Televisions are difficult to place in multibed rooms. Television sets are too high or too distant for easy viewing, or there is no place to put them because all surfaces are used or inappropriately located.
      a. Consider removing the televisions from the rooms.
      b. Consider smaller, personal television sets for individuals.
      c. Consider putting televisions on top of dressers or shelves and using Lazy Susans or similar devices to direct the sets toward the viewers.
    2. Televisions are too loud; they disturb roommates or can be heard in the hall.
      a. Inexpensive, wireless devices available through health catalogs or electronics suppliers permit individual volume control at very little cost. Closed-loop systems are also available for use in larger areas or with multiple listeners.
      b. Consider placing smaller televisions on bedside stands so the volume may be lowered.

you might personalize the areas behind each bed. Conversion is sometimes the best course of action (Figures 4–11 and 4–12).

3. Four-bed rooms. Some four-bed rooms are fairly generous in space beside the bed and for a social area. The problems that arise relate to providing space for solitude and acoustic and visual privacy. Four-bed rooms are sometimes more acceptable for short stays, when people have similar needs and are sociable. Four-bed rooms sometimes can be converted into three-bed rooms or into combinations of singles and two-bed rooms (Figures 4–13 to 4–16). This will, of course, reduce the bed count unless an addition is planned elsewhere. Retain an architectural firm to study your particular plans, window placements, and options.

Fig. 4–6 Wardrobe types. Wardrobes can look like closets, yet they avoid the need for sprinkler heads.

- To provide a better view, relocate or replace existing windows with windows of a different type (Figure 4–17). In making new bedroom windows, consider lowering the sill to 24–30″ (61–76 cm) from the finished floor.

TOILET AREAS

Toilet rooms are central to dignity and caregiving. In far too many facilities, the room configuration, size, fixture placement, doorway width or door style have created additional reliance on diapers or pads for people who are incontinent. Current medical and nursing literature support a more proactive toileting program and more upright toileting for improved elimination, hygiene, and skin care. While this requires a revolution in staff training, it also requires adequate toilets.

Fig. 4-7 Combined dresser and desk unit. Increase bedroom storage by replacing the desk with a series of drawers. If one end corner is rounded and does not have base cabinets, it can be used as a writing surface.

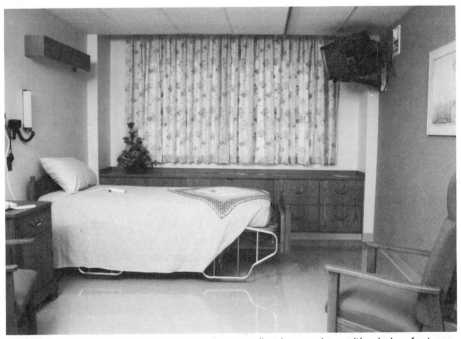

Fig. 4-8 Bedroom window treatment. Improve first impressions with window features and wall decor. A neat valence above vertical blinds provides easy maintenance and a more residential appearance than vertical blinds alone. Wider valences sometimes reduce glare as well. Other amenities shown here include shelves, tackable wall surfaces, and border prints that develop flat walls or vertical surfaces into more interesting, residential surfaces. (By Eden Design Associates, Inc., Carmel, Indiana.)

Table 4–3   Improving Bedroom Appearance Through Interior Design

A. FABRIC ITEMS
  1. Drapes
     a. Try vertical blinds, even though they look less residential than drapes. They are available in fire-rated fabrics.
     b. Use secure hardware, perhaps mounted as a ceiling track. Consult a drapery store or designer.
     c. For opening drapes, consider wand devices or methods other than pull cords.
     d. Use a valance at the top of the window to individualize rooms, even though the drapes themselves might be similar. Valances can also be used with vertical blinds, which are sometimes called "verticals" (Figure 4–8).
     e. Return individual drapes to the proper place by labelling both drapes and rod with an identification code (room and location key).
     f. When replacing window coverings, meet flammability regulations. Note also that some verticals are made out of dense, noise abatement materials.
  2. Privacy Curtains
     a. Consider the ensemble effect of privacy curtains, window curtains, bedspreads, and other furnishings (Figure 4–9). Use people with design coordination training as needed. Label curtain and rod or track to assist in identification and matching after laundering.
     b. Colorful and coordinated curtains made of fire-rated materials are displayed at many larger health facilities conventions.
     c. Simple, muted, bedside curtains in a textured weave may blend well with colorful window curtains. Cubicle curtains should sometimes be the same color as the wall to make them less apparent in an otherwise residential room (Figure 4–1).
  3. Bedspreads
     a. Consider whether bedspreads might be brought from home or individualized in some other way. If you try this approach, you must develop procedures for laundering and meet flammability standards and state requirements.
     b. It is not necessary that all bedspreads within the same room match. It is sometimes more important that residents are able to identify an area of the room as their own. You may obtain a coordinated look through color, materials, or an interesting blend of patterns.
  4. Chair upholstery. Problems with chairs that are loose, tattered, or falling apart must be resolved.
     a. Investigate whether residents can bring chairs from home.

(continued)

Table 4–3 (*Continued*)

       b. Consider refurbishing dilapidated chairs. Some vintage chairs are sturdy and worth refurbishing. (See "Chairs and Seating" in Chapter 6.)

       c. Not all residents are incontinent, and most incontinent people need not have an entire chair made of nonabsorbent materials. Backrests, armrests, and chair sides and back view may look conventional. Seats may be removed and cared for as needed.

B. WALLS AND WALL COVERINGS

  1. Glare or shiny paint. Glare is discomforting to the vision of older people and staff members.

       a. Repaint with nonglare paints.

       b. Matte-finish wall coverings of all types are preferable to reflective surfaces.

  2. Dirty walls or apparent discoloration

       a. Clean and repaint if walls are dirty.

       b. Discoloration may suggest problems like moisture, smoke, lamps that are too close to the wall, poor quality paint, or paint over an oily or soiled base or over wall covering adhesive.

  3. An accent wall (one that is decidedly darker or bolder than the others) makes the room appear small.

       a. Keep all the walls within a single room light and of similar tones.

       b. Do not alter rooms that look small if the colors reflect the occupants' choice.

  4. Bold, vibrant, or controversially bright walls sometimes diminish individuals and their possessions. These colors and patterns are often not chosen by residents.

       a. Consider allowing residents to choose the room color and a border of strippable vinyl.

       b. Select colors that allow people and their possessions to be the focal points.

       c. See Chapter 6 for recommendations on color, pattern, and personalization.

C. FURNISHINGS AND CLOSETS

  1. Damaged or mismatched dressers or bedside stands

       a. Replace damaged furnishings as needed.

       b. Consider leasing furniture if purchase poses problems.

       c. Explore used or discount furniture sources, such as hospitals, other nursing homes, and manufacturers' outlets. You can find advertisements for these in nursing home magazines, or contact your national nursing home purchasing plan for additional sources and contacts.

Fig. 4–9 Bedroom interiors. Bedspreads may match walls and window coverings but vary them from room to room to avoid monotony and to improve the identifiability of individual rooms.

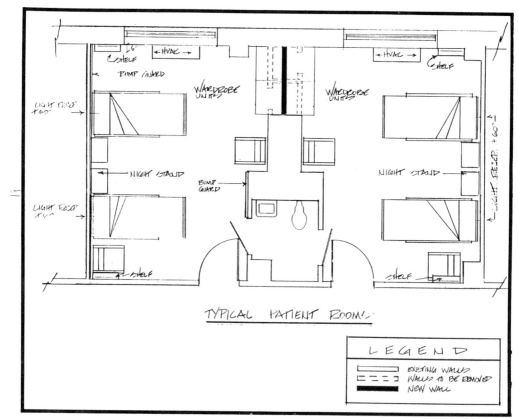

Fig. 4–10 Standard two-bed room with closet modification. To increase clothing storage areas, add dresser drawers and wardrobes with adjustable shelves and poles to two-bed rooms. (By Eden Design Associates, Inc., Carmel, Indiana.)

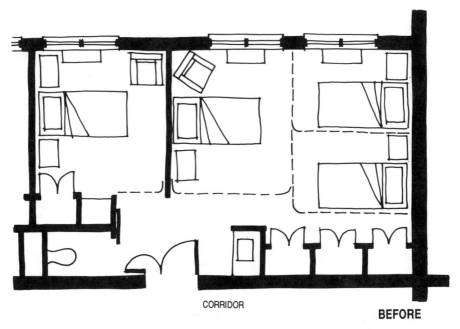

Fig. 4–11 Before renovation of three-bed room. A combination of improvements may be possible for narrow room configurations, such as this triple with adjacent single rooms. (By Timothy C. Boers, Boulder Associates Architects, Boulder, Colorado, for Hooverwood Jewish Home, Indianapolis, Indiana.)

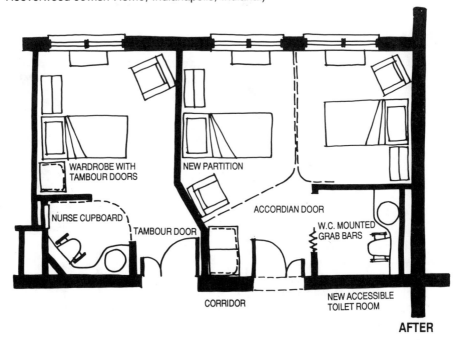

Fig. 4–12 After renovation of three-bed room. Irregular partitions and variations on privacy curtain placement made possible this conversion to three singles with an additional, more accessible toilet room. The tambour door on the bathroom (left) resembles a roll-top desk on its side. (By Timothy C. Boers, Boulder Associates Architects, Boulder, Colorado, for Hooverwood Jewish Home, Indianapolis, Indiana.)

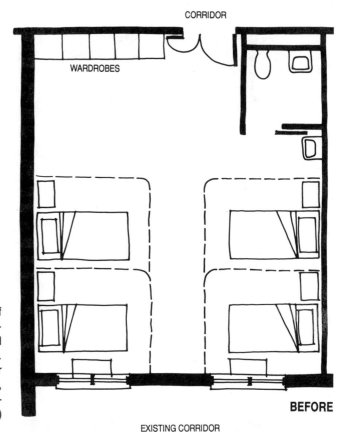

Fig. 4–13 Before renovation of four-bed room. This typical four-bed room has a consolidated wardrobe area and shared toilet. (By Timothy C. Boers, Boulder Associates Architects, Boulder, Colorado, for Hooverwood Jewish Home, Indianapolis, Indiana.)

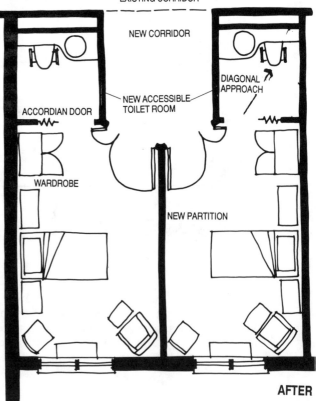

Fig. 4–14 After renovation of four-bed room. The four-bed room here has been converted to two single rooms, each with a toilet room. The indented corridor can be used to minimize the storage of carts in the hallways, thereby reducing the institutional appearance of corridors during morning care. (By Timothy C. Boers, Boulder Associates Architects, Boulder, Colorado, for Hooverwood Jewish Home, Indianapolis, Indiana.)

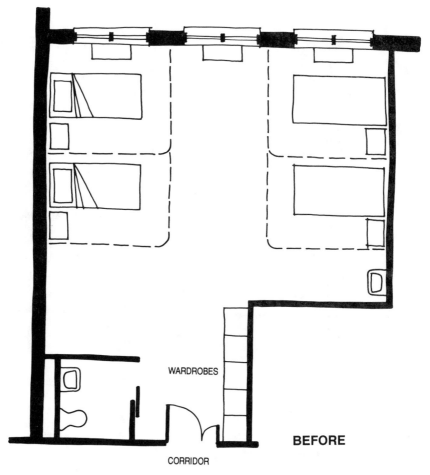

WARDROBES

BEFORE

CORRIDOR

Fig. 4–15 Before renovation of four-bed room with challenging windows and systems. Odd numbers of windows or a single large window surface pose special renovation challenges. Heating and controls require separation as well. (By Timothy C. Boers, Boulder Associates Architects, Boulder, Colorado.)

Common Problems

- The toilet areas do not have sufficient space to allow wheelchair users to transfer themselves independently or with one or two staff members assisting (Figures 4–18 and 4–19).
- The handrails are ineffective.
- The toilets are too low or too high for most people (less than 15″ or more than 18″).
- Visual privacy is compromised in the toilet areas.
- Commode chairs are widely used.
- Four or more residents share one toilet.
- The toilet areas are difficult to clean.
- The air is stale or malodorous.
- The toilet areas look stark.

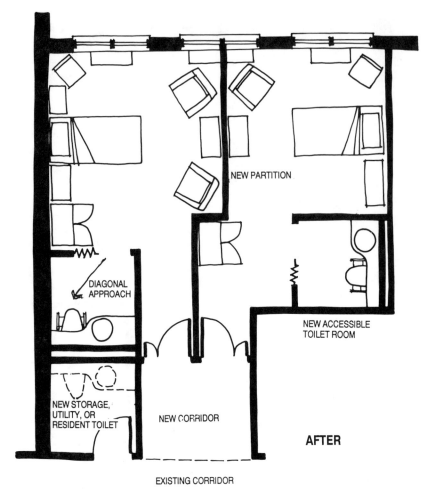

EXISTING CORRIDOR

Fig. 4–16 After renovation of four-bed room with challenging windows and systems. Window placements such as this one may require several approaches: replacement of the window, dual heating systems (or partitions that open cleverly), and an irregular wall divider. The result is two rooms and additional utility space. Toilets can sometimes be added to the corridor side in rooms less amenable to added bathrooms. (By Timothy C. Boers, Boulder Associates Architects, Boulder, Colorado, for Hooverwood Jewish Home, Indianapolis, Indiana.)

Special Problems

- The toilet rooms are clustered ("gang toilets").
- There is an insufficient number of toilets, or they are not located where needed.
- There are tubs in the toilet room, the tubs are unusable, and the floor area is too small for transfers (Figure 4–20).

Objectives

- To encourage resident independence and reduce staff time by providing easily accessible toilets with fixtures and doors that residents can operate without assistance (Figure 4–21).

Fig. 4–17 Bay windows. Bay windows that are low enough for window seats increase usable room area without adding to floor space. (By the Architects Collaborative, Cambridge, Massachusetts, for New York State Veterans Home, Oxford, New York.)

- To accommodate the need for visual privacy in toilet areas.
- To provide an appropriate number of toilets for the population and to locate them where they are needed.
- To reduce staff time by selecting materials and fixtures that are quickly and easily cleaned.
- To improve the appearance of toilet areas and minimize odors.

"By-statements" or responses to these objectives may be selected from among the approaches, as appropriate.

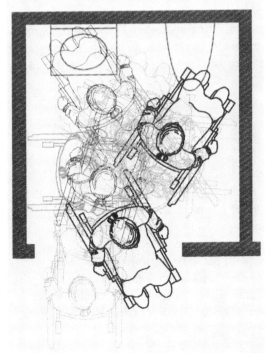

Fig. 4–18 Functional access. Wheelchair users rarely make a complete circle to turn around. Computer modeling and anthropometric research can be used to describe the shape and factors that assist mobility. (Model by L. Hiatt and Dale Tremain, Ellerbe Beckett, Minneapolis, Minnesota.)

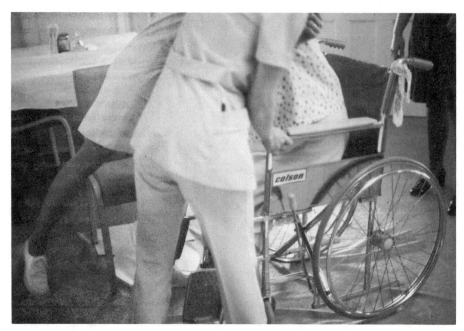

Fig. 4–19 Demonstrating a two-person transfer. Some people cannot easily stand by themselves, and due to body mass or available space, they may require a two-person transfer. Toilet and tub rooms must accommodate these more complex requirements.

Approaches

While you are in the planning stage, consult with members of the nursing, housekeeping, and therapy departments. They may be able to identify problems with the existing toilet areas and to offer helpful suggestions for the future design. After you have developed a plan, test it out in a mock-up or in one toilet area. Obtain staff reactions before making widespread changes. Changes in toilet rooms may involve asbestos risks. Work with architects and professionals licensed to offer options for renovations where asbestos must be contained.

Social Solutions

- Develop a formal program of systematic toilet training for all levels of care. A toilet training program is as much for the staff as it is for older people who are vulnerable to incontinence.
- Train staff members in efficient transfer techniques, including methods for working in existing toilet rooms. Using clothed staff or resident models, take still photographs to illustrate safe methods of transfer. Make these photographs available to temporary staff members. Train residents to work with the existing toilet room features.
- The widespread use of commode chairs often signals poor toilet facilities. Problems may include distant location, inaccessible toilet rooms, an insufficient number of toilets, and poor handrail configura-

Fig. 4–20 Before renovation of small bathroom with underused tub. Some nursing homes have tubs in many bathrooms that go unused because older people need help to get in and out, and there is insufficient space for staff assistance and transfer devices like lifts.

tion. The ultimate solution rests in correcting these underlying problems, not in adding more commode chairs.

- Commode or portable toilet chairs are not a satisfactory solution to toileting problems. They may be helpful in the short term, however, by providing an accessible toilet near the bed with sufficient space for a safe transfer. They also provide an appropriate height for safe toileting, and they offer support on both sides of the toilet where it is needed. Most bathrooms offer support on only one side, although there are alternatives (Figures 4–22 and 4–23).
- When commode chairs are used, privacy must be a constant consideration. Do not use multiple portable toilets in sight of each other. Ideally, other residents should not be in the room when the toilet is being used. Shield the user with privacy curtains or similar screens.

Fig. 4–21 Accordion doors. Placed on closets or bathrooms, accordion doors are easier than swing-style doors for residents to open and close.

- Do not overlook safety and hygiene issues when commode chairs are used. Make sure that residents have access to the call system and that staff members do not abandon them if they need assistance. Proper disposal and sanitation of the commode are essential. Develop specific routines to minimize contamination, odor, distance, and time. Also develop procedures for resident and staff handwashing.
- If two or more users share one toilet room, consider creating grooming areas elsewhere, like in the bedroom or in a niche in the shower room or hallway (Figure 4–24).
- Minimize odors by flushing toilets immediately after use and airing out toilet rooms when residents are away from the area. Clean the floor thoroughly; consult suppliers regarding appropriate methods for your flooring. Ceramic tile grout is more likely to retain urine odor than is sheet rubber designed for toilet room floor use, and it must be carefully cleaned. Check the aroma of cleaning supplies. A chemical need not smell harsh to work effectively.

Fig. 4–22 Options for toilet safety hardware. New devices respond to the needs of older people for various types of support not typically provided by fixed, wall-mounted single-side hardware: (top left) bars on either side of the water closet; (top right) swing-down, U-shaped bar behind toilet with comfortable arm rests; (bottom) other options, including fixed, wall-mounted bars and floor-mounted devices.

Physical solutions

- If there are too few toilet rooms (fewer than one toilet for every four residents, for example), consider adding toilet areas or reconfiguring existing rooms to increase their usefulness. Toilet rooms can sometimes be created from hallway closet areas or in multibed rooms. With today's residents becoming increasingly vulnerable to incontinence, providing toilet rooms is a key to optimizing toilet training.

Fig. 4–23 Toilet room with rails mounted on the water closet. Because few older people use side or parallel transfers, hardware that works like chair armrests eases their use of the toilet. A simple border print or some artwork may transform a utilitarian toilet room into a space that supports the time spent here. (KKE Architects/Spaces Interiors, Minneapolis, MN for River Garden, Jacksonville, FL.)

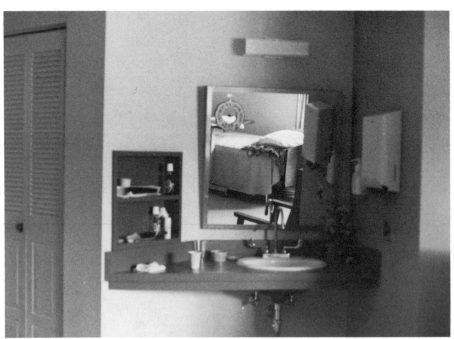

Fig. 4–24 Sink in bedroom. In some states, a sink must be added to the bedroom when more than two people share a toilet. The sinks may be more useful when designed to fit the room's decor. Here, sink, vanity, mirror, and sundries are provided. (Sponsor designed, Presbyterian Home of Central New York.)

An insufficient number of toilets reinforces the use of underpads or diapering and "briefs," which is ultimately less desirable than incontinence management through upright toileting.

- In individual toilet rooms, consider the best ways to use the floor area. Sturdy, toilet-mounted handrails may clear some floor area for a two-person transfer. Alternatives to solid, swing-style doors may increase independent use and facilitate use with wheelchairs.
- If you are planning new toilet rooms, consider the following:

  1. Place both sink and toilet fixtures on the same wall and directly opposite the opening to minimize the steps and turning required and to optimize space for transfer.
  2. Make the opening as wide as possible (even 4 feet, 1.25 m, or more) to minimize wall damage.
  3. Place the opening diagonally across from the toilet to facilitate wheelchair use if less than full width doorway is possible (such as when allowing folding doors to collect to one side).
  4. Allow at least 18″ (46 cm) from the edge of the toilet to any wall or projection to enable staff members to maneuver in a two-person transfer. Some minimum standards require only 18″ from the center line of the toilet to the wall. This generally does not allow adequate space for staff members to provide the necessary assistance at the person's side.
  5. Use sturdy accordion doors; these are easier than rigid doors for people in wheelchairs to open.
  6. Place the sink in a banjo-shaped counter that is securely attached to the wall and can be used to lean on (Figure 4–25).
  7. Use a toilet with a recessed base, which is easier to clean.
  8. Include good ventilation and appropriate air change and pressure relationships in the design plans.
  9. Provide a secure vanity with leg room beneath. Make space available above the vanity for grooming and other supplies to keep the counter clear.
  10. Provide a storage area for staff supplies or utensils and even goods like diapers. Consider, for example, the space between the studs of the wall in an area that will not interfere with safe transfer. This storage area is sometimes called a *nurse server;* it frees the bedside stand for resident use and may also encourage handwashing by staff.

- Improve the appearance of toilet areas through the judicious use of wall coverings, lighting, mirrors, and shelving. When refurbishing, use nonglare paint, vinyl wall covering, or border prints for decoration. A lighting level of 60 to 80 foot-candles is best for these areas. Wash or replace lens covers, and choose indirect lighting sources. Select a mirror that fills the entire area behind the sink and adds to the residential quality of the space. This is preferable to a tilt-style

Fig. 4–25 After renovation of small bathroom with underused tub. Remove underused tubs to make space for better wheelchair access and perhaps a larger, more contemporary sink. If the tub is located along a corridor wall, a portion of the space may be used to create corridor storage, such as for clean linen. A larger mirror, a storage area, and a vanity were added here. Ceramic tile was replaced with sheet rubber flooring, and the lighting was improved throughout the toilet room by using one long fluorescent fixture. Note that when the vanity covers the tanktop toilet, it is divided and hinged for easy access to the water closet for repairs. Grab bars are better on each side of the water closet, though this is not supported by some state regulations. (By SFCS, Inc., Roanoke, Virginia.)

mirror. Or use a lower mirror that is visible to those in wheelchairs. Provide recessed shelves of an appropriate height for grooming supplies.

- Improve safety of toilet areas through the following techniques:

  1. Repair floors when necessary.
  2. Provide secure, toilet-mounted handrails on both sides of the toilet, if space permits, and a well-blocked, wall-mounted, horizontal bar to be used as a balancing surface (see Figure 4–22a). The latter is sometimes helpful when removing and replacing undergarments.
  3. Relocate any dispensers that are in the way of residents or staff.
  4. When replacing floors or adding new toilet areas, select sheet rubber flooring rather than ceramic tile. If ceramic tile must be used, seal the grout against odors.
  5. Tailor toilet seat height to the needs of residents; their feet should touch the floor when seated. This may require the use of seat extenders to increase the height of the toilet.
  6. Avoid placing showers or tubs in unsupervised areas, such as toilet rooms adjacent to bedrooms. Most nursing home clients

require assistance with bathing. Accessible showers and tubs require more space than is usually available in bathrooms for one or two residents. The floor must also be kept dry, which presents other requirements. This is why bathing areas are often planned for individual use by 5 to 15 different people, with staff supervision.

- Minimize the time staff members spend cleaning by improving the lighting in toilet areas and sealing the grout on ceramic floors. (Consult a contractor or hardware store for recommendations. Look for products like Ardex™.)
- Minimize odors by consulting with a mechanical engineer or licensed specialist regarding the air handling system. Cleaning, filter changes, and minor adjustments sometimes result in great improvements. Remember that cover-up aromas do not solve odor problems and, if used, should not smell worse than the odor source itself.

BATHING ROOMS

Bathing rooms have developed an image of store rooms or worse. These spaces should be transformed for staff ease and resident experiences. Health club spas are a better role model. A key to the transformation may involve better fixtures, newer chair-style lifts, and better space planning. Usually, attention to aesthetics, air quality, and storage of clean and soiled utilities completes the transformation process.

Common Problems

- Bathing areas have inadequate humidity control or ventilation.
- The shower heads are fixed and cannot be directed easily.
- Shower facilities are poorly designed; staff members get wet.
- Bathing aids such as lifts are unavailable or difficult to operate or do not fit client capacities.
- There is insufficient space for the easy movement of wheelchairs.
- There is no space to store clean and soiled linens or grooming aids; too much space is used for equipment.
- Bathing areas compromise privacy.

Special Problems

- Bathing areas do not meet the special needs of some residents (for example, those who are obese, cannot balance easily, or require prone bathing).
- Residents are afraid of bathing.
- New bathers and lifts do not fit in existing spaces.
- The bathers are all centrally located, causing congestion and compromising efficiency and dignity as people travel to and from their rooms.

Objectives

- To provide a safe, private, hygienic, efficient, and pleasing bath or shower for every resident, three to seven times per week (with appropriate skin lubrication).
- To reduce the hazards of bathing, including the risk of falling.
- To increase the comfort and efficiency of the staff.

Approaches

Examine current bathing techniques and analyze more effective ways to use the bathing area. Pay special attention to undressing and dressing procedures (do they respect the modesty of residents?), the disposal of soiled linens (are they stored in vented areas or odor-free containers?), transfers and lifting (are they done safely?), grooming and hair washing and drying (are they done before leaving and efficiently?), and toileting (is privacy respected?).

Evaluate new bathing and showering equipment carefully. Consider resident characteristics; time commitment of the staff; water availability; preferred approaches to bathing; frequency of baths; staff and resident preferences, concerns, and comfort; and available features to increase comfort, like whirlpools, fast water flow, ease of entry, and familiarity. Some clients may not do well in a seated tub, so options for semiprone seating or shower tables may be necessary for particularly frail populations.

Social Solutions

- Remove all unnecessary items from the bathing areas. Consider the best location for clean and soiled linens, personal grooming supplies, and other items that must be stored there.
- Look for opportunities to use small items that can personalize and humanize bathing, such as individual bath brushes or sponges; bubble bath, special soaps, or skin creams; and a vanity with an easy to use (hotel-style) hair dryer. Explore safety devices that do not look institutional (Figures 4–26 and 4–27). Try a transfer bench to ease residents over the edge of a traditional shower or tub with a ledge or high sides (Figure 4–28). Use a chest-high privacy curtain to keep staff members dry while assisting residents (Figure 4–29).
- Work with the staff to develop methods for respecting the dignity of residents. Determine the number of baths that must be given at one time or in sequence and identify ways to optimize privacy.

Physical Solutions

- Have moisture and ventilation problems checked by a trained and certified professional.
- Consider using a hand-held shower, instead of a fixed shower head, to direct water appropriately and keep staff people dry (Figure 4–30).
- Make sure the shower has scald control to prevent residents and staff

Fig. 4–26 Tub safety. Hardware placed on the outside edge of the tub helps people to get in and out. (By Lumex and others.)

members from being burned during bathing. This can often be handled least expensively at the central water heater. If additional heat is needed for clothes washers or sterilizers, use temperature boosters on those appliances.

• Consult a certified expert regarding ways to achieve a curbless shower with appropriate water drainage. Instead of ceramic tile

Fig. 4–27 Zig-zag bar for showers or standing in tub. Hardware of this type responds to users of different heights and in different positions. It prevents people from sliding more effectively than straight, vertical bars.

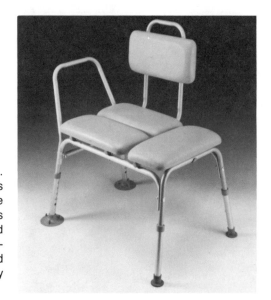

Fig. 4–28 Shower or tub transfer bench. Showers with difficult rims and tubs with edges often present obstacles to efficient and safe care. Transfer benches with adjustable legs provide a surface for sitting, swinging legs, and getting into tight shower spaces. They also allow staff members to dry bathers while seated and to conduct transfers on dry floor areas. (By Lumex and others.)

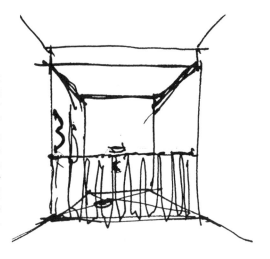

Fig. 4–29 Improved shower privacy without wall. Small showers can be enlarged with stock fixtures, such as those made by Silcraft™, or through fabricated shower units. To keep staff people dry, a partial-height privacy curtain often works better than a built-in wall because the curtain allows staff people to provide the assistance residents need. The larger shower is used in conjunction with a shower chair and hand-held-style shower. (Illustration by Dale Tremain, Ellerbe Becket, Minneapolis, Minnesota.)

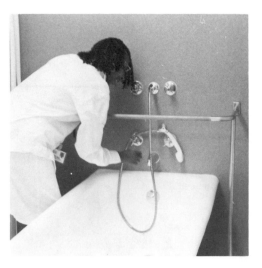

Fig. 4–30 Hand-held showers. These attachments offer options for personal care using traditional tubs and showers.

flooring, look into nonslip sheet rubber products, such as Forbo™, Endura™, or R.C.A. Mondo™. Make sure sales representatives supply adequate training to staff on the upkeep of these floors.

- Evaluate various models of bathers and lifts according to specific client needs. Available models include conventional tubs or conventional tubs raised; prone tubs with side or back chair lifts; box-style, front-entry bathers (seated) with or without lifts or chair transfers that convert to bather seating (such as NOA™); and tilt styles with side entry (such as Parker™) and full tub tilt (such as Arjo™ clam shell).
- Measure the actual equipment and lifts (or obtain measurements from the sales representative or manufacturer) and estimate the space required for their operation to determine whether they will fit within the available space.
- When tubs have been added to older bathing rooms with mechanized lifting aids, the overall effect is sometimes a motley collection of fixtures: underused showers or tubs and a crowded area around the newer or more accessible tub. Consider reconfiguring such spaces for optimum effectiveness. Pay particular attention to newer devices for transfer and lifting that can also be used in the tub. These may be safer and take up less space than the old swinging, sling seat devices that recall dunking stools.
- Provide privacy between the toilet and bathing areas with a privacy curtain in a ceiling track or, preferably, an appropriately designed and ventilated enclosure.
- Build a small grooming area with a low mirror and hanging space for personal items.
- Ensure adequate lighting. Indirect, water-protected, nonglare fixtures that provide at least 60 foot-candles are preferable.
- Add a safe heat lamp or heating element.
- Use nonglare vinyl wall covering or nonglare paint to give the bathing area a fresh look every two to four years.
- Introduce coordinated colors with waterproof wall hangings, washcloths, or other personal bath items.

NURSING AND STAFF
WORK AREAS

Staff effectiveness is far more likely with a well thought out (not necessarily massive) team center or nurses' communication station. Similarly, design of other staff work areas should incorporate an understanding of the special duties, especially morning responsibilities, of nursing assistants.

Common Problems

- One staff station serves nurses, nursing assistants, unit clerks, physicians, and other allied health professionals.

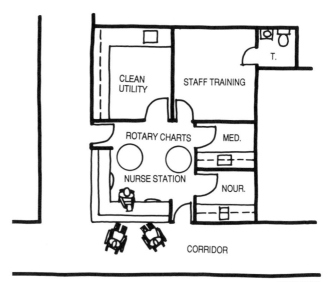

Fig. 4–31 Layout of typical utility and nursing station. Most nursing stations are a series of areas and rooms. Clean utilities, break rooms, training rooms, medications, and nourishments may all be located behind the information and communications work areas. Rotary or "drum-style" charts are also typical. The space sometimes has soiled utility and equipment storage facilities and lockers tucked in behind the counter. (By Timothy C. Boers, Boulder Associates Architects, Boulder, Colorado.)

BEFORE

- The area was not designed to accommodate the responsibilities and number of people who use the area.
- The station does not work equally well for all shifts.
- The staff area is too small or too large.
- Fixtures, equipment, or work materials expand horizontally, consuming floor and work surface areas; walls and vertical surfaces are not effectively used (Figure 4–31).
- Nursing assistants do not have direct access to the utilities and supplies they need. For example, they must go behind a counter or through one work area to use the amenities they require (Figures 4–31 and 4–32).
- There is no satisfactory place for staff meetings or quiet charting. The nurse in charge does not have an office, and there is no secure place to store private possessions such as purses, sweaters, or hygienic supplies (Figure 4–32).
- There is no pull-off area for older people or others to use when communicating with staff members across the counter. Conversations are heard in the corridor, and those approaching the counter block traffic or complicate circulation.
- Staff members are encouraged to gather or linger in work areas. They have difficulty getting their paperwork done due to the traffic, circulation, and unpredictability of contacts with residents, visitors, or housekeepers who pass by the nursing station (Figure 4–32).
- The charts were not designed for long-term care, or they are stored in units that are fixed in location or require 360° of access (Figure 4–33).
- Inadequate chairs or impediments under the counter result in uncomfortable seating.
- There is continuous noise.

Fig. 4–32 Before reorganization and renovation of service core. The utility functions sometimes need reconfiguration. In this example, the nursing station blocks several rooms used by nursing assistants. Bathers are small and difficult for wheelchair transfer, and small shower cubicles are virtually unused. The consulting room has become a locker room, break room, meeting room, and charting room as well as the only viable place for private consultations. The sun deck is rarely used.

1. Double Room
2. Single Room
3. Toilet
4. Stairs
5. Corridor
6. Living Room
7. Porch
8. Quiet Room
9. Wheel Chair Storage
10. Nurses' Station
11. Telephone Booth
12. Telephone Room
13. Consult Room
14. Work Room
15. Clean Linen
16. Soiled Linen
17. Janitor's Closet
18. Shower
19. Training Toilet
20. Bath
21. Trash Room
22. Equipment Storage
23. Dining Room
24. Pantry
25. Sun Deck
26. Elevator
27. Trash Chute

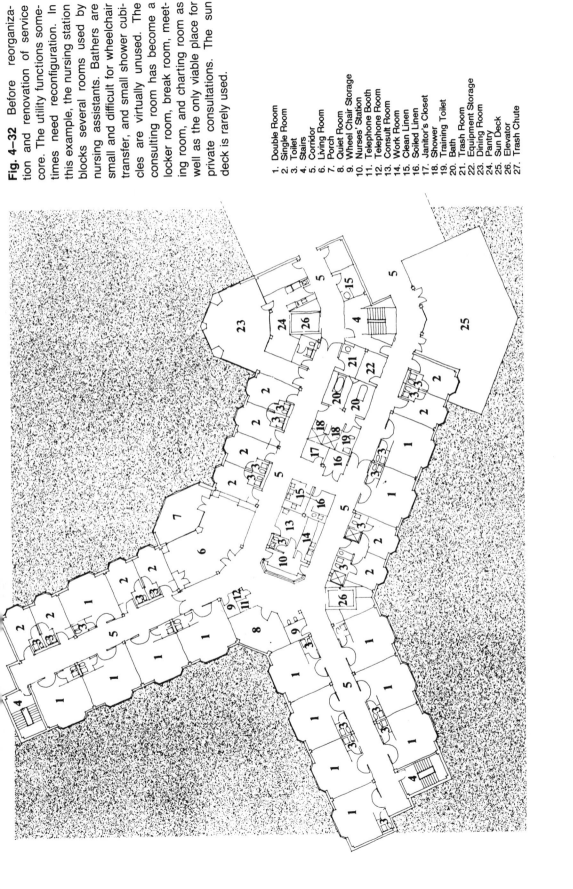

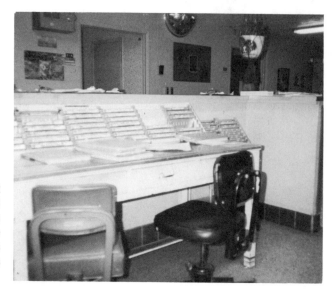

Fig. 4–33 Before refurbishment of typical nursing station. Tired case goods, tattered chairs, charts designed for short stays in acute care units, and high counter tops are difficult features for caregivers of older people.

- Lighting is inadequate.
- The call system requires too much space; it is difficult to reach and compromises available work space.
- Panic and fire safety annunciator panels dominate the visual image of the area.
- Notes, signs, and clutter dominate the visual image of the area.
- The front of the station is chipped or damaged; the station and nearby walls present a poor appearance.

Special Problems

- Glass petitions divide older people from staff members, often resulting in more noise due to the reverberation of glass and the exertion required for staff and residents to communicate.
- The counters are too high.
- The location of the staff area is too prominent (dominating the imagery) or too removed (difficult to find) relative to the facility's philosophy of care.
- Residents are unevenly or haphazardly assigned to provide morning care or answer calls. That is, primary or equitable patterns of nursing assistant assignment are impossible.
- Two staff teams work in one station.
- The station doubles as reception desk and information center for the entire facility.
- Staff territoriality or views result in resistance to a discussion of possible changes or alternatives.
- Staff members differ on options for the best use of the station.

Objectives

- To develop a station that reflects the facility's philosophy of care and projects the desired image while effectively meeting the needs of residents.
- To provide an area appropriate to the interdisciplinary needs of all those who must use the space.
- To divide the station into zones based on staff access needs, with the goal of minimizing unnecessary traffic, interruptions, and walking distances.
- To provide efficient methods and spaces for charting and storing records and to provide charts that are capable of managing the necessary information.
- To reduce the noise generated in this area that disrupts the unit or interferes with staff activities.
- To provide task lighting that does not impede the sleep or activity of residents in nearby rooms.
- To organize the appearance of the station by finding subtle areas for information panels and annunciators.

As in other sections, add to the objectives as necessary and develop appropriate approaches to these objectives or formulate "by-statements" from suggestions such as those offered in the following approaches.

Approaches

Establish policies regarding how nurses and nursing assistants will work, how they will be assigned to residents, and how they will accomplish record keeping and call responses. Consolidate activities when possible. Differentiate the functions that must occur at or behind the station and those that are best located near resident rooms (for example, the storage of linen). Price alternative charting systems, seating, lighting, and features to consolidate functions, and compare the value of minimal rearrangement and full renovation.

Social Solutions

- Meet with a core group of staff members to discuss options for improving the function of work spaces. Separate work spaces from staff gathering areas. Show examples of possible decentralization.
- Train nursing assistants to interact with residents rather than "homing" to the staff station.
- Consider hiring a ward clerk for paperwork.
- Examine unused areas; identify areas that might be made available through better organization, use of double-locking medicine carts, built-in storage, relocation of break rooms, or reconfiguration of bathers, for example.

Fig. 4–34 After refurbishment of typical nursing station. The front of the nursing station has been covered with noise- and abrasion-absorbing fabric. The back surface also absorbs sounds. A ceiling valance indicates the location of the station, which was formerly difficult to detect from a distance, and protects people in nearby rooms from light from the station. (Jewish Home and Hospital, Kingsbridge, Bronx, New York.)

Physical Solutions

- Purchase portable, notebook-style charts that can be stowed against a wall in wheeled carts or pushed into quiet charting areas or meetings.
- Improve all work and storage areas through cupboards or built-ins designed around the present paper flow needs.
- Cover the back wall and front of the station and the area across from the station with noise-abatement materials that are fire-rated for placement on walls (Figure 4–34).
- Consider increasing writing or seating areas by providing only one point of entry (Figures 4–35 and 4–36).
- Discuss the options for staff stations that do not look institutional (Figure 4–37).
- Provide an area where residents can communicate with the staff without blocking the corridor (Figures 4–37 to 4–39).

UTILITY SPACES

As clients have become more frail and incontinent, the need for and placement of proper utility areas have become critical. Visit the average nursing home on any morning and the corridor has become a virtual supply depot and disposal alley. Solve these issues, and both efficiency and image are likely to improve.

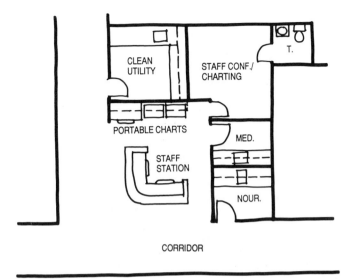

CORRIDOR

AFTER

Fig. 4–35 After layout of a formal, office-style nursing station. This traditional refurbishment involved recessing the station from the corridor, optimizing space use with portable charts on rectangular carts, and eliminating one of the two entry points. The counter has been lowered to allow wheelchair users to approach it without reaching staff papers. (By Timothy C. Boers, Boulder Associates Architects, Boulder, Colorado.)

Common Problems

- The utility rooms for clean and soiled linen are distant from the rooms where linen is handled.
- Staff members must go behind the nursing station to get to utility rooms (Figure 4–32).
- The air in utility areas is stale or malodorous.
- Storage areas are disorganized (Figure 4–40).
- Carts fill the corridors, creating obstacles and an institutional appearance.

Special Problems

- Soiled linen is improperly handled.
- The wheels on carts or bins are noisy.

Objectives

- To provide the appropriate equipment and space for the type and amount of soiled linen generated.
- To minimize the distance staff members must travel by providing

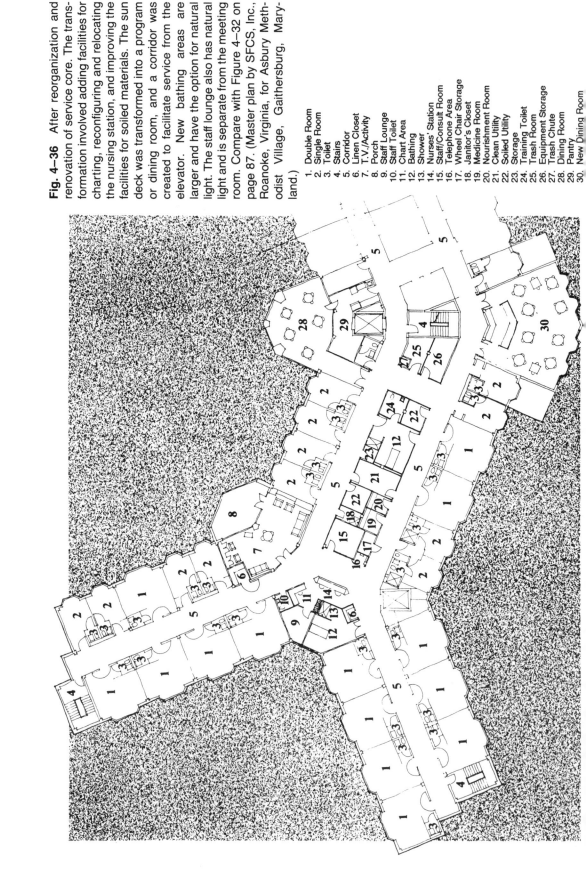

Fig. 4–36 After reorganization and renovation of service core. The transformation involved adding facilities for charting, reconfiguring and relocating the nursing station, and improving the facilities for soiled materials. The sun deck was transformed into a program or dining room, and a corridor was created to facilitate service from the elevator. New bathing areas are larger and have the option for natural light. The staff lounge also has natural light and is separate from the meeting room. Compare with Figure 4–32 on page 87. (Master plan by SFCS, Inc., Roanoke, Virginia, for Asbury Methodist Village, Gaithersburg, Maryland.)

1. Double Room
2. Single Room
3. Toilet
4. Stairs
5. Corridor
6. Linen Closet
7. T.V./Activity
8. Porch
9. Staff Lounge
10. Staff Toilet
11. Chart Area
12. Bathing
13. Shower
14. Nurses' Station
15. Staff/Consult Room
16. Telephone Area
17. Wheel Chair Storage
18. Janitor's Closet
19. Medicine Room
20. Nourishment Room
21. Clean Utility
22. Soiled Utility
23. Storage
24. Training Toilet
25. Trash Room
26. Equipment Storage
27. Trash Chute
28. Dining Room
29. Pantry
30. New Dining Room

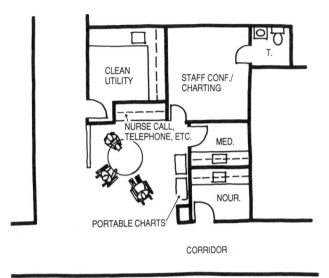

CLEAN UTILITY

STAFF CONF./ CHARTING

T.

NURSE CALL, TELEPHONE, ETC.

MED.

NOUR.

PORTABLE CHARTS

CORRIDOR

AFTER

Fig. 4–37 Residential-style nursing station. The intention here was to provide areas for conversation, private charting, and conferences, and the effect was a noninstitutional nursing station. The charts were shifted to tall, wheeling racks of notebooks, and the call system was moved away from the conversation area to a computer. Seating and table areas are available to older people and staff during the daytime. (By Timothy C. Boers, Boulder Associates Architects, Boulder, Colorado.)

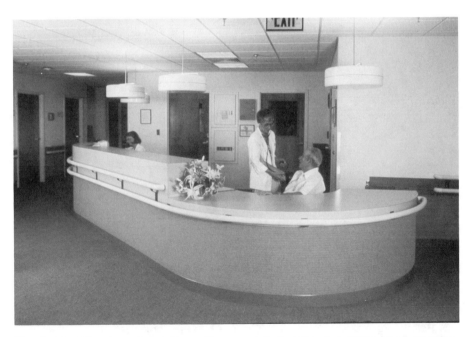

Fig. 4–38 Bilevel nursing stations. No one nursing station is suitable for all organizations. The bilevel model shown here provides higher areas with partial security for writing and a lower area that invites interaction. Residents round the corner and pull out of the main hallway to speak with staff members. (By SFCS, Inc., Roanoke, Virginia.)

Fig. 4–39 Low-profile nursing stations. By lowering the profile of a nursing station or information desk, eliminating the glass, and providing space for wheelchair users to approach without reaching papers, the facility offers an interactive image.

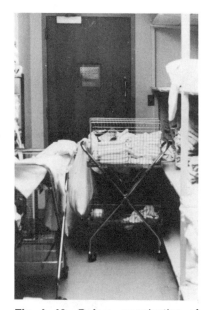

Fig. 4–40 Before organization of clean linen room. The key to making better use of small areas is to organize storage and use all of the available wall space.

Fig. 4–41 After organization of clean linen room. Shelves, storage bins, good lighting, and a commitment to maintain order increase the effectiveness of storage areas.

local facilities, such as utility areas, where they are needed (for example, near bedrooms, toilet rooms, and bathers).
- To develop and use techniques that minimize odor.
- To minimize the presence and distracting noise of utility containers.

Approaches

Ask staff members for suggestions regarding the most difficult aspects of materials management. Look at staffing patterns in terms of the span of control: How many people are nursing assistants responsible for serving? Now that primary nursing models are gaining acceptance, nursing assistants, especially in morning care, are assigned to give primary activities of daily living (ADL) assistance to a group of six to twelve people (usually in clusters of 6, 7, 8, 10 or 12 persons). By considering the span of control of nursing assistants to older people and where the linen is produced or needed, you can determine the best locations for utility areas. The number of residents and their location may also explain why carts are found in locations distant from centralized facilities.

Social Solutions

- Locate clean materials as near as possible to the nursing assistant's immediate work area (that is, in or adjacent to bathrooms or in hall cupboards). If structural changes are required, they must meet fire and life-safety standards.
- Analyze how soiled personal linen is handled and explore ways to minimize odor. Are containers covered or do covers help reduce odor transmission? Would more frequent pickups help? Discuss with suppliers options for the chemical treatment of soiled items to reduce odor (not to cover it up). These may include enclosing linen in plastic bags before storing it.
- Air out utility areas when residents are not present.
- Organize clean storage areas to improve stacking, replacement, and use of out of season items. This will not only consolidate storage and offer more space but should add to staff efficiency.
- If carts must be used, perhaps they can be colorful and more effectively designed. Both institutional supply houses and "closet stores" in many municipalities have good ideas for such vehicles.

Physical Solutions

- Build or develop places for clean linen storage adjacent to where the linen is used (that is, near the bed or bathing area).
- Increase the effectiveness of ventilation in areas where soiled linen is stored. Engage a trained and certified engineer to assess and develop a cost plan for ventilation improvements.
- Reconfigure space to optimize the flow of traffic (Figures 4–36 and 4–41).
- Consider cart size in relation to storage areas.

• Look at new product lines for disposables, refuse management, and storage. Information is often available at conferences and in hospital or nursing home management magazines.

SOCIAL AREAS, DAYROOMS, AND ACTIVITY AREAS

Common Problems

• There is an insufficient number of social areas and lounges.
• Overcrowding makes socializing difficult.
• Social areas are too distant to be convenient for residents and staff; consequently there is a lack of supervision.
• Social areas seem sparse or barren.
• Social areas seem busy, cluttered, and heavily designed.
• Social areas go unused.
• The furniture arrangement makes social areas difficult to use (Figures 4–42 to 4–44); the chairs are lined up around the perimeter of the room.
• Televisions play constantly or there are other monotonous stimuli.
• There is not enough to do.

Fig. 4–42 Traditional large multipurpose room. Common dayroom challenges include glare, inadequate space for wheelchair users, vintage living room furnishings, and stark or cluttered walls.

- The activities rooms are distant from the unit and offer crafts or other events that are not attended by frail, cognitively impaired, or less mobile residents.
- There is insufficient storage for activities on and off the unit.

Special Problems

- The social areas double as dining rooms.
- No bathrooms are located near the social areas.
- The shape of the space makes socializing or watching difficult.
- Smoke makes the social areas unpleasant.
- The space is behind closed doors, which makes it psychologically and physically difficult to enter.
- Some staff people and residents assume that the best space to socialize is in front of the nursing station.
- Activities are encumbered by inadequate seating, including the excessive use of recliner chairs; inadequate areas with doors that close to provide a quiet place for activities; and an inadequate match between the natural interests of residents and the environment's capacity to support those interests.

Objectives

- To provide a variety of social options, in at least these options from solitude to opportunities for two or three persons, from family sized groups of 4–8 to discussion class sized groups of 9–12 to large group assemblies.
- To offer places and unique furniture arrangements appropriate for social gatherings of these different sizes (Figures 4–45 to 4–47).
- To stimulate conversation by offering changing scenery and interesting variations in the spaces, decor, and people that residents encounter (Figure 4–48).
- To facilitate conversation through the arrangement of furniture by grouping chairs at slight angles or around tables, rather than lining them up or placing people more than a "handshake's distance" apart.
- To recognize the need for solitude by offering (but never imposing) areas where people can be alone.
- To offer visual privacy by recognizing the need of residents to control access to their space, except in an emergency. When this need cannot be satisfied in the bedroom, visual privacy may be afforded in a suite or room that is reserved for whatever use the resident and family have in mind.
- To provide opportunities for solitude and privacy without endangering residents by ensuring that residents and staff members can easily contact one another and will communicate at prearranged times.
- To design resources for social areas that are appropriate for residents by requesting their input and responding to their reactions. These

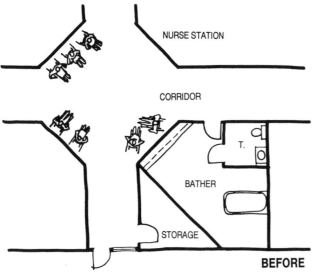

Fig. 4–43 Before renovation of nurses station. In many facilities, older people gather in the corridors near nursing stations. This sometimes indicates a lack of supervised seating located nearby. (By Timothy C. Boers, Boulder Associates Architects, Boulder, Colorado.)

Fig. 4–44 Before rearrangement of medium-sized social area. Social areas are often filled with too much furniture given the proportion of wheelchair users. Chairs may block televisions or be grouped around the perimeter. Low end tables, coffee tables, and traditional "motel" desks sometimes go unused. The space often looks disorganized and crowded, even when only one or two users are present, and it is often difficult to get to the windows to enjoy the view. (By Timothy C. Boers, Boulder Associates Architects, Boulder, Colorado.)

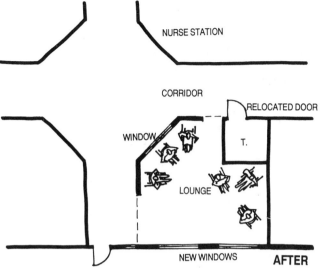

Fig. 4–45 After conversion of utility area to small seating room. Underutilized or "found" spaces sometimes may be converted into social areas. An unused bather that was unnecessary to meet code requirements was converted into the lounge and adjacent toilet shown here. Windows were added to bring natural light into the lounge and adjacent areas. Note also the diagonal chamfered corners; these can reduce wall damage at tight intersections. (By Timothy C. Boers, Boulder Associates Architects, Boulder, Colorado.)

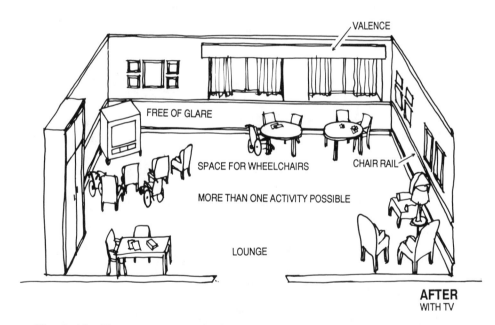

Fig. 4–46 After rearrangement of medium-sized social area. The room was reorganized to facilitate socializing, and the windows were changed. Zones or areas of activity were created based on an understanding of what people want to do and will do. Tables were added to organize socializing, and unused furnishings were removed to provide more space. Storage facilities were included, and the walls were designed to look inviting, even when there are few people present. A chair rail protects the wall and gives the space character. Vertical blinds and a valance help to reduce glare, and the television is located in a glare-free corner. The space now works for wheelchair users. (By Timothy C. Boers, Boulder Associates Architects, Boulder, Colorado.)

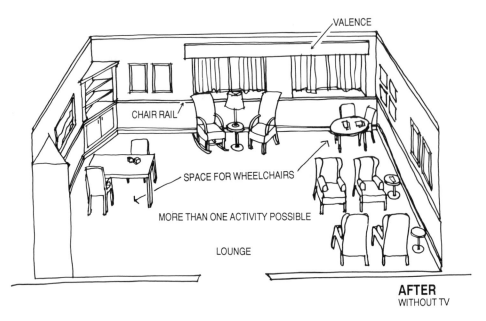

VALENCE

CHAIR RAIL

SPACE FOR WHEELCHAIRS

MORE THAN ONE ACTIVITY POSSIBLE

LOUNGE

AFTER
WITHOUT TV

Fig. 4–47 After rearrangement of medium-sized social area. If older people are not watching TV, and its noise and presence dampen conversation, the room may be organized for more participatory options. Clusters of seating, rocking, use of corner cupboards to define space and provide props for conversations or memory development groups are all readily available. (By Timothy C. Boers, Boulder Associates Architects, Boulder, Colorado.)

Fig. 4–48 Focal points and seating arrangement. Placing tables in front of a window improves conversation options. The resident and visitor sit closer, the table covers some of the symbols of frailty, and the surface provides many opportunities. The view serves as a conversation stimulus, as well.

resources may include familiar furnishings, objects, and visitors. There should be items for residents to touch, use, or otherwise enjoy.

- To provide furnishings that are appropriate for a frail population by taking care not to overfurnish, by using sturdy tables that will not cause residents to trip, and by choosing chairs that are suitable for the activities they will support.
- To create comfortable settings for conversation by minimizing noise, glare, and unpleasant odors; improving lighting; and selecting interesting focal points.
- To offer effective activities, programs, and pastimes for the entire population and places to hold those activities, with minimal transportation time.

Approaches

Observe existing social areas, and discuss them with residents and staff people from all three shifts. Consider each social space individually. Decide how it might be used, what it needs, and what it does not need (or what needs to be removed or alleviated). Consider designing each available area for a different purpose. If an underused space must be made more attractive, consider ways of adding improved toilet facilities nearby or bringing increasing activity to the space, perhaps in conjunction with activities, nursing, or food service. Work with staff members on plans for bringing caregivers and therapists to the dayrooms or onto the units.

Social Solutions

- Arrange furniture to support groups of varying sizes, the specific users, and the activities in each space. For example, a large 25' by 25' (7.6 m × 7.6 m) room may be subdivided into four smaller areas, each with a slightly different character (Figures 4–46 and 4–47). Use tables to increase activity and facilitate conversation. Place them in front of a window to provide a further stimulus to conversation (Figure 4–48). Bookshelves or high-back (wing-style) chairs help divide large areas into smaller ones (Figure 4–47).
- Provide staff members with their own gathering spaces so that they will not dominate the areas intended for residents.
- Schedule activities or snacks in social spaces to increase their use; consider playing the television only when residents request it.
- Schedule staff members to provide informal programs or care in the social areas.
- Make the social areas more comfortable by reducing glare and noise. (See "Lighting" and "Noise Reduction" in Chapter 5.)
- Recreation staff people might work with the nursing staff and visitors to provide varied social experiences for all residents as an alternative to offering only solitude or large group experiences.
- Name each space in relation to the formal and informal social events

that occur there (library, parlor, family room, porch, etc.), even if the shapes of the rooms are similar and only the furnishings and seating arrangements vary.

- If the nursing station is treated as a major social area, consider the following:

    1. Are staff members concentrated at the nursing station when they might be decentralized and working with smaller groups of people?
    2. Could some other events be readily created that would be as interesting as staff routines?
    3. How could residents' needs (such as toileting and social contact with "verbal and healthy" people) be fulfilled in other gathering places?
    4. Are programs being brought to the units or to individuals who are frail, mentally impaired, or otherwise less able to get to other areas of the building?
    5. Should the area be renovated (Figures 4–43 and 4–45)?

    The nursing station is sometimes accepted as an adequate gathering place. However appropriate and stimulating that may be for some residents, the social contact that results should probably be supplemented with other experiences that engage older people with each other, with staff seated at eye level, or with family or visitors in other than institutional routines.

- Assign a therapeutic recreation staff member to the unit with a work station and regular presence in the area. In large facilities, decentralize the staff. Use volunteers for larger events, such as parties, and encourage staff members to focus on the hard-to-reach clientele.

Physical Solutions

- Provide several types of spaces, including social areas that are separate from dining rooms.
- Build additional social areas, if necessary, considering the best location, such as on or near the unit or in the lobby (Figures 3–6 and 4–49).
- Use the information provided in Appendix C to compute the size of the social area that is needed. Be sure to allow enough space to hold programs and informal gatherings.
- Develop social areas from underused areas of the building, with appropriate fire, life-safety, and human comfort considerations. Social areas have been developed from unnecessary bathing rooms, former laundries, store rooms, and underused offices, for example (Figures 4–36 and 4–45).
- Minimize glare and optimize lighting in relation to the programs and informal gathering that occur in the area.

Fig. 4–49 Adding on a social area. When adding a social area onto the front of a building, it is possible to incorporate features and details from the original building. The columns shown here work to organize seating and define gathering areas. They also provide interesting focal points in the space. (By SFCS, Inc., Roanoke, Virginia.)

Fig. 4–50 Activities room basics. A new activities room combines accessible hand-washing with cooking and storage facilities.

Fig. 4–51 Activities room display. Combining storage with display as shown here offers bystanders a look at projects, a view into the activities room, and information on the schedule. (By Dale Tremain, Ellerbe Becket, Minneapolis, for Charter House, Rochester, Minnesota.)

- Organize an activity room around the preferred activities of the residents, including music, exercise, baking, gardening, outings, and sensory stimulation programs geared toward cognitively impaired people (Figure 4–50).
- Provide ways of orienting people toward activities, such as combining display cases and storage (Figure 4–51).
- Develop devices that serve as room dividers and on-unit storage (Figures 4–52 and 4–53).
- Use computers to generate activity calendars. Give residents and families their own copies, and generate larger copies for display. If office workers handle this task, the recreation staff will be free to develop programs for cognitively impaired people.
- Develop on-unit spaces with doors for group programs that may generate noise; add doors to existing spaces on the unit.

DINING ROOMS

Common Problems

- The food arrives cold.
- Residents must wait a long time for meals.

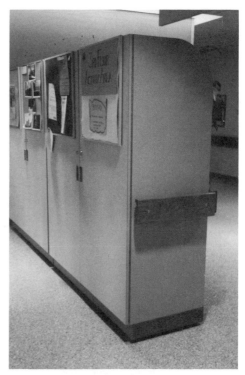

Fig. 4–52 Storage devices double as room dividers. Baycrest (Toronto, Ontario) has developed ways of combining storage units and dividers; they feature an added handrail mounting surface. Opening the doors creates a mini environment that could provide a backdrop for programs like music or art.

- More people have mechanical diets (that is, usually soft foods run through a blender) than might need them if the food were prepared differently, if there were different eating tools, such as Teflon™ coated spoons, or if there were greater assistance with dining.
- People eat alone in their bedrooms because (1) there is inadequate space for everyone to dine at one time; (2) the dining room presents views of people who are eating clumsily; or (3) the dining experience is painful as a result of noise, glare, clutter, or confusion.
- The dining room is on a different floor or at a great distance from the residents. Staff time, waiting, and special arrangements are required to bring residents there.
- There is no natural aroma associated with the meal, or aromas come far ahead of the meals themselves. In the first case, natural digestion is not aided; in the second, people become restless when they are hungry and can smell a meal but must wait a long time for it.
- The dining room does not look like a dining room.
- People don't speak much in the dining room.
- The circulation is inhibited or the space is cramped.

Fig. 4–53 Family room from lounge. Giving a standard lounge some character may involve using every nook and cranny and building in surfaces to support programming. This otherwise spare room is transformed by a piano, sideboard, rockers, and glare-controlling mini-blinds. The valence covering the shades helps to soften the hard materials of the room. (Sholom Home, St. Paul, Minnesota.)

Special Problems

- There are no nearby bathrooms.
- The dining room does not smell good.
- People dine in their bedrooms because there is no adequate dining area convenient to the unit.

Objectives

- To provide nourishing meals in a timely fashion by optimizing the way foods are delivered.
- To ensure that hot foods are hot, cold foods are cold, and all foods look conventional by using appropriate cooking and delivery systems.
- To offer residents choices during the meal by providing appropriate storage and service areas to offer alternatives to the main course and beverage, condiment, and other menu choices.
- To provide residents with comfortable social experiences by offering everyone the option of eating at a table with one to three other people.
- To offer opportunities for conversation and contact by using tables of no more than 48″ across.

- To provide an environment that is sufficiently free of noise to allow people with slight hearing loss to understand normal conversation by using noise-abatement materials where possible, by minimizing the noise of equipment, and by separating the dining room from the food preparation and dishwashing areas.
- To minimize the likelihood of spills by adopting such dining room features as chairs that fit properly under tables, eating utensils designed for the grip and balance capacities of older people, and vessels that are stable and easy to use.

Approaches

Staff members must work with specialists, such as occupational therapists, physicians, dieticians, and others, to develop the best dining plan before addressing dining room questions. To identify problems, observe the dining room prior to and during several meals, including breakfasts; observe some weekend meals. Discuss and review the needs and preferences of different users. For issues related to food quality, temperature, delivery, and staffing, consider engaging a food service consultant who specializes in similar facilities. National associations publish directories of such specialists; many appear at conferences on long-term care. Make sure to visit their projects or at least speak to line staff who have worked in a kitchen the specialist has designed.

Social Solutions

- Develop a special dietary plan with the assistance of interested physicians, the dietitian, nurses, and nursing assistants (or whoever is involved with feeding residents). The plan should include suggestions for optimizing self-feeding, safe yet familiar eating methods and foods, seating and table arrangements, and any tips that facilitate effective and comfortable dining.
- Arrange the dining room to optimize aisle space and room features (Figure 4–54). Try arranging tables like diamonds on a playing card, at an angle with respect to the wall. This configuration creates more aisle space and minimizes the potential for residents to back into one another.
- Develop dining areas in places that optimize staff time, particularly time for nursing. If residents dine on the unit, however, give them some opportunities to go elsewhere for variety.
- Arrange to have some aspect of the meal (bread, salad, juice, or appetizers, for example) delivered when the residents arrive in the dining area. If the trays are late, the meal can still begin.
- Consider ways to bring natural food aromas to the unit to stimulate digestion before sitting at the table. Could bread, desserts, soups, or other foods be warmed in nearby serving kitchens if there is no natural food aroma?

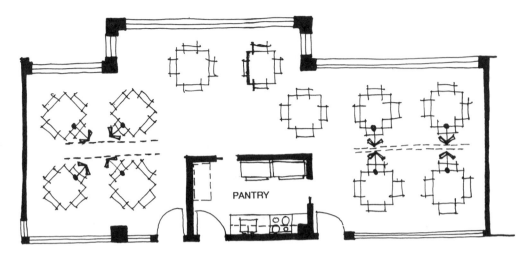

Fig. 4–54 Dining arrangements. Placing tables at an angle with respect to the wall often increases the amount of aisle space. (By Timothy C. Boers, Boulder Associates Architects, Boulder CO.)

Fig. 4–55 Exterior addition of new corridor for dining area. The new staging and waiting area created by adding an exterior corridor to the building increases the access of all residents to windows. (By SFCS, Inc., Roanoke, for Westminster Canterbury, Richmond, Virginia.)

Physical Solutions

- Provide a dining area that is adequate for the number of people who will use it and the mobility devices they need, using the type of information provided in Appendix C. If necessary, add on to the building to accomplish this (Figure 4–55).
- When remote dining rooms are planned, develop a separate serving kitchen to facilitate service, minimize noise to the dining areas, optimize food temperature, and provide storage for beverages and condiments (see "Pantry" in Figure 4–54).
- Select furniture, shelves, plate racks, or other features to reinforce the dining function and improve the appearance of the area (Figures 4–56 and 4–57).
- Provide more equal access to windows and improve circulation into and around the space by moving the corridor to the exterior (Figure 4–55).
- Use noise-abatement materials on the walls, tables, and floor to minimize noise (Figures 4–58 and 4–59).

Fig. 4–56 Dining room decor. Dining room refurbishments often involve working with walls, window coverings, noise-abatement materials, and lighting. The lighting shown here comes from three sources: daylight, decorative chandeliers, and recessed indirect light. The plate rack provides dining "cues" and offers the major source of identification for the room. (Simpson House, Philadelphia, Pennsylvania.)

Fig. 4–57 Dining room appearance. Although an open serving area and chandeliers may be acceptable in a residence for older people, alternatives are necessary in a nursing home due to the number of people who have difficulty seeing, moving, hearing, and managing. Several residential features and furnishings, including wall coverings, room proportions, decorative furnishings, and attention to color and texture, can be retained in the health care environment. (By Dale Tremain, Ellerbe Becket, Minneapolis, for Charter House, Rochester, Minnesota.)

OUTDOOR AREAS

Common Problems

- Outdoor areas are underused.
- Doors or entries are difficult for residents or staff to negotiate. The doors are heavy or narrow; the entries have ramps or sills.
- Sun, glare, and unpleasant temperatures are a problem.
- Courtyards are too enclosed or bare.
- Bench-style seats are difficult for older people because they lack armrests.
- There is too much seating and too little room for wheelchairs.
- Toilet rooms are not available or are inconvenient to outdoor areas; there is no running water to drink or to use in outdoor activities.

Fig. 4–58 Noise sources. Transmission of noise is common when the food preparation area opens onto the dining room. Closing the window, setting up a separation partition, and using less noisy utensils may help to reduce background noise.

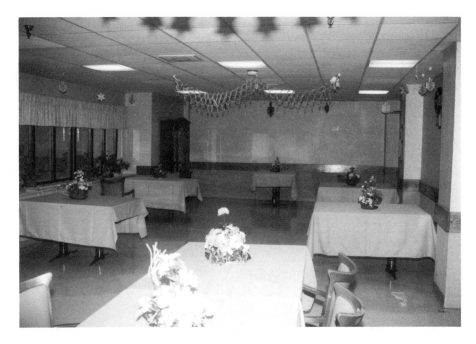

Fig. 4–59 Noise abatement in dining room. Although simple in appearance, the tackable wall covering (above and below chair rail), tablecloths, and drapes help to reduce noise in this nursing home dining room. (Jewish Home and Hospital, Kingsbridge, Bronx, New York.)

- There is little to do or see outside.
- The area cannot easily be supervised.

Special Problems

- People cannot or do not get outside.
- Much money was spent on some outdoor areas that do not fully benefit all residents. For example, there is a wandering garden, but few people use it.

Objectives

- To provide access to familiar and natural resources through outdoor areas that are easy to use and supervise.
- To offer amenities known to improve the comfort of residents, such as protection from glare and insects.
- To make outdoor areas accessible to those in wheelchairs.
- To provide comfortable seating that is easy to use.
- To offer tables and surfaces for activities as an extension of other facility programs.
- To ensure the safety of residents through perimeter security that does not dominate the imagery or experience of the space.

Fig. 4–60 Garden for wanderers and others. This garden, although fenced, is filled with interesting features and irregular pathways. The features attract attention and minimize the feeling of confinement. (Motion Picture and Television Studio Retirement Center, Woodland Hills, California.)

- To provide focal points, such as activities or unpredictable sights, and features that people of all ages will enjoy.

Approaches

Meet with staff, residents, and their families to establish priorities. Inventory the natural resources of the building to determine the advantages and drawbacks of various outdoor areas. Look for views, activity, glare, extreme temperatures, natural phenomena, and accessibility.

Social Solutions

- Educate staff members and families about the importance of bringing residents outside.
- Run a staff drill on the use of doors and practice methods of working with existing outside features, including ramps, locked doors, and umbrella tables. Practice with staff in wheelchairs.
- Work with special departments to help bring people outside, like

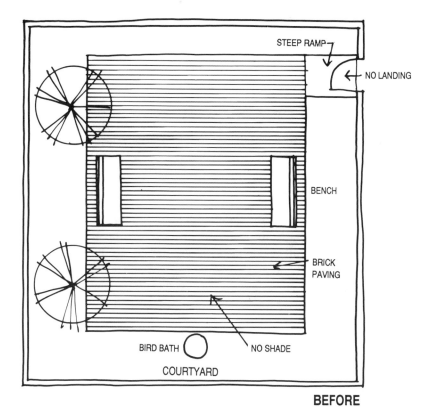

BEFORE

Fig. 4–61 Before renovation of outdoor area. Outside areas are often enclosed with problem doorways and ramps. Pathways are sometimes difficult to traverse. Shade may be unavailable, and the seating may be limited to distant benches. (By Timothy C. Boers, Boulder Associates Architects, Boulder, Colorado.)

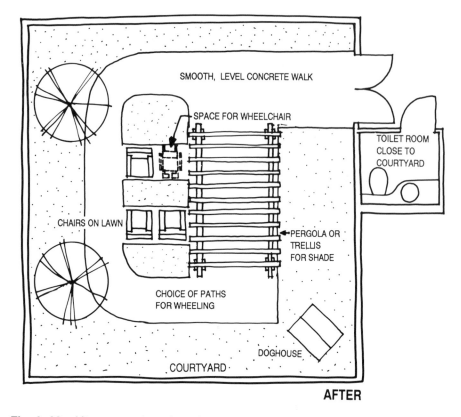

AFTER

Fig. 4–62 After renovation of outdoor area. New double doors improve entry and egress. Smooth walkways and areas planned for wheelchairs and regular seating facilitate use. Shade, focal points (animals or plants), and accessible toilet facilities improve the comfort and usefulness of these areas. The net effect should be a varied space. (By Timothy C. Boers, Boulder Associates Architects, Boulder, Colorado.)

food service, therapeutic recreation, and volunteer services. Assign volunteers to the people who have the most difficulty getting outside.

- Provide all residents with appropriate clothing and protection, including sunshade and sunscreen, for weather conditions.
- Do not restrict the use of wandering gardens (areas with special security and touchable amenities) to people with dementia. Allow residents from all levels of care to use them (Figure 4–60).
- Open windows and air inside spaces (before residents use the area) to provide fresh air when getting outside is difficult.

Physical Solutions

- Provide on-unit outside areas.
- To improve accessibility, provide doors without ramps or sills (Figures 4–61 and 4–62).

Fig. 4–63 Outdoor area with a ramada. This overhead trellis creates a shady area that is conveniently located close to the building. The overhead slats do not unduly darken nearby rooms, which in this case are offices. Tables and chairs increase the likelihood that outdoor areas will be used. (Chandler Health Care, Newtown, Pennsylvania.)

- Provide shade, perhaps by using a ramada (wood slats at an angle), awning, or gazebo (Figure 4–63).
- Attend to such necessities as toileting, drinkable water, and a call system or telephone. Locate new areas where staff members can easily supervise them (Figure 4–36).
- Develop interesting pathways, functional seating, zones for various users, and activities and highlights, such as a smelling garden, pet visiting area, or orchard.

5
Systems

Building systems (climate control, lighting, plumbing, communications, and security, to name a few) are often at the root of a facility's functional problems. Many sponsors are reluctant to undertake systems changes, however, because such changes usually involve the entire building and are perceived as having little visible marketing appeal. In fact, though, systems contribute to the quality of life in a nursing home and are probably the major determinants of whether an environment appears institutional or residential.

Systems assessments should usually be undertaken by licensed professionals. Professional assistance will also be needed to plan appropriate options for improvement. This work is often done by contractors or licensed specialists because of the intricacies involved.

This chapter introduces four building systems (lighting, noise abatement, odor control, and communications) and outlines the criteria to consider when designing for older people. Each section lists the problems that facilities commonly face, offers objectives, and suggests various approaches. These lists are not intended to be exhaustive. The objectives are offered as starter lists; add your own as appropriate. Likewise, you should personalize the approaches to suit your particular needs.

LIGHTING

When there is insufficient light, older people often give up on an activity and redirect their energies. Glare, however, tends to be painful. Some people may tear or squint; others may complain of headache or general malaise. Good lighting design may go a long way to optimizing the residual vision of older people and may improve color discrimination.

Common Problems

- Too little illumination
- Uneven illumination
- Lighting that is inappropriate to its task (for example, night lights that are too bright for sleeping and reading lights that are poorly located)
- Glare (that is, reflection, flashing, or blurring of details due to the appearance of white light)

Fig. 5–1 Lamps for various functions. Lamps manufactured today have a variety of functional, safety, and durability features. The Nightengale™ shown here is designed as a table lamp. It has an easily operated paddle switch at its base, night light, plug-in receptacle, indestructible and easy-to-clean shade, and UL/CSA certification. A trendsetter for the industry, the fixture comes with a five-year warranty. It is available in custom colors by Adjustable Fixtures, Milwaukee, Wisconsin.

Objectives

- To identify shadow areas that may pose problems for walking or other functions by looking for darkened areas on floors in bedrooms, toilet rooms, and other spaces accessible to residents.
- To optimize the light needed to see special items such as signs by using nonreflective lettering, background materials, and surfaces.
- To light tasks appropriately by providing fixtures with sufficient wattage where needed. (See Figure 5–1.)
- To identify glare that might pose problems for walking, table activities, viewing, or close-range tasks (such as grooming, telephoning, and reading institutional signs) by walking through the facility and looking for "flashes" or pools of bright, reflected light.
- To overcome problems with uneven lighting and glare by providing appropriate levels of lighting and fixtures with appropriate diffusers or lens covers.
- To eliminate exposure to bright, unshielded light sources, including chandeliers, by using shades, specially treated bulbs, or other appropriate means.
- To minimize glare problems by purchasing and installing nonglare

surfaces, such as matte-finish table tops and counters, objects, and wall coverings.

Approaches

- Analyze the areas where close-range tasks are performed. Table 5–1 lists the recommended lighting levels for a variety of activities and spaces.
- Measure lighting levels. Photography stores often rent meters that measure lighting levels. As a rough indicator, if a space has too little light to photograph with a 35-mm camera using 400 ASA film at a speed of 125 without a flash, there is too little light for older people.
- Try these social interventions: move people to the best locations for close work, manage glare by using the available window coverings before holding group meetings, and speak with residents about their individual needs so that they may be seated accordingly.
- Some studies suggest that light from an incandescent bulb is better for reading than fluorescent light; however, further research is needed. Fluorescent light may be more tolerable when the source is shielded or indirect (that is, when you cannot actually see the bulb because it is hidden with a diffuser, in a cove, or behind a valance).

NOISE ABATEMENT

Noise is one of the most serious problems in many nursing homes, yet many sponsors are not aware of the issue. It contributes to agitation and stress and minimizes the capacity of older people to understand conversation. Noise in

Table 5–1 Recommended Lighting Levels

Activity	Location	Recommended Level (foot-candles)
Reading	Social services, library, halls, chapel, bedside, activities room, staff station, offices, signs[a]	50–100
Facial recognition	Dining areas, hallways, doorway to room, staff stations, offices, lobbies, elevators	50–60
Grooming	Bathroom, bedroom (dresser), tub room, shower area, salon	50–100
Selection	Activities room (games, projects), dining areas, telephones	50–100
Directions	Hallways (room identification), maps, name lists, directories	50–100

[a]Older people who use magnification (magnifiers or corrective lenses) require higher levels of lighting. "Low-vision" professionals assess and prescribe for individual needs. The American Foundation for the Blind (15 West 16th St., New York, NY 10011) publishes a directory and offers further information on low-vision services, devices, and clinicians.

Fig. 5–2 Noise abatement. By using noise-abatement materials especially designed for application on walls (and fire-rated for vertical placement), the noise generated in one area, such as this open seating space, is less likely to reverberate off of the walls.

dining rooms (Figure 5–2), nursing stations, bedrooms, and entries or lobbies negatively influences behavior.

The objective of noise abatement is to minimize background noise. The ideal noise level is about 20 decibels before conversation. Audiologists have devices for measuring ambient noise.

Common Problems

Equipment

- Deafening loud speaker systems interrupting concentration
- Noisy and continuous call systems
- Door buzzers
- Noise from ice machines, cleaners, elevators, or other motors
- Noisy fans or heating and cooling systems

Induced

- Music played continuously that impedes hearing and understanding conversations
- Radios and televisions playing selections of questionable interest to residents
- Lack of familiar sounds that are meaningful to and selected by the residents and have natural qualities of vibration and resonance, as from music and live performances

Related Resident Issues

- Shouting to be better heard
- Withdrawal or nonparticipation due to inability to hear
- Difficulty sleeping due to noise
- Calling out continually (not satisfied by traditional staff responses)

Objectives

- To offer for most of the day an acoustical environment that facilitates natural conversation in public areas by reducing noise.
- To offer at night an environment that is free of machine noise and human conversation that is not initiated and requested by the older person.
- To allow residents to select the types of sounds available in their rooms by asking them and their families what they would like to hear.
- To allow roommates to exercise individual preferences by offering appropriate listening devices.
- To provide a varied acoustical environment by arranging for live performances.

Approaches

- Identify the source or sources of the noise.
- Move or change those sources that are not essential.
- Use doors and windows to close out noise. Place noisy items (such as ice machines, typing equipment, vending machines, dishwashers, and laundry equipment) behind closed doors when possible. Close off the kitchen from the dining room to reduce noise.
- Select quiet fans, and use heating, air conditioning, and ventilation systems that do not produce noise when possible.
- Schedule noisy services, such as vacuuming and floor cleaning, when most people are away from the area.
- Be sensitive to noise. Move residents to the quietest areas available. Make sure the gathering areas are away from such noise producers as dish rooms, offices, and television sets.
- Check the noise reduction coefficient (NRC) when you purchase such items as wall coverings, floor surfaces, vertical blinds, and room dividers. Sales representatives and manufacturers generally have this information in their detailed specifications.
- Try baffling to mitigate the effects of hard walls (cinder block or ceramic) or windows (a major source of reverberation and noise). Baffling involves using materials that are vertically fire-rated for use on the walls. Baffling is often successful behind nursing stations. Noise-abatement materials such as drapes, acoustical blinds, and heavy shades may be used to mitigate noise in large expanses of

windows. Room dividers made of improved materials absorb noise while subdividing large areas for small-group activities. Brand names of baffling materials include Softwall™, Knolls Furrows™, and J.M. Lynn™. You must check state regulations; some states may not approve these materials, although they have satisfied American Standards Testing Materials requirements.

ODOR CONTROL

Nothing deters visitors like stale air or odors from bodily wastes. Ironically, many cover-ups are as objectionable as the source odor itself. The objective should not be an odor-free environment (any more than it should be a wholly bright or totally silent one). Instead, try to fill the facility with pleasant, natural aromas.

Common Problems

- Excrement odors
- Pungent cleaning chemicals
- Odor cover-up
- Stale, unmoving air
- Smoke

Objectives

- To provide fresh air by making sure that air circulates and changes regularly throughout the facility.
- To optimize good aromas and eliminate unsatisfactory ones by developing and implementing new procedures for managing clean and soiled materials more effectively.
- To improve individual body odor by improving resident hygiene. (An astounding number of facilities bathe older people once a week or less—though "bed baths" or washcloth cleansing may be more frequent.)
- To improve smoke management by developing smoking policies and by using equipment that ventilates the building.
- To provide pleasant odors by exposing people to natural smells and by responding to their preferences for particular aromas. This may involve observing, listening to reactions to aromas during daily care, and working with family members.

Approaches

- Work with mechanical engineers to ensure that air circulates and changes regularly in all areas of the building. You may need to vent some areas directly to the outside rather than recirculate the air. This is particularly true when staff members stow soiled materials in areas

Table 5–2 Linking Spaces, Features, and Desirable Aromas[a]

Location	Aroma
Bathing room	Aftershave, cologne, skin cream, make-up, bubble bath, gentle-fragrance herbal soaps
Toilet room	Fresh air, cleanness
Dining room	Breads and desserts (especially before meals to aid natural digestion), coffee or breakfast meats in the morning
Bedrooms	Fresh laundry, airiness
Program areas	Popcorn for movies, cocoa for evening events, strawberries for spring birthdays
Dayrooms or lobbies	Fresh flowers, outdoor smells
Porches or outdoor areas	Fresh earth, plants and flowers, natural and distant odor of pets
Windows, orientation, and geographic reinforcement	Rural: seasonal, harvest, spring; waterfront: fresh sea air; suburbs: fresh grass, barbecue; urban: ethnic foods

[a]Personalize this list using your knowledge of residents and the area. Recognize the possibility that residents may prefer their own choice of aromas.

that were poorly designed for circulation. The air pressure in bathrooms or program areas can sometimes be adjusted so that it is positive or negative relative to some adjacent space, thereby improving the air quality.

• Analyze potential sources of acceptable and unacceptable odors. Identify the source and location of the odor and the times when it is worst. Be sure to obtain information in the early morning and on weekends.

• Determine how each negative odor might be eliminated. Pay particular attention to negative odors from urine and feces, smoke, cooking fats, strong cleaning chemicals, and body odor.

• Consider ways to release or accommodate enjoyable aromas. People benefit from exposure to pleasant smells, such as freshly baked goods, culturally meaningful foods and seasonings, fresh fruits and vegetables, popcorn, light aftershave or cologne, and baby lotion. Table 5–2 lists some desirable aromas that are linked to particular areas.

COMMUNICATIONS

Communications systems are essential for those older people who can use them. Though these devices are required, many older people who are very frail and/or cognitively impaired cannot use traditional devices. New technologies or alternate means of communication need to be developed for the future.

Common Problems

Call Systems

- No system exists at all, or the system is not located where residents spend most of their day.
- The system was designed for a different purpose.
- Residents cannot reach or operate the system easily.
- The system requires or involves two-way conversation, and residents cannot speak easily on voice systems or do not hear well.
- Staff members use the system excessively to the detriment of the residential environment.
- Calls are not answered quickly enough to satisfy residents or families.

Public Address Systems

- The system is operated too often, is too loud, and dominates the acoustical environment, causing residents to become confused by the noise.
- The system crackles or is otherwise difficult to hear.
- Piped-in music is played continuously.

Other

- There are no amplification systems that selectively assist hearing-impaired people with chapel services, group meetings, or television programs.
- Telephones are inaccessible or lack privacy.
- Exit door signal systems are deafeningly loud or staff do not respond quickly.

Objectives

- To increase the efficiency of staff communication by using devices that direct requests to the proper staff without interfering with the functions of other staff or residents.
- To use piped-in music appropriately by being selective about where and when it is played.
- To increase options for residents to communicate with the outside by offering telephone services that are responsive to their financial and hearing or health needs.

Approaches
Try these techniques to improve the social environment:

- Train staff members to respond in person rather than call to each other. Train the staff not to listen into rooms unless there is resident

or family permission for some short-term or overriding life-safety
issue.

- Help the staff recognize how stressful inappropriate noises can be to
older people.
- Use the public address system selectively (for example, just for fire
or emergency information) and use telephones for routine communications. Mute the bells on phones. Lower the volume of the public
address system, and make sure it is free of static.
- Direct staff people to take residents to telephones regularly, without
waiting for residents to ask.
- Assign staff people to particular exits on a rotating basis so there is
clear-cut responsibility for the door alarm. Implement a parallel
system for substitutes (that is, those from medical pools).

Try these techniques to improve the physical environment:

- Use telephone or other portable call systems for remote areas. Speak
with a communications expert about the possibilities for your facility
and location.
- Explore the newer, digital call systems that allow variations in how
individuals and rooms are connected to the nursing station or other
backup points.
- Make sure the call system is audible but not dominating. Speak to
the manufacturer if the tone is deafening or otherwise unacceptable.
- Consider ways to make the call system easier for older people to use.
The simplest systems do not require two-way conversations and do
not offer a confusing variety of buttons. If the call system is difficult
to reach, consider longer cords and Velcro™ attachments to the chair
or bed or another appropriate device. In bathrooms, make sure the
call system can be reached from the toilet and from the floor by
using heavy-grade string and eyelets or another appropriate system.
In new installations, consider systems that cannot be yanked from the
wall or that can easily be reconnected because of their modular
design.
- Provide lighting-based signal systems for residents who are hard-of-
hearing. Check catalogs and health magazines for sources, and
contact your local society for hearing-impaired people for additional
information.
- Evaluate public address systems and repair or replace them, if
necessary. There should be public address systems in function rooms
for announcements, programs, and activities like bingo. For many of
these events, portable (wireless) microphones or those with long
cords will improve the ability of the staff to offer programs and of
residents to hear the speaker.
- Consider pocket-sized pagers for directors of nursing, department
heads, and frequently needed staff people to minimize the use of

public address systems. Silent pagers are available that vibrate or become slightly warm and thus do not disrupt meetings.

- Play piped-in music in resident-use areas only when it is requested by the residents or when the space is not being used for conversation and listening. If families complain about the lack of continuous background music, explain that music is not played constantly because it affects the ability of older people to hear conversation, and many object or call out as a result. You might suggest music be available to individuals on their request or in places that serve as second dayrooms. These policies might be detailed in an information sheet for visitors.
- Ask the phone company or resource groups for people with hearing impairments to identify closed-loop or other portable amplification systems for auditoriums or meeting rooms and for listening to television.
- Offer an accessible telephone for residents in an area designed for loud but private conversation. Speak with the phone company about appropriate amplification for public and individual phones.
- Consider alternatives to door buzzers so deafening that they frighten residents.
- Use conferences, trade shows, magazines, and local sales representatives to help identify better solutions to communications problems.

6
Interior Design

The thinking about interior design for older people has changed in recent years as a result of two developments. First, these changes represent the awareness that most older people stay in nursing homes for more than a few days. It is estimated that 25% of all nursing home clients stay for 18 months or less, but 75% stay substantially longer (3 to 5 years).* Whether their stay is measured in weeks or years, the environment is increasingly significant because of the inevitable confinement. Second, these changes also reflect the realization that interior design may profoundly influence specific behaviors. These include ability to communicate and interest in communicating (even for residents who are not vocal or fully verbal), reaction to others, ability to focus or sustain attention, comfort, mobility and balance, and orientation and wayfinding.

Even when architectural and structural changes are not possible, many objectives may be reached through interior design. Through interior design, environments for older people should optimize sensory function. With improved lighting, the increased capacity of environments to promote normal conversation, and the thoughtful use of the visual and tactile environments, the older person may find it easier to respond to the stimuli of this form of communal living.

Interior design involves struggling with many paradoxes. First, good design incorporates some variety; however; the environment should look coordinated without being matched. Second, good design involves visual cues; however, visual stimulation, such as color, can easily be overemphasized or underplayed. Third, good design should include landmarks and features that reinforce direction; however, some popular ideas of the past, such as color coding or boldly colored doorjambs, are too abstract for most older people to use, and they fail to evoke a specific response related to spatial identification.

This chapter examines six important issues in interior design: color, patterns, floor coverings, chairs and seating, decorating the walls, and wayfinding and signs. As in previous chapters, the lists of common problems, objectives,

---

*National Center for Health Statistics. 1986. Nursing and related care homes as reported from the 1982 National Master Facility Inventory Survey. *Vital and health statistics*. Series 14, No. 32. DHHS Pub. No. (PHS) 86-1827. Public Health Service. Washington, D.C.: Government Printing Office.

and approaches presented in each section are not intended to be exhaustive. Personalize each list to suit your particular needs.

COLOR

For many people, selecting the colors for a nursing home is more confusing than ordering wine. They assume there is a formula for success, when in fact there are no exact rules for choosing appropriate colors. For years, even designers of health care facilities sought the one perfect hue that would unlock the potential, joy, or reverie of staff and residents. Unfortunately, there is only so much you can do with color. Although color can be quite valuable, it will not guarantee restfulness or liveliness, improve eating, overcome memory loss, or produce staff efficiency.

Older people perceive colors and color combinations differently than younger people do. Bear these differences in mind when selecting colors for a health care facility:

- Older people often see less variation in colors of the same grayness or intensity.
- Older people sometimes confuse colors such as blue, green, and violet and find them difficult to name.
- Real-life colors may not match the colors that older people recall. For example, someone may say, "They don't make Wedgwood blue like they used to."
- Color is very abstract. Most older people cannot identify their door from the color of the jamb alone. This is particularly true when the same hue is used on other doorjambs or when the resident did not choose the color. Older people sometimes find familiar objects in the room or next to the door to be more helpful for identification than color alone.
- When an individual ages, the lens of the eye often becomes yellowed. (In some people, it becomes a yellow-brown.) Some evidence suggests that this influences the naming and perception of colors.

Common Problems

- Colors are monotonous
- Wall color dominates possessions or people
- One color scheme has been used, dating facility
- Wall colors do not accommodate or blend with floor or health equipment
- Wall colors are too bright or dark, making spaces seem smaller
- It is difficult to change colors or get a fresh look by shifting color blends every few years
- Lighting is so poor that existing or preferred colors cannot be readily distinguished

• Those who select colors are inexpert or lack experience necessary to respond to the different constituencies involved.

Objectives

• To provide pleasure or enjoyment. This may be accomplished in a number of individual ways: by incorporating more input, greater variety yet better continuity, and/or by having a plan.
• To elicit a positive initial reaction to a setting or area that can carry one through new or unfamiliar experiences by using color combinations (perhaps with professional guidance or with the input of someone who combines colors that are pleasing to most of those involved in planning).
• To provide effective backgrounds for artwork or personal items so that those items will be noticed by keeping most walls light and simple.
• To reinforce other evidence that someone cares about the facility and, by association, its people by freshening color combinations every few years in most areas.
• To offer various experiences within the environment for those who cannot get out often.

Approaches

Social Solutions

• Respect individual color preferences, but remember that relying on one person's preference for a whole social setting can be misleading.
• Allow residents to select wall color or an accent (such as a border print, bedspread, or window covering), especially when their stay is measured in months or years.
• Reinforce the selection of personal items, including clothing, that reflect preferred colors.
• Encourage a participatory program of selecting, hanging, and reviewing artwork for bedrooms or nearby hallways.
• When choosing colors, ask residents to select from actual samples rather than just name their preferred color. Provide as large a sample of the color as possible (at least 12″ by 12″, 30 by 30 cm). Small chips mislead most people.
• Educate designers and family members about color distortion in older people, and modify procedures for color selection accordingly. Designers and those who make selections involving color must have access to this type of information long before they design, shop for, or acquire items for the facility.
• Consider staff color preferences for areas that they use, including spaces such as laundries, utility rooms, break rooms, and entry corridors. With their preferences accommodated, it may be easier to

support the choices of residents, especially when residents and staff members come from different age groups (stylistic eras), cultural backgrounds, or income levels.

- Make an organizational commitment to change some areas over time, tempering trendiness with the comfort of familiarity.

Physical Solutions

- Look at the facility in terms of the overall variety in tones. By varying color schemes, rather than seeking a single color palette or combination of colors, you can respond to individual differences and stimulate through change.
- When selecting, matching, and combining colors, consider the equipment or features of the building that cannot be changed, and explore options for making them work for you. Visit the facility or view a videotape of it to help you incorporate the existing features in any planned changes. Wheelchairs, cubicle curtains, chair seats, floors, and even some bedside furnishings may give the facility a "calico" image. Give these items special attention so that they do not appear to be thoughtlessly mismatched. The "given" features of an environment can sometimes be changed, such as by reupholstering wheelchair seats in vinylized or appropriate fabrics or by using neutral hardware and flooring to allow greater freedom for easily changed surfaces like walls.
- Go to a paint store and study paint strips or look at an interior design book with a good section on color to release your imagination. Note that color samples are often arrayed from light (nearly white) to dark (nearly black) regardless of the name of the hue.
- Use contrast to emphasize important features and to improve visibility. Contrast helps older people to distinguish foreground from background, and it can effectively be used to differentiate floors and walls by making the edges clearer. Decide which features should stand out from the background. These might include art, food on a plate, and personal items. Use contrast to optimize the visibility of what residents need to see (Figure 6–1). Contrast involves the juxtaposition of differences. To appreciate existing contrasts, upgrade lighting. For example, place a dark object against a light background to increase the contrast and make the object more visible. This suggests that walls should not be overpowering, intense, saturated colors. Brightness may be better used for small items like changeable features: drapes, commode seats, pillows, and handles rather than for large surfaces or floors.
- Learn to use a gray scale to improve contrast where you want particular features to stand out. This involves learning to work with variations in color saturation or value. Many institutions tend to vary the hue (the color itself) but not the value of the color (its darkness).

Fig. 6–1 Use of contrast. How can items be made to stand out from the background? In this bedroom, small pieces of art and personal items are readily visible because they are placed on very light walls. Call system and oxygen hardware blend into the darker "head wall." The moderate tone and light pattern of the drapes serve to frame the view beyond. A simple white bedspread shows off the resident's personal coverlet.

Facilities that are all bright colors (crayon tones, for example) or all vanilla colors (creamy mauve, peach, aqua, etc.) cause fatigue, especially when every room is similar in other ways, as well.

- Be wary of color trendiness. One year all institutions were white, then they were all light green, then they all used seasonal colors (red, orange, green, and yellow). The late eighties were marked by mauve (light pink with beige or violet overtones), and the early nineties may see the reintroduction of teal (evergreen or dark turquoise), peach tones, and some brick red. By applying trendy colors to durable surfaces, including cabinetry, floor covering, and major furnishings, you run the risk of dating the building.
- Consider making some rooms feel different, perhaps by using patterns or by working in lighter values than elsewhere.
- Consider keeping large areas like walls light, so that art stands out. You might want to select artwork and wall color together so that they complement each other.

PATTERNS

Many institutions in recent years have shied away from decorating with patterned materials and have chosen solid-colored walls, furniture, and floors instead. For many people, the patterns recede to the background on large surfaces, such as lounge walls. The pattern is more noticeable when it is located in the resident's personal area, when it conflicts with the resident's tastes, and when it camouflages important information that must be distinguished from the background. Patterns can be difficult to use effectively, but they need not be avoided. The literature on patterns for older people is spare, and the topic warrants additional research.

Common Problems

- A large, bold, contrasting, or repetitive pattern used in a relatively small area dominates the space, the activity, the individual, and his or her possessions. Older people look out of place in such an environment.
- A particularly bold pattern used on a wall where something else is meant to be the focal point (for example, personal memorabilia or a television) draws too much attention to itself and causes confusion.
- Patterns on floors appear to be objects and give the sensation of instability or faulty balance.
- Patterns that seem to vibrate or "take on a life of their own" contribute to a sense of confusion or uneasiness (Figure 6–2).
- Wavy lines appear to move or look like flames.
- Dominant pattern features resemble prisons, cages, fences, or other inappropriate images.

Objectives

- To use some patterns to stimulate a sense of variety, identification, or other perceptual pleasure by offering the option for patterns in

Fig. 6–2 Disturbing patterns. Particular floor and wall coverings give the illusion of movement or vibration.

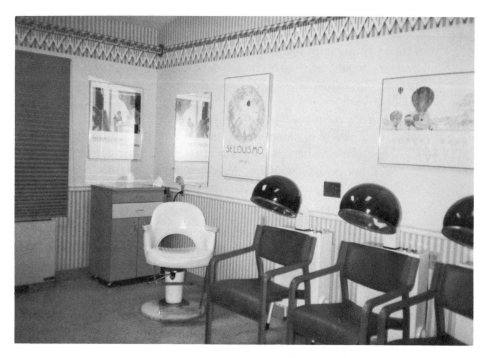

Fig. 6–3 Serendipity in interior design. Spaces that are occupied infrequently and by choice can take on a spirited look through the use of wall coverings and bold art if care is taken to color coordinate the fixed items and the finishes. The chair colors helped to determine the tones used here (a dark but pleasing blue-gray). The overall effect of the salon is neither traditionally feminine nor necessarily anticipated. Striped, patterned paper may work when it is not at eye level or on the ground and when it is offset by large areas of solid color. (Sponsor designed by Jewish Center for the Aged of Greater Saint Louis.)

bathrooms, bathers, dining rooms, salons, activity areas, physical therapy spaces, lobbies, and possibly in bedrooms. (See Figure 6–3.)

- To use patterns that allow objects to be displayed on the wall by using a small strip of a border print at ceiling or chair-rail level that is offset by solid-colored areas.
- To consider wall covering patterns in relation to what will be displayed so that the pattern does not dominate the art.
- To select a combination of color and pattern that is appropriate to the function of the room by considering the activities that take place there and the gender and cultural experiences of the users and by giving some rooms an individualized identity.
- To give the environment a sense of security and depth by considering wall covering with a textured appearance.
- To improve the practicality of patterned materials by selecting them on the basis of cleanability and availability of replacement stock.

Approaches

- Consider what imagery would support an area. Think about whether the pattern will date the area unnecessarily. Consider using art and objects to transform the space.
- Use a designer who understands the perceptual needs of older people to help select pattern and color combinations.
- Look for fire-rated materials. While this may seem obvious, it is surprising how many organizations and designers still are not attuned to flammability requirements.
- Look for strippable border prints or removable adhesives. These allow you to give the building a fresh look or to personalize rooms with a minimum of work.
- Obtain pattern samples of a sufficient size to determine the reaction of those who will live, work, and visit in the decorated area.
- Try out patterns where they will be used with the expected daytime and nighttime lighting.
- Consider decorating one or more areas in nontraditional ways. The beauty parlors, a visiting room, an office, or a hobby shop are good candidates for special treatment.

FLOOR COVERINGS

Many sponsors have tried to establish their image through their choice of floor coverings, sometimes giving more attention to their floors than to their walls. They chose floor surfaces for their glossy appearance and used them to bring pattern, color, and style into their facility. For older people, the functional objectives of flooring are somewhat different. Pattern and style would be better developed through wall decorations or flooring that is not used for pedestrian traffic, such as living room areas.

Common Problems

- Floors are not level or even, contributing to tripping hazards.
- Floor materials change, and a transition strip, threshold, or other impediment to free movement is present in any of the following areas:

  —Bedroom to bathroom
  —Hallway to bedroom
  —Shower area to shower stall
  —Lounge to outside area
  —Front entry to outside area
  —Hallway to offices

- Floors must be cleaned every day. The population is likely to soil them quickly.

- Too many people fall, and there are different opinions regarding the use of floor materials to reduce injuries and maintain efficient mobility.
- Shiny floors are seen as an indicator of good care. In fact this is not true. Shiny floors may increase the likelihood of falls, and they often require valuable staff time.
- There is a reluctance to use carpetlike materials.

Objectives

- To provide nonslip floors by selecting materials wisely and treating or cleaning them appropriately.
- To have floors that are easy to traverse by minimizing changes in grade, patterns, and anything else that is an obstacle to vision or movement.
- To contribute to noise abatement by using flooring materials that absorb sounds.
- To save staff time by selecting flooring that is easily cleaned in as few processes as possible and that is safe while being cleaned.
- To choose flooring that will continue to look good by considering durability, wheel traction, and the types of traffic that it receives.
- To provide flooring that contributes visually to a sense of stability and balance by minimizing features that resemble steps, such as highly contrasting stripes or designs, and that make it difficult to concentrate, such as glare, busy or bold patterns in highly contrasting colors, or patterns that appear to vibrate, like plaids or pin dots.

Approaches

- Study the new materials and options. Consider the new carpetlike, nonwoven floor surfaces. They absorb noise, can be cleaned with the appropriate equipment in fewer steps than ordinary floors, and many are surprisingly easy to walk or shuffle on. For new toilet rooms, tub rooms, or other wet areas, look at alternatives to hard ceramic tile, including sheet rubber.
- Meet with sales representatives to learn about cleaning options that minimize burnishing or waxing.
- Select materials that are free of glare and contribute to a visually secure floor surface.
- Consider using wheelchair tires made of harder materials than the usual soft rubber. They are easier to propel on flat or low-pile carpet or resilient floor surfaces.

CHAIRS AND SEATING

Seating for older people is a nursing, physical therapy, and management concern that too often has been overlooked. If no one takes responsibility for

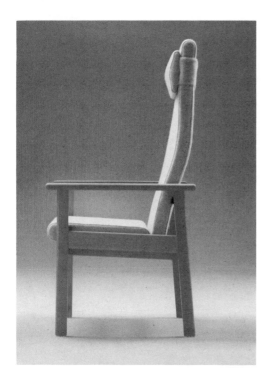

Fig. 6–4 Room chair. Modular furniture, contemporary in appearance, offers a variety of choices in materials and features. Chair by Globalcare, Marlton, New Jersey.

fitting chairs to people, it is sometimes because the facility does not view the fitting of wheelchairs or chairs as a responsibility of caregiving. Many of the chairs we associate with older people are neither designed for them nor suited to the health care environment. Chairs should not be viewed as cosmetic devices or decorations any more than lighting fixtures should. They become an environment for many older people, and they are basic to the daily health care needs and medical equipment of the facility. They must be selected for each individual and updated in accordance with changing needs, just as a prescription would be kept current. (See Figure 6–4.)

Common Problems

- People sit in chairs for many hours during the day; although most nursing requirements urge a regular change in the type of seating, in practice, this often does not happen.
- Many people sit in chairs that are too low or too high, too wide or too narrow, or too deep from front to back. Many chairs are designed without armrests or with armrests that are too high, too low, too spindly, too sharp, or pointed at the ends.
- In poorly fitted chairs, people "learn" poor posture, which sometimes leads to digestive problems.
- Restraints are inappropriately used to hold people in chairs that do not fit their contours or meet their needs.
- Chairs are often selected on the basis of their appearance and price.

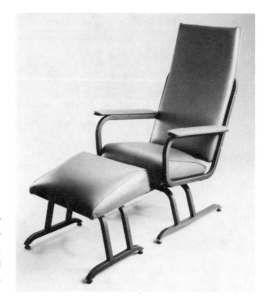

Fig. 6–5 Highback rocker. A few chairs offer safety, motion, and advanced fire retardancy (Option 133 as per California's technical requirements). This locking platform rocker and other chairs by Nemschoff, Sheboygan, Wisconsin.

Objectives

- To select chairs that fit individuals by measuring people when purchasing new chairs or by "trying on" existing chairs to determine which fit best.
- To meet the seating needs of different people by acknowledging that their needs vary and that there must be a variety of chair sizes and styles to suit everyone.

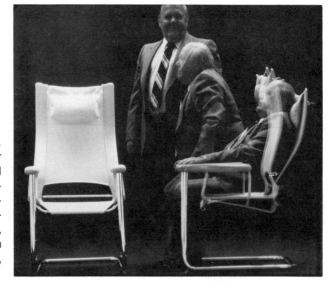

Fig. 6–6 Motion while sitting. New chairs designed just for older people, like the Warren and Rose chairs by Add+Interiors, offer bouncing motion and breathable fabrics. These two chairs respond to a wide variety of needs, from residential living to health care. Chairs by Add+Interiors, Los Angeles, California.

- To minimize seating fatigue by encouraging movement in chairs that bounce, rock, or swivel and by moving people to different seats every hour or so. (See Figures 6–5 and 6–6.)
- To minimize the use of restraints by providing chairs and chair coverings that do not cause sliding.
- To increase comfort by selecting chair surfaces that allow air to circulate rather than surfaces that become hot or clammy.
- To offer chairs appropriate for various activities by selecting chairs that encourage forward motion or have straight backrests for use at tables, and chairs with armrests and slight backward inclines or straight backs for relaxing and conversation.
- To reduce tipping and falling by using chairs that are well balanced and not too large at the base and that have no protruding chair legs to trip residents.
- To support the sitter's legs by ensuring that the feet make contact with the floor or are supported by a footrest.
- To eliminate or reduce the use of reclining chairs by providing chairs that support the upper body and by developing exercise programs that increase appropriate motions and minimize contractures and other conditions that often result in the use of reclining chairs.

Approaches

- Good chair selection involves knowledge of the available chairs, measurement of the individual, and understanding of the chair's use. For example, will the individual be leaning back and relaxing or sitting forward to see or to use implements at a table? Will the chair be used for locomotion? Table 6–1 identifies some of the measurements that must be considered in selecting chairs for specific uses. Table 6–2 lists some common seating difficulties.
- Inventory chair problems in each room. This might be a good project for a trained intern in administration, nursing, or occupational or physical therapy, perhaps alongside a designer.
- Make a commitment to remove unsafe chairs and to repair those that can be repaired.
- Train staff on proper positioning, chair allocation, and chair use.
- Encourage people to bring a chair from home for their room if the chair is fitted to their present needs, in good condition, and made of fire-safe materials. Stuffed chairs can be flammable and contain toxic materials. Sandel™ makes fire-resistant fabric that can be used to wrap foam or other cushions to provide a protective barrier against smoke and fire. (See Appendix D, page 227.)
- Survey the number of chairs in each area with respect to present population needs.

Table 6–1 Selected Seating and Chair Measurements[a]

Seating Feature	Chairs for Dining & Table Activities	Chairs for Talking & Waiting	Chairs for Relaxing
Chair or Sofa Seat			
height (during sitting)	17–18″	17–17.5″	17–17.5″
depth	17.5–18″	18–19″	18–19″
width	16.5–18″	16.5–17.5″	16.5–17.5″
slope	.05″	1″	1.5″
shape	level, flat	flat	flat
density	firm	moderately firm	moderately firm
front edge	flexible/firm	flexible/firm	flexible/firm
Arm Rests			
height	7.5″	7″	7″
length	seat back to past front edge	seat back to past front edge	seat back to past front edge
width	2–3″	2–3″	3″
width between	18″	18″	18.5″
slope	horizontal	horizontal	horizontal
shape	uncurved/flat	uncurved/flat	uncurved/flat
density	firm/padded	firm/padded	firm/padded
front edge	rounded but firm	rounded but firm	rounded but firm
Back Rest			
height	13.5″	14″ (+)	17″ (+)
width	12.5″	13.5″	14″
slope (inches from vertical)	2″	3.5″	5″
shape	16–18″ radius	16–18″ radius	16–18″ radius
Tie Rail			
height	13–15″	13–14″	12–14″
placement	directly under chair seat	directly under chair seat	directly under chair seat
Upholstery			
materials	nylon, vinyl, nylon/polyester, vinylized cotton fire rated	nylon, vinyl, nylon/polyester, treated cotton & cotton blends fire rated	nylon, vinyl, nylon/polyester, treated cotton & cotton blends fire rated
treatments	stain resistant (Scotchgard™ and Teflon™), fire retardant, water resistant	stain resistant (Scotchgard™ and Teflon™), fire retardant, water resistant	stain resistant (Scotchgard™ and Teflon™), fire retardant, water resistant
cushions	firm and dense fire retardant, i.e., Sandel™ no welted seams	firm and dense fire retardant, i.e., Sandel™ no welted seams	firm and dense fire retardant, i.e., Sandel™ no welted seams

prepared by: Joan A. Pease
      Principal
      Partners in Planning
      85 So. Bragg St.
      Alexandria, VA 22312

[a]Source: Joan A. Pease, Consultant in Retirement Housing, Partners in Planning. Abstracted from Human Factors Data, Anthropometric measurements of older people. Washington, Government Printing Office, 1962. Data such as these would benefit from additional and more recent corroboration.

Table 6–2 Common Seating Problems

Problem	Implications and Examples
Poor positioning	Slumping
Lack of body strength	Difficulty in standing and transfer due in part to "learned" poor posture
Poor digestion	Incomplete digestion and constipation due to poor positioning and lack of motion (restrained motion)
Sleepiness, fatigue	Body slumps, oxygen supply to brain is reduced due to compression of diaphragm
Feet not in contact with floor; legs dangle	Seat too high; may experience edema (water build-up in lower extremities) due to dangling legs
Seat too slippery or soft	Sliding out of chair
Feeding problems	Not close enough to the table
Lack of space	Chair bases or legs are too large or protrude
Shoddy or worn appearance	Chair materials are worn
People seated for too long; seating not varied	Pressure sores, restlessness; some chairs should allow safe motion
Chairs all one size	People vary in size, and chairs must fit them
Chairs tip easily	Greater dependence on staff for assistance in transfer or greater vulnerability to falls
Sharp edges on armrests	Bruised forearms likely
Chairs too low (less than 16″ from floor)	More assistance required getting up and out
Chairs not fitted to people	People likely to be tied in or restrained
Chairs lack structure to support lower back	Lower back ache; lumbar fatigue
No armrests	Sliding
Recliners used for much of the day	Too much pressure on lower spine and buttocks, resulting in vulnerability to skin breakdown

- Examine the use of recliners and bulky geriatric wheelchairs on an individual basis. Consider alternatives, particularly for newly admitted people, and work toward minimizing the improper use of these chairs. (See Figure 6–7.)

WALL DECORATION

Decoration should give a facility personality and convey the value placed on all residents, staff, visitors, and the community.

Common Problems

- The walls are bare and stark, and no one knows what to put on them.
- The walls are decorated at regular intervals with a particular style of

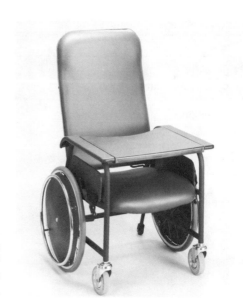

Fig. 6–7 Alternative to geriatric wheelchair. A high-backed chair with large wheels, like the one shown here, can be used in place of large, bulky geriatric wheelchairs. Wheelchairs should be prescribed. This model by Lumex™.

Fig. 6–8 Before refurbishment of cinder block walls. Cinder and ceramic block walls have been used in many nursing homes. These materials are often difficult to change and decorate, and they have been associated with increased noise.

painting at a specific height. Although there is something on the walls, they do not look distinctive. There is little variety.

- The decorations look fragile or homemade (for example, cutouts, magazine pictures, and posters).
- Items are not touchable.
- Wall decorations are not looked after; they are askew, scattered, disorganized, or in poor repair.
- There is no place to hang things, or the surface makes hanging items difficult. (See Figure 6–8.)
- Items cannot be seen by wheelchair users or are not within eye level.
- Artwork does not relate to the wall covering or color, or it is dominated by it.
- There is no place for residents to individualize a wall area.
- There is no system for rotating or rearranging items.
- Staff members disagree about the type of art that will interest residents.
- Some people believe that art overstimulates memory-impaired people.
- Items on the wall should be fire rated for vertical placement, but they are not.
- Wall murals have become dated, or the image no longer suits the purpose of the unit.

Objectives

- To develop a plan for using art that does not result in a formal, repetitive, and unvarying set of acquisitions by recognizing individual preferences in subject, size, style, color, and amount of art and by considering how items are hung or displayed.
- To recognize that art is for residents, families, staff, and other community members by involving these individuals in the selection of items for the areas they are most likely to use.
- To consider using art to reinforce other program goals by selecting wall decorations that match the particular characteristics of residents. Some examples are outlined in Table 6–3.

Approaches

- Ask a cross section of residents, staff, and community members to consider the objectives for an art program.
- Explore new sources of art, such as libraries, historical societies, galleries with items on loan, local artists, and resident artists.
- Look for new types of art, like touchable and washable pieces, art made from vertically fire-rated materials, sculpture, and pieces that are particularly large.
- Consider the meaning of art for different groups and in different locations: personalization in bedrooms; first impressions in entries, elevator lobbies, and intersections; cultural identification, geographic

Table 6–3 Matching Artwork with Client Needs

Characteristics of Population	Appropriate Art
Alert, physically able	Permanent display in some areas, changing display in others; encourage personalization
Cognitively impaired	Use resident and family involvement to choose art that cues or reinforces memories; personalize room with things donated by family; select safe, touchable items that cannot be ingested, easily pocketed, or lost
Heavy care	Place art in areas inhabited by older people; mobiles or touchable items; items near bed or on ceiling; familiar, comforting images; items that help people judge reality: clock, marked calendar, plant that blooms
Behaviorally expressive	Art that helps dissipate stress and agitation, such as touchable, vertically fire-rated carpet and scenes that tell a story; watch resident reaction and adapt accordingly
Rehabilitation	Manipulable or hand-held objects; items placed sequentially to encourage ambulation or wheeling
Staff members	Culturally reinforcing, personally selected for office, break area, and lockers
Families, including children	Interesting, meaningful; representational or abstract; intergenerational interest

relevance, and intergenerational interaction for residents, staff, and visitors.
- Explore ways to frame, organize, hang, or display art to reduce the apparent length of corridors.
- Add a step to the selection process for wall covering to consider what will be displayed on the walls.
- Consider alternatives to wall murals, such as large painted scenes on fire-rated canvas or another surface that can be removed when necessary (for example, when adjacent areas need repainting).

WAYFINDING AND SIGNS

As institutions grow and sprawl, information that helps residents, staff, and visitors has become essential. Because older people have unique ways of perceiving space and signs, their needs may go beyond those of the general public.

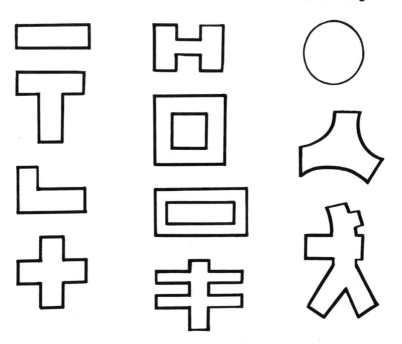

Fig. 6–9 Wayfinding. Initial studies indicated that building size and configuration contribute to confusion. Simple outline buildings (left column) were found to be less disorienting than those with several intersections (center column). The most disorienting buildings in this study appeared to be those that lacked distinctive intersections and familiar right angles (right column). (After Hiatt, 1985.)

Common Problems

- The building layout is inherently confusing. It is round or has several angles and grids; it is not laid out with simple right angles (Figure 6–9). In certain areas, people cannot find their way to known destinations or cannot retrace their steps. This often results from the ambiguity of the intersection.
- The building appears stark and repetitious in terms of color, textures, surfaces, glare, windows, corridor vistas, and doorways.
- The walls are made of cinder block or similar glazed block, which is repetitious, contributes to disorienting noise, and provides a surface that is difficult to decorate.
- Visual features of the environment, such as glare, nondifferentiation of floors and walls (Figure 6–10), or inappropriate emphasis on repetitive features (Figure 6–11) inhibit wayfinding.
- The corridor is old and has a number of exposed features, including pipes and sprinkler heads, that are visually confusing.

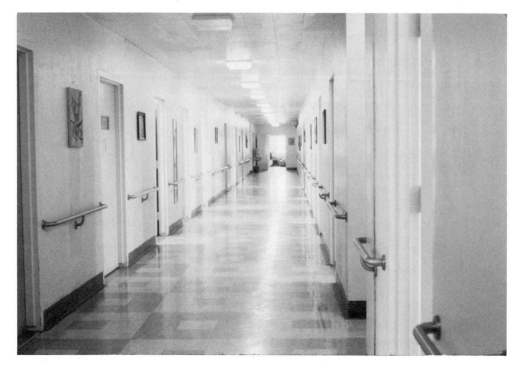

Fig. 6–10 Corridor problems. Common corridor difficulties include nondifferentiated floors and walls. Glare, lack of distinguishing visual features, and the appearance of length all complicate the perception of hallways and the ability to move easily.

- Policies forbid personalization and the use of wall areas for landmarks or tackable surfaces, thereby limiting variety.
- Signs are unavailable or illegible due to size, quality, or location, or they do not use the names by which places are commonly known.
- Abstract cues such as color coding are not clearly understood or used.
- People have had little practice in getting around the building, including retracing steps.

Objectives

- To minimize confusing features in new construction, such as mirrored walls, glare, acute angles at corridors, and repetitious unit entry points, by using design features and materials that are unambiguous, free of glare, and familiar and by optimizing the use of right angles.
- To facilitate identification by providing surfaces along the hall, beside the door, and in the bedroom for the display of personal items and by transforming cinder block into a more residential surface that can be decorated.

Fig. 6–11 Emphasis on inappropriate corridor features. Dark door jambs, sharp contrast between sections of the wall, and dominating floor patterns or tiles often date a facility and convey an institutional image.

- To provide a system of clarifying where one is by providing simple maps and simple word signs to indicate the location and name of places.
- To minimize confusion at points known to be troublesome by improving lighting and signs and by considering the best placement of information.
- To provide information at intersections about what is ahead, to the left, and to the right by creating appropriate signs.
- To provide information in formats that are relevant to the particular needs of residents by using large-print, high-contrast lettering for those who do not see well, personal objects as cues for those who are mentally impaired or who prefer to use objects as landmarks, and the language most likely to be understood by residents.
- To organize signs by placing them at eye level and in some predictable location, like on the wall next to the handle side of a door.
- To communicate information about the organization as part of the

Fig. 6–12 Corridor refurbishment. Blending door jamb with walls, and then using different floor and baseboard colors may help to organize corridor appearance and provide an appropriate background for art. Walls do need to be different from floors in terms of coloration. Distinguishing the floor from the walls, even with a slender baseboard, may help people to walk more steadily.

sign system by providing maps that identify departments (administration, business, clinic) and hours of access.
- To assist residents in wayfinding by giving them practice.

Approaches

- Analyze a simple floor plan of the building to determine the locations of intersections, entries, exits, elevators, and parking lots. (See Figure 6–9.) Determine whether there is sufficient information to and from these locations by asking people to give directions and by reflecting on the questions they raise.
- Ask staff and residents to identify the most confusing locations within the building and to recall places that visitors, residents, and new staff ask about most. Then develop the appropriate signs or landmarks to facilitate the use of these areas.
- Look for visual features that draw attention to unnecessary details, thus causing confusion. Try to create a more unified corridor with

Fig. 6–13 Before refurbishment of vintage corridor. This 1884 retirement facility features corridors with high ceilings, brick walls, and exposed sprinklers. Slight variations in proportions and use of materials will transform it. (By Lewis and Rogers, Fort Washington, for Ralston House, Philadelphia, Pennsylvania.)

Fig. 6–14 After refurbishment of vintage corridor. Dark, flat-finish paint helps to hide ceiling hardware and mechanical systems. New, horizontal fixtures improve lighting. Glare-free carpeting and attention to wall and doorway colors convey a very different image. (By Lewis and Rogers, Fort Washington, for Ralston House, Philadelphia, Pennsylvania.)

the appearance of a backdrop or household hallway. Minimize the confusing effects of long corridors by painting door jambs the same tone as walls (Figure 6–12). Minimize visual disturbances by "painting out" pipes or other features (Figures 6–13 and 6–14).

- If there are closets, storage rooms, or staff areas that need not be called out to residents, consider camouflaging them by minimizing the emphasis placed on the doorway. Consider placing identifying signs well above eye level. Residents can then generalize that low signs are resident-use areas, and high signs are utility areas or off-limits.
- Look for alternatives to cinder block as a wall surface. These include covering walls with paint, sheet rock, or full panels of tackable surface and wall coverings (Figure 6–15).

Fig. 6–15 Tackable wall coverings. Cinder or ceramic block walls can be covered with materials that aid noise abatement, offer different textures, and provide a surface for changing decoration. (Presbyterian Home of Central New York.)

- To help distinguish individual rooms, provide tackable surfaces for personal items. Ideally, these surfaces should not look like small, framed cork bulletin boards. When the background surfaces for doorside decorations are themselves designed, they can help distinguish rooms along a linear corridor (Figures 6–16 to 6–20).
- Many older people cannot remember their room according to door or door jamb color because this information is too subtle and abstract. Color coding may help cluster a group of rooms, however, and break down the apparent length of a corridor, making it easier to remember the general appearance of one's room from the distance.
- Use a simple awning or other doorway treatment to improve the recognition of offices or other areas along a lengthy corridor (Figure 6–21).
- Position signs and artwork at eye level. High, overhead signs are

Fig. 6–16 Tackable surfaces camouflaged as wall coverings. When planning a system for personalizing bedroom door areas or using individualized landmarks, remember that some collections may be dense, others spare, and others nonexistent. The self-healing, tackable wall covering shown here provides a generous surface for decoration next to the door and looks almost like vinyl or fabric wall covering when undecorated. Displays can be changed without requiring wall repairs. A light backdrop increases the contrast, assuming most objects are dark or bright. This doorway has been recessed, making the displays more visible and giving the corridor a streamlined appearance that may be easier for maintenance.

decorative but may be out of the viewing range of older people who have difficulty looking up (Figure 6–20).

- Make sure signs are legible. Raised lettering on signs often chips or creates shadows. Incised, nonglare, highly contrasted lettering may be more readily visible than raised letters (Figure 6–22).

- Most older people do not read Braille, but many have vision impairments. Large letters, 1½″ to 2″ high (depending on the viewing distance and the number of letters), may be easier to read for more people than Braille. If a resident is helped by Braille, it should of course be provided.

- Make activity calendars and clocks (aspects of environmental information) part of the decor. If you discover that digital clocks are unfamiliar to some older people or difficult for them to use, consider more traditional time pieces for public areas.

Fig. 6–17 Displays to reduce visual clutter. Small framed bulletin boards or displays applied directly to doors are sometimes perceived as patchy and cluttered. Displays must look good from a distance, even though individual items may be recognizable only at close range. Here, distinguishable shapes like quarter moons are placed beside each door. There is one for each person in the room, and they are assigned to match bed placement. These tackable backboards lend order to small items, because from a distance they create their own arrangement, thus helping to distinguish bedroom doors from utility doors and organizing the corridor.

Fig. 6–18 Improving traditional bulletin boards. Oversized square or rectangular boards may look more residential when their colors match or blend with the wall and when the edging is narrow.

Fig. 6–19 Memory lanes. The creative use of bulletin boards or similar display features gives the corridor a sense of variety and aids room identification. Objects next to the door may be more readily recognized than colors or name labels alone.

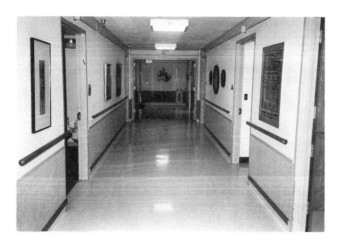

Fig. 6–20 Arranging artwork. Varying the placement of artwork along a corridor may improve the appearance of the corridor. Note the organization and style of frames and the effect of using large mat boards to increase the significance of the smaller pieces.

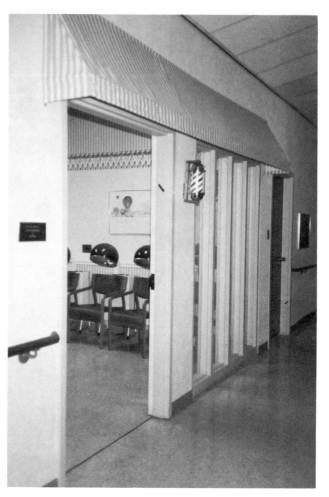

Fig. 6–21 Use of landmarks and canopies to emphasize special areas. Features can work together to distinguish a particular room from other areas and to provide a landmark when viewed from the distance. A valence or small awning placed over a doorway will serve this function, but care must be taken not to impede fire safety and call systems. Three-dimensional features, like the familiar barber pole, further distinguish the space and dress up an otherwise unvaried corridor. The awning pattern shown here is carried as a border print through the room along the same sight line. (Sponsor designed by Jewish Center for the Aged of Greater Saint Louis.)

- Develop simple, nameable landmarks that can be used in giving oral instructions, and place them at critical points. Good items to use as landmarks include a large clock, an easily described object (such as a bell, hat rack, or painting), and a distinctive furniture arrangement (Figure 6–23). (See also Figures 6–16 to 6–20.)
- Name corridors for local streets so that intersections in the building are similar to those residents have used outside.
- Train staff to give simple oral instructions that are free of color information, because older and younger people may see colors differently.
- Give people actual practice or "orienteering" experience so that they understand the building layout, location of key resources, and location of directions. You may need to repeat this information several times.

Fig. 6–22 Print legibility. Contrast and a simple roman lettering style increase the visibility of signs that are meant to be read up close.

Fig. 6–23 Furnishings as landmarks. Familiar or special furnishings, placed near the entry to a unit, may help distinguish the entry and serve as identifiable landmarks from the distance while encouraging closer inspection. (By SFCS, Inc., Roanoke, Virginia.)

Fig. 6–24 Telling the story to visitors. Today's nursing home is more vigorous about marketing and providing information to the public. The unit shown here was developed by a local cabinetmaker to display current events, information on special programs, pamphlets, and applications. Items of greater interest to children may be displayed at the bottom. (Evergreen Manor, Oshkosh, Wisconsin.)

- Allow residents to walk alone or to wheel themselves to develop their skills, when feasible.
- Tell the public about what you are doing. A well-designed and well-used kiosk will help visitors become acquainted with your programs and resources (Figure 6–24).

7
Special Design Issues for the Mentally Impaired

Since the early seventies, when the issue of design for cognitively impaired older people began to appear in the literature, our awareness of the nature and size of this population has broadened. Our perception of their abilities and the variety of their impairments are changing, as is our approach to this population.

Planning effective design for the mentally impaired is often a special case of planning good design for all people. The more responsive the environment is to the needs of older residents, the more likely it is that the environment itself will adequately serve people who are cognitively impaired. This population, as a whole, tends to be more vulnerable to the weaknesses of existing long-term care design, including inadequate space, confusing features, lack of culturally meaningful cues or objects, and features that distance or otherwise inconvenience staff members, making them less readily available. Mildly to moderately impaired people are particularly vulnerable to the cuing effects of the environment. The presence of noxious stimuli (such as glare, noise, and odors), poor traffic patterns, inadequate texture, and insufficient access to the outside may be particularly difficult for these populations. The environment also significantly affects more severely impaired people, whose physical needs predominate over their mental needs. For this population, effective seating, comfort, textural variety, and even items for room personalization may be resources in individualized contact.

Renovation is important when the environment as a whole has risky features, inappropriate stimuli, or inadequate social areas. Renovation may not require the construction of a new or special building for the mentally impaired. A program center will sometimes provide an adequate basis from which to develop enriched, personalized activities. If additions will be made for people with dementia, a program center or in-house day-care program should probably be included in the planning.

This chapter addresses some of the issues that you must consider when designing for older people with cognitive impairments, who may have varying characteristics and needs. It begins with a discussion of the common problems that nursing homes face, offers some objectives to get you started, and then suggests approaches that might work. As in previous chapters, these lists are not intended to be exhaustive and you should personalize each to suit your particular needs.

Common Problems

- The population is considered monolithically, as though all mentally impaired people were the same: all wander, all are risky, and all are incapable of appreciating their environment. In fact, none of these generalizations is founded on empirical research. Sponsors must decide which of the following client groups to serve and how:

    1. Those who are not overtly impaired
    2. Those with conventional cognitive deficits, such as slowed response rate, but who are free of diseases like Alzheimer's
    3. Those with vacillating behavior that may be something other than cognitive impairment (for example, people with abreactions to medications, electrolyte imbalance, undernutrition, or other conditions that may be reversible)
    4. Those with underlying emotional difficulties as a primary behavioral diagnosis
    5. Those with mild dementia
    6. Those with moderate cognitive impairment
    7. Those with severe cognitive impairment

- Facilities respond to the needs of the cognitively impaired with architectural drawings rather than programs. A facility needs a program first. (Some architects assert that a program *is* an architectural response.) The program must include a series of population, staffing, and scheduling features that may be developed and documented by those involved with the services and operations of the facility.
- Institutions often try to make macro-level environmental changes (such as special units, wandering gardens, and interior pathways or loops for safe motion), while overlooking important micro-environmental features (such as noxious stimuli like glare, noise, and uneven lighting). Micro-environmental features (that is, elements of interior design and items that come in contact with the individual) are often valuable program resources.
- Facilities fail to provide features that support attention span. The following, for example, should be accommodated:

    1. Improved lighting
    2. Separation or elimination of distracting traffic in areas meant for concentrated behavior, such as eating or group work
    3. Noise abatement
    4. Basic physical comforts, including appropriate temperature, free-

dom from drafts, supported feet, comfortable seating, and appropriate management of incontinence

5. Aromatically pleasing environments

- Institutions search for a single, perfect model of the proper size, with specific anticipated features and a particular use of interior space. They fail to recognize the need for examples, research, modification, and more research before developing even a series of options. A single model is unlikely. This is good news for existing facilities.
- It is assumed that mentally impaired people need specially built facilities. In fact, if nursing homes were free of features that cause problems for most older people and staff, they would be more appropriate places for the mentally impaired.
- Rather than adapt a multidimensional approach to meeting the needs of mentally impaired people, some facilities limit their focus. They provide one major design feature and expect it to serve all or many of the mentally impaired. A multidimensional focus involves developing a program with ramifications for medical services, nursing coordination and treatment, nursing assistants, therapeutic recreation, dietary staff, housekeeping, social services, families and volunteers, pharmacy and treatment services, administration (risk management), and allied health (physical and occupational therapy).
- Facilities overlook or take for granted basic issues affecting the quality of life. Here are five examples:

1. They do not consider privacy to be an important need of mentally impaired people on the assumption that it will isolate them. In fact, private time may promote social time.
2. The significance of personal appearance is overlooked. Although grooming may be familiar for some people, it must be encouraged. This may be because facilities for hair care are distant, or staff people have no knowledge of or facilities for convenient grooming, dressing, and related aspects of dignity for those who are incontinent.
3. People are too often left without human contact or sources of vestibular and tactile stimulation. Vestibular stimulation includes touch and movement such as rocking, gentle vibration, or other systemically experienced contact.
4. Until recently, physical restraints were viewed as a necessary attribute of care and mandated by medical orders, even though a growing body of research questioned the value of body holders and the use of traditional chair-tables as restraints. Restraints may encourage injury, skin breakdown (due to the lack of freedom of movement), and even falls. Some research favors better positioning and fitting of chairs to people.
5. Choices are denied to mentally impaired people because of a lack of knowledge of how to offer them options. Since dementia is

associated with limited skills of abstract reasoning, such as planning, choices must be offered in relation to immediate options. This minimizes the need to draw upon recent recall, which is usually limited.

- There is little to cue or stimulate memory for familiar facts. (Familiarity is defined here by the resident's life history.) A variety of things (such as objects, memorabilia, decorations, textures, foods, clothing, patterns, and colors) encourages resident recollections and stimulates conversations between residents and staff members.
- Facilities do not understand or accommodate the need for repositioning and motion. There should be appropriate options for gross and fine movement and for exercising coordination skills. There should be individualized plans, furnishings, and environments that support movement while ensuring that it is safe.
- The environment often does not respond to an individual's need for emotional support. Emotional support may involve providing places where one can shift one's mood from inward to outward or from frustrated to expressive, for example. There should be places, natural and contrived, that encourage a full range of emotions. They should allow touching, venting frustration, individual exploration, a sense of mastery, and the experience of familiar emotions related to music, listening, responding to soft animals or wondrous babies, slapstick humor, and the like.
- Older people with various forms of dementia can be distracted by the presence of too many people. An optimal number has not been established and probably varies with individuals, capacity differences, and social norms. There should be places for small groups of varying sizes to gather for social activities. Larger spaces may be appropriate for groups involved in exercise, music, performances, parties, and events where individual behavior is not expected. Note that some people may not function well in larger groups.

Objectives

- To respond to variations in mental impairment in the population by developing different programs and design that respond to people of varying needs and capacities, including residents who have (1) no evident impairment, (2) mild impairment associated with slowed responses, (3) mild impairment associated with dementia, (4) moderate impairment, and (5) complex needs.
- To wrap design around specific program features by creating a program concept first, then considering whether the program requires a specific unit or place.
- To identify the population's needs by analyzing the following: the existing population, the demand for services by new applicants, the best utilization of existing staff members and programs, the best

utilization of existing design (including location, facilities, natural perimeter security, and unit size), and features for programming.

- To make an informed decision by studying all of the available options for serving the mentally impaired, including the development of an in-house care program that may or may not be related to a special residential area of the building.

Approaches

- Conduct a facility inventory to identify potential hazards for those with unpredictable behavior. Develop a plan to overcome these risks. Consider creating a secure area for free and unrestrained movement by combining door security and site amenities to minimize the risk of encountering traffic. Consider also adopting telemetric, wearable alert systems that allow individuals to move but that trigger an alarm when they pass a particular point (preferably well in advance of the front door).
- Optimize the sensory environment. See "Lighting" and "Noise Abatement" in Chapter 5 for suggestions on reducing noxious stimuli, such as glare and noise.
- Simplify the environment by eliminating distractions from the activity in progress. At mealtime, for example, attention should focus on eating, and the dining environment should be free of television, noise, excessive motion, and behavior unrelated to meals. Group activities should take place in an area without distractions, with appropriate objects for discussion, and with few other stimuli. This approach is especially valuable for people with moderate impairments.
- Provide options for exploration. Create places where people can roam, operate items, and handle objects, for example. These areas will provide appropriate stimulation while serving as a place to release excess energy (Figure 7–1). This is another valuable approach for those with moderate impairments.
- Use artwork or other objects to evoke memory and stimulate responsiveness. For the severely impaired people, provide textured items to hold and touch. For all levels of impairment, try personal items in rooms, aroma, and objects to stimulate activities of daily living (such as clothes laid out on bed to encourage self-dressing).
- Provide landmarks for wayfinding. See "Wayfinding and Signs" in Chapter 6. This approach is especially beneficial for mildly and moderately impaired people.
- Provide opportunities for residents to go outside for fresh air. This approach will help those with all degrees of impairment.
- Provide variety in environments so that when a person is caught in a "mood rut" changing place can be used to encourage normal mood changes. Often new faces, fresh air, different sized rooms or a new ambiance support the shift from dejected to benign.

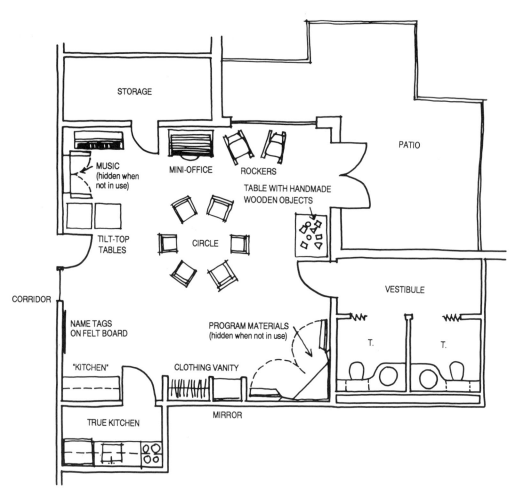

Fig. 7–1 Energy outlet room for dementia care. Rooms like this one offer concurrent activities and features to cue possible activities. Certain areas may be opened and closed, and people can change their orientation as they would in a stage set. Nearby bathrooms, staff areas, a resident-use kitchen, and outdoor areas complete the space. An open area at the center is used for formal discussions, and it allows people who cannot sit to participate while moving around the room. The items here were selected to encourage exploration; appropriate items include a roll-top desk, racks of familiar clothing, a vanity, rockers, tables with objects like fine woodwork for caressing, and windows with views to the outside. (By Timothy C. Boers, Boulder Associates Architects, Boulder, Colorado.)

- If your facility is small, consider blending dementia day care with care for residents who live within the institution (Figure 7–2).

Example How much programming and space needs to be allocated to people with dementia? Assume that 50% of a nursing home's population is cognitively impaired and that 50% to 75% of those people may benefit from group programming. (Those who demonstrate complex physical needs but do not re-

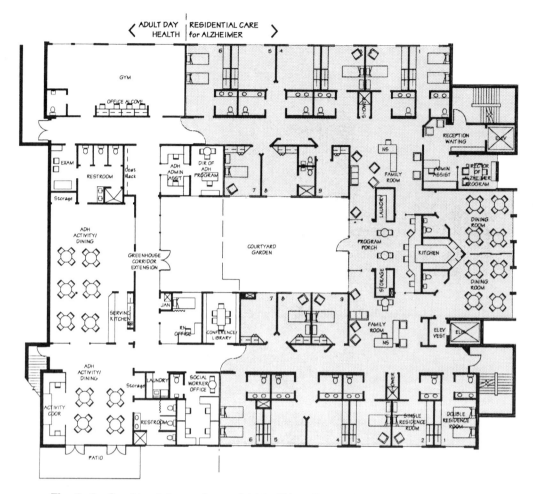

Fig. 7–2 Combined day and overnight facilities. Sponsors increasingly seek to combine day programs with overnight facilities. This study plan for Pacific Presbyterian Medical Center offers a series of small gathering places (shaded areas distinguish inpatient from day care), dining area, a familiar counter area, program spaces, and living rooms. All have niches for exploring and wandering. This renovation plan was developed for a traditionally designed nursing home. (By Barker Associates, Palo Alto, California.)

spond in group situations may benefit from one-to-one contact that emphasizes sensory interaction, touch, comfort, bathing, aromas, fresh air, etc.) This should offer some indication of the demand for a dementia care program.

In-house programs can be developed in unused space, in space that is created from a dayroom, a series of bedrooms, or storage facilities, or in space that is added onto the building. The "program center" or energy outlet room may be directly related to a unit, or it may be centrally located. Be sure to provide transportation to the center for those who require the amenities it offers. If it is far from the dining area, you may want to offer the option of meals in this center. In new construction, it may be valuable to create an

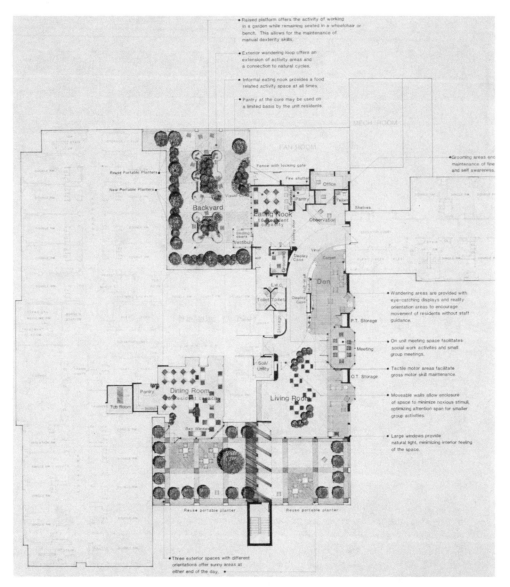

Fig. 7–3 Creating a dementia program space by building a room on a rooftop. Residents from two adjacent wings will jointly attend in-house day-care programs in this multifaceted program space. The areas were developed based on the program created by staff members and on a profile of prototype participants. They include a staff center, a kitchenette for staff use (residents can look in over a familiar kitchen counter), a small snack area, grooming facilities, a formal living room and adjacent area for roaming, small niches for observation and visiting, a large and flexible area for such activities as exercise and music, individual exploration areas to be decorated in response to resident interests, storage facilities, and options for going outside. In this model, most residents dine back on their unit. This area was sized and planned for sixty users and has noise-abatement properties. (By Whelan and Associates, New York, with Korsunsky Krank Erikson, Minneapolis, Minnesota, for Jewish Home and Hospital, Kingsbridge, Bronx, New York.)

observation area (using two-way rather than one-way glass) where visitors can observe what is happening without entering the room. We are not typically troubled by the thought that older dementia care participants may watch those staff or family members who watch them during a meeting or tour as long as visitors do not continually enter the space used for dementia programs.

The space itself should stimulate thinking and offer options, yet have some controllable qualities. Like the little niches in Figure 7–3, it should be possible to close off certain areas (minimizing extraneous stimuli) or use doors or screens to help organize attention span. A key to success is understanding that not all people will participate by sitting down. Some will meander around the perimeter, occasionally stopping to join in, occasionally standing still before one of the tables. Designing the space is much like planning for a three-ring circus, a Montessori classroom, or a participatory museum.

The amount of duplication of on-unit services will vary, as will the space requirement for a meaningful program. The staff may come from nursing, therapeutic recreation, social services, and volunteers. There are roles for all allied health professionals, including occupational and physical therapists. Successful programs usually involve a designated program leader with a strong link to administration.

8
Typical Questions and Replies

The following are actual questions raised during recent renovation and refurbishment projects. They are grouped according to topic. The responses may be of interest to others.

COST

Question. How do costs for new construction compare with costs for renovation?

Reply. Construction costs vary tremendously by area. In 1989, the cost of new buildings ranged from $62.00 to over $100 per square foot, depending on location, labor availability, and labor source. Renovations are so varied in actual cost one must actually describe and price each project on a job by job basis. Prices may run from $40 to $100 per square foot.

Renovation is often far more expensive than anticipated. The hidden costs include asbestos containment or removal and the expansion of heating, air conditioning, and other systems into new areas. Many states have established a limit on the cost of changes that can be made. When expenditures approach that amount, they must be reviewed by a cost-containment or architectural plan review group, and any noncompliant areas of the building must be brought into compliance with applicable state regulations. For older facilities, this can mean adding plumbing and changing door widths, resulting in increased costs.

PLANNING

Question. Why not just tell us how big to make it and list the features we need without all the theory? As an administrator, I don't need to be involved.

Reply. An important goal for renovation is to improve the fit among design, users, and services. When designers and their clients agree to "skip the generalities," the resulting project often revolves around features that fail to meet this objective. If there were just one way to handle such issues as privacy, design for the mentally impaired, and outdoor areas, the design process would be much simpler. Unfortunately, there is no one way.

If design team members have trouble with the planning process, consider working with planning specialists prior to developing schematic or concept drawings. This process is too important to sidestep. The cost of jumping into a project without first clarifying the givens, the population, the service and management patterns, and the design options is likely to be quite dear.

Question. Doesn't planning make a project more cumbersome than necessary?

Reply. No. Planning does take time, but it is worth the investment when you remember that you will live with the result for years. Good planning often makes a project go faster and run more smoothly; poor planning often slows a project down.

Question. Isn't design primarily a cosmetic issue?

Reply. No. Design affects the quality of service a facility is able to offer, and good design helps a facility operate efficiently. When you consider that labor represents the major proportion of a nursing home's life-cycle costs, you realize that good design is an investment in sound operation.

Question. What specifically does good design do for an operation?

Reply. Good design may

- Attract staff, residents, and their families
- Communicate your concept of service to outsiders and help market your facility
- Increase staff productivity and resident independence
- Increase the comfort of residents and visitors
- Help retain staff
- Reduce the cost of consumables
- Serve as an adjunct to a wide range of programs, including effective morning care, odor reduction, better service for the mentally impaired, and reduced risk of falling

Question. Should we involve the existing population in the planning process? How?

Reply. Residents should certainly be involved. They are a terrific source of information, and they enjoy roles ranging from participating in focus groups that help define projects to serving (from a safe distance) as sidewalk supervisors.

Early on, initiate resident discussion groups about the proposed project. Topics might include how the project may affect resident payment rates, when it will be completed, and what else the residents would do, given the chance. Provide residents with the opportunity to review written and illustrative material about the proposed project.

Mid-stage, give residents the chance to examine small-scale models or to experience mockups including full-scale two-dimensional plans of a proposed room or area.

During construction, keep residents involved with the project and apprised of its progress by making the following available:

- A gallery of construction photographs or videos
- Ongoing administrative reports on the project's implications for the immediate lives of residents
- Safe, supervised tours or video trips of interior and exterior changes, when appropriate
- Occasional question and answer sessions with the project manager

After construction, give residents the opportunity to ask questions of the management and design team. Include them in a systematic evaluation of what works and what does not work (the post-occupancy evaluation).

Question. How do you respond to a staff member whose attitude is, "Why ask me?"

Reply. Staff members of many different departments have information that is extremely useful in making design improvements. While many may not have specific information regarding all of the available problem-solving approaches, some will identify the route to solutions, and others will be virtual encyclopedias of information.

Staff members are asked to contribute to the planning process because they may have insights on the following:

- The givens
- The population, from a functional point of view
- The operation of services, including schedules, staffing, work flow, and areas needing change
- Where design has failed in the past

You need not implement all suggestions literally, but it is very helpful to address valid issues raised and praise staff for valued input.

Question. How might we respond to questions such as, "Why hasn't anyone asked me before this?"

Reply. Most older buildings were designed without suggestions from staff members because there was concern that their input would be unreasonable, impractical, or obvious. Although this concern is occasionally well founded, most of what has been learned about good design has come from staff people. As a result, many top managers now recognize the significance of working with all of the staff to obtain information about the health care facility as a residence for older people, as a work area, and as a place that provides many other services.

Question. How much time will the planning process take?

Reply. If the facility has a good planning and decision-making process in place, most participatory planning will involve short meetings and some reflection on operations. The time, from several hours to a few weeks stretched over one to three months, is usually well worth the result.

Question. Will my ideas be implemented or used?

Reply. Planning involves obtaining many ideas. Some will be implemented, some will not. No promises can be made. Unless you voice your suggestions and substantiate them, however, it is unlikely that they will be implemented.

Question. I am a staff member who has not been involved with the design decisions thus far. How can I be heard?

Reply. If the facility is involved in a planning process, there are several ways to make a difference. You may need to illustrate that you have information not previously considered. Try these techniques:

- Use the "to . . . by" statements described in Chapter 3 to clarify your needs.
- If you work in direct contact with residents, be well versed on the population. Information describing the number and characteristics of residents and a schedule of your work with them will be helpful.
- If you are knowledgeable about a service area, such as maintenance, housekeeping, or food service, consider the operation in terms of how it might be more effective. What do people require to do their jobs and to cooperate with the improvements planned?
- Show how your idea might improve the efficiency of the facility. Information that demonstrates financial savings is especially compelling.
- Be willing to write your thoughts down. Your participation may at first be confined to memos and well-substantiated recommendations. Be ready to participate when asked.

ARCHITECTURE AND ARCHITECTS

Question. What is special about designing for older people?

Reply. Designing for older people involves an understanding of the people themselves and the many "filters" through which their needs are met. Codes, management, and staff may all serve as filters. Stereotypes of older people and their families may also serve to filter out effective design solutions.

Designing for older people is special because it requires knowledge about their functional capacities that is not intuitive. In fact, there is little about design for older people that can be gleaned from personal experience with one or two older family members. At no other time in life are people more diverse.

Question. If nursing home clients are indeed older and sicker than in the past, why does design matter?

Reply. It is true that older people now enter nursing homes with increasing numbers of concurrent conditions, but they are not necessarily more likely to require bed stays. Today's residents require systematic care directed at their needs. This does not mean, however, that they have no capabilities. In fact, they may have much untapped potential. Even bedridden residents require attention that can be supported through good design. Good design can optimize residents' vision, hearing, mobility, agility, endurance, attention span, speed of response, comfort, safety, dignity, and social interaction, among other things.

Question. Can design for older people be interesting?

Reply. Design for older people must accommodate their special functional needs, but this does not mean that the process cannot be creative or rewarding. Effective design is well appreciated. It is quite satisfying to release the potential in older people and their caregivers by making a difference in walking distances, effective allocation of space, or the available stimuli, for example.

Question. What are the common failings of architectural design for nursing homes?

Reply. There are many:

- Design sometimes focuses on one or two features (for example, the visual qualities of the environment or a "wandering loop") without attending to the full range of design issues.
- Codes are overlooked or consulted too late; personal meetings with regulatory officials are set late in the process rather than earlier.
- Regulations are seen as the guide for good design. Regulators and reviewers have insufficient operational data to use when reviewing a project or arriving at mutually understood outcomes; the written rules function as *de facto* clients.
- Clients are given insufficient cost information by designers or estimators to usefully participate in the decision-making process.
- Equipment selection is made too late in the process; as a result, items do not fit in the designed or renovated spaces.
- Out-of-date texts and facilities are used as models for design; hospitals are used as models of service delivery in nursing homes.
- The design program is weak. For instance, it produces only a room list with square footage, rather than recognizing that other information is needed from the start. Size must be determined by function, equipment, and configuration of the room.
- The design or building shape may result in social areas that are too small to furnish and use effectively or that have angular walls, making them difficult for people to fit in because they sit in square or rectangular chairs or at square or rectangular tables.

- There is impatience with the planning process, questions of staffing, and details of utility.

Question. Where do you find a qualified architect?

Reply. Begin by listing, perhaps in the form of questions, everything you know you want done. Consult the *Journal of Long-Term Care,* which publishes a list of architects who notify the American Institute of Architects that they work in the field of aging. Speak with friends and associates about the architects they have used, the types of services they received, and the cost. Determine how the firm works. Some have a personal service orientation; others use a pre-established approach to design issues. Find one that suits your preferences, and determine whether the firm would be willing to work with you. Do not be swayed by the number of similar projects the firm has completed. Do look for familiarity with applicable regulations. The most appropriate firm for you may be new to this type of design. Finally, look for someone with whom you will enjoy working. Renovation involves visual creativity and the ability to listen. The design team you choose must have these qualities and be cost-conscious, too.

Question. What do you do when architects or consultants disagree?

Reply. Try these methods:

- Listen to the differences. Different people sometimes respond to different sets of information. There may be value in accommodating these differences.
- Ask for substantiation. Examine the reasons behind the opinions, and identify the research that supports them.
- Ask the specialists to consider the other's point of view: "Under what conditions might you adopt this recommendation?" When underlying factors are resolved, a single conclusion can sometimes be reached.
- Check whether anyone is holding the project back or restraining the best options for older people and staff. Specialists sometimes give opinions in areas in which they have no qualifications. Watch for opinions that are not corroborated by empirical research (for example, a staff member who strongly opposes something without adequate current experience). Watch also for designers who place the exterior appearance of the building ahead of the interior operations, suggesting that the layout does not matter.
- Do not relinquish decision-making authority to outsiders. Designers and consultants should give you options, and you should make the final decision (preferably not alone). Projects that get into trouble often have design team members who presume that operational issues are insignificant.

INTERIOR DESIGN

Question. Should facilities for older people really concern themselves with interior design?

Reply. Good interior design can make as much difference to older people as nearly any other aspect of supportive care. This is a field where you can make a qualitative (not just a sensory) difference.

Question. What are some examples of interior design issues in a typical nursing homes?

Reply. Common issues in interior design for older people include the following:

- Color and appearance
- Seating, chair selection, and sources
- Lighting, low-cost fixtures, and lenses (diffusers)
- Spatial arrangement; furnishing dayrooms and dining areas
- Orientation and wayfinding, signs, and landmarks
- Acoustics, noise abatement
- Design for mentally impaired people
- Better use of corridors and reduction of their apparent length
- Carpeting and floor covering options

Question. What are the common challenges related to interior design for nursing homes?

Reply. The greatest challenge for nursing homes is to find a good interior design firm that is knowledgeable in aging, product sources, life-safety issues, and cost effectiveness, and can make the environment look and feel terrific.

Those who are new to the field of interior design for older people must avoid several common pitfalls, including these:

- Considering the look of an area without fully understanding the functional needs of its users
- Treating color in the abstract, that is, without considering the interactive effects of light, texture, surfaces, and existing or planned features, including equipment, artwork, and seating
- Focusing on the visual attributes of the environment to the exclusion of texture, aroma, and acoustics
- Overlooking data on the population's characteristics (mobility, agility, and incontinence, for example) in selecting furnishings, finishes, and fabrics. This often results in overfurnishing or choosing inappropriate, nondurable, difficult to use, or labor-intensive furnishings. The ultimate result is a disinclination on the part of the nursing home to use interior designers in the future.
- Lack of consideration of fire- and life-safety requirements, including seismic considerations when appropriate

- Ignorance of new materials and adequate alternatives
- Insufficient product testing and evaluation. Testing may involve covering the floor of one or two rooms in a material proposed for use and evaluating its durability, ease of cleaning, and potential mobility.

FAMILIES

Question. Whose needs should be considered first: the residents' or their families'?

Reply. Designing for older people involves satisfying many paradoxes. Instead of designing exclusively for either residents or their families, try to be responsive to both groups. A key to effective design is to understand the different audiences that address design. Give each group something, and see that no one is alienated by the final results. The ultimate users are, of course, older people and staff members. When a conflict arises, give their needs priority.

Question. How can we convince family members of the wisdom of doing something differently?

Reply. Families often respond favorably when they are consulted in advance and when things are done in the best interest of the residents. When given sound explanations, they can be strong supporters of new environments or different ways of offering care. Show that the proposed changes have a sound basis and that a peer group of family members has been involved. Offering publications or other documentation can often be effective.

Do not be intimidated by families. Being a family member or older person does not confer special knowledge about gerontology or effective design. You may need to explain concepts and features through meetings, explanatory readings, and direct contact of family members and trusted staff.

Question. What types of design appeal best or market most effectively to family members?

Reply. Sponsors and designers are often alike in making sweeping generalizations about how families will react to various design or program changes. The simplest and safest way to determine their preferences is to ask them. The focus groups I have met with cite these types of design changes as the most appealing:

- Features that clearly improve the quality of life for residents in some way, for example, improved privacy, appearance, arrangement, choice over schedule, or safety
- Features that increase the ability of family members to communicate effectively or have satisfying visits, such as pleasant areas for visiting or easy things to see or do in the nursing home

- Features that provide a sense of security and comfort for older people
- Features that minimize the time staff members require to respond to requests for assistance or that convey staff presence and availability
- Features that improve the condition of whatever group is perceived to be neglected, such as people with Alzheimer's disease or related disorders, those who are terminally ill, people who might benefit from rehabilitation, or those who call out or are incontinent

Individual facilities may, of course, have pressing needs in other areas that would greatly alter their priorities.

9
Review Agencies,
Record Keeping,
and Costs

In the United States, health care institutions are regulated by the state in which they are located, and they operate under licenses issued by that state. There is no single federal set of standards. Many expansion projects and most renovations that nursing homes undertake involve some form of state review. Some states require a Certificate of Need or a similar license to proceed. Some mandate a series of reviews as the project progresses that might involve architects, engineers, and health care or gerontology program people. A few states also hold cost reviews.

During the last three decades, state regulations have shaped many of the features we now associate with nursing home design. The earliest regulations concerned fire and life safety. Regulations that emerged from the United States in the late fifties dealt with staffing, as well. In the sixties, states created minimum standards in more areas, including activities staff, the hours between meals, and written procedures.

It is useful to obtain information on the applicable state or regional review process and the applicable regulations before beginning the work. Knowing how to explain the plans before a review board and how to support your proposals with documentation and cost estimates will help you obtain approval.

WORKING WITH REVIEW
AGENCIES

There are several things to keep in mind as you approach a major renovation project. First, the nursing home will undoubtedly be governed by regulations of some sort. It is unlikely that a facility can be built or substantially modified in any state today without being subjected to some form of design review. Policies vary, however, with respect to the amount of capital investment that can be made without review.

Second, fire, life-safety, and related regulations vary considerably from one area to another. In the United States although some fire codes are fairly standard across the nation, most states do have unique nursing home regulations.

Variations among states include minimum property standards. For example, some regulations require the construction of a minimum of 370 square feet (34.4 square meters) per bed; others support minimums of over 500. States also vary with regard to minimum room sizes. In some places a double-occupancy room must have at least 80 square feet (7.5 m^2) per person; in other places, the minimum is 100 (9.3 m^2). (Neither 80 nor 100 square feet per person will provide a functionally accessible room, however, based on traditional furnishings and wheelchairs.)

Third, when undertaking renovations, it is often necessary to bring the full facility into compliance with state regulations if the cost of the project exceeds a particular amount. States vary with respect to the capital cost expenditure that will require full compliance.

Finally, few places have formal procedures for working with review agencies to develop responsive program and design regulations. Notable exceptions include New York, Florida, Minnesota, Virginia, Tennessee, and Ontario and other parts of Canada. Some states are developing procedures for working with sponsors to understand the population, service, cost, and design implications of existing buildings.

Limitations of Current Regulations

Many existing regulations are clearly outmoded or otherwise inappropriate for today's nursing home population. It helps to understand the genesis of and rationale behind existing codes when seeking a variance for your facility or attempting to change regulations that trouble the entire industry.

Candid policy makers admit that few of the regulations in effect today are based on current empirical research on older people or on operations-based post-occupancy evaluation of similar projects. Even requirements for room size and staffing have been based on limited research. We lack tremendous amounts of information on what older people and the acts of giving care require. Sponsors themselves are sometimes reluctant to conduct research because they assume that the more they know, the more it will cost them. This assumption is faulty. The more we know about the characteristics of older people, the more effectively we can tailor the design of the environment to meet their needs. Design that increases resident independence and decreases costs of staff labor contributes to the overall efficiency of the facility and is economically beneficial to everyone.

Nursing home regulations borrow from other industries—most notably from hospitals. Hospital codes, unfortunately, are not good models for nursing home regulations because they are based on the needs of a population that spends most of its time in bed. In addition, most existing regulations do not reflect holistic concerns. For example, they do not address ways of balancing protection and freedom of movement.

Many regulations come into being as a result of some concern or tragedy. That is, a particular set of circumstances often triggered specific regulations. Understanding the genesis of existing codes will enable you to work with policy makers on their current relevance. Let's look, for example, at the codes requiring all bedroom doors to be within view of a nursing station. There are at least three possible origins for this regulation. It might be traced to (1) hospital care, where a patient's ability to get out of bed was significant information for physicians and discharge planning, (2) the days before the adoption of call systems, when people tossed shoes into the hall to signal their need for assistance, or (3) the days before smoke and fire detection, when someone had to monitor the bedroom door for life safety. Are these regulations still relevant today? Do we expect the nursing station to be attended at all times? And what do we expect the nurse to see? Perhaps it is time to rethink monitoring.

The characteristics and needs of nursing home residents have changed since most regulations were drafted. One way to combat outmoded regulations is with current data on the population. Information such as mode of ambulation, assistance needed, and equipment involved in care may help make a case regarding appropriate regulations and design. The data must encompass projections regarding populations of the future.

In many states, the regulations were written in the form of minimum requirements, but they are being administered as though they were maximum requirements. Some applicants meet resistance in using their private funds for design changes, even when such changes offer operational savings. In the worst cases, sponsors cannot increase the square footage of their facilities with their own funds, even when additional space would improve the efficiency of services and operations. States like New York have begun to lead the way by providing options for "institutionalized" improvisation. That is, if you provide your own funding and can prove that the proposed change will improve patient or resident care or staff efficiency, provide needed research or education, or meet the complex care requirements of clients with brain damage, dementia, or other disease, you may be permitted to increase the square footage of your facility.

Implications

The limitations described above have become sources of frustration for responsible sponsors interested in making a difference through design. It is possible to meet all the requirements of the code without fulfilling the basic needs of older people. Good examples of this are handrails in bathrooms and halls that do not accommodate how older people actually reach for and lean on surfaces. Many regulations also fail to adequately address lighting, glare, and noise-abatement issues. Improvements must be made in the review process:

1. The communication among state review boards and sponsors, architects, and designers must be improved. We need ways to come together to deliberate about the population, cost sources, labor issues, and design options. For example, what are some acceptable

options for handling exit security and fire safety on units serving people who are confused? These and other questions need to be researched to suggest appropriate options for facilities of different sizes and vintages and for populations of varying risks. Procedures for studying existing regulations and systematically working toward the best minimums and supportive guidelines are sorely needed. Regulations should reflect the vibrant growth in research on aging, products, and operational costs. More research must be conducted, and many regulations must be questioned. Everyone involved in the design of long-term care facilities will benefit from conversations carried out in the spirit of mutual need for knowledge and effective design.

There must also be procedures for bringing sound arguments regarding innovative concepts to a forum for review. In some states, the process is sluggish, and to ask to vary from the norm is to guarantee delays that escalate construction costs. During the eighties, architects, consultants, large sponsors, and developers looked for places willing to accept innovation in order to study the results of efforts to optimize design. A few states have made it somewhat easier to try new ideas. Tennessee's Certificate of Need (CON) process, for example, allows documentation and oral presentation of projects, and New York funded a series of research-worthy projects in 1990 with the objective of stimulating design and technological improvements.

2. There must be more systematic post-occupancy reviews and more environmental analyses of existing facilities; they will provide a better understanding of which design features work and why. We already have the facilities; we simply have not yet developed financial mechanisms or incentives for studying them. A notable exception is the Environmental Design Research Association (EDRA), which continues to stimulate post-occupancy evaluation. Its annual conference proceedings often include articles on methods of evaluation, criticism, and issues in participatory planning.

3. There should be industry voices (long-term care professionals and architects) to present product needs to manufacturers so that they will provide products that facilitate caregiving. In Ontario, Canada, the government has funded the production of an interesting newsletter called *Windows*, which reviews and evaluates technology related to consumer needs and gerontology.

RECORD KEEPING

Good documentation is often invaluable for sponsors planning renovation projects. Your proposal will be strengthened when you support it with written records. Particularly helpful is documentation of precedents set in other facilities. It is also important to maintain records of decisions made during the planning process, to obtain facility drawings for the use of designers and architects, and to maintain files with product information.

Written Support during the Application Process

You must know how to present your proposal in terms that the review agency will understand and accept. In general, if you base your arguments on what is beneficial for older people, sound operations, and long-term financial stability, you will find common ground with the agency. It also helps to be well versed in product safety, fire, and earthquake issues. Although some sponsors and some health departments have made great headway in bringing "quality of life" issues to each other and to the attention of state review agencies, it is sometimes still difficult to use these arguments when presenting a specific project concept. If you decide to try such an approach, be prepared to use financial and efficiency arguments, as well.

Sponsors who structure their explanations around generalizations rarely meet with easy success. It is unlikely that an approach like the following would be well received:

> We want to offer more space because we believe in dignity and privacy.

A better approach would be to combine arguments for increased efficiency with quality of life issues. The following approach, for example, might be successful:

> With just an 18% increase in space, we would be able to increase the options for resident self-care, decrease the time staff members must spend with residents maneuvering wheelchairs, and contribute to better options for the use of space, such as improving privacy—which appears to improve social behavior according to some social science literature.

To ensure the success of your proposal, substantiate your plans with written documentation. This material may be appended to formal applications or brought to meetings and used as handouts. You will find the following types of information valuable:

1. A clear statement describing your plans
2. The alternatives you have explored and their advantages, drawbacks, and costs
3. The effects your proposal will have on operating budgets, including maintenance, consumables, labor, and occupancy. Ideally, you should show operational savings.
4. Precedent information, including the following:

   - The sponsor's name, address, phone, size, type of sponsorship, and level of care
   - The architects, designers, or manufacturers involved
   - Research articles on the value of the feature
   - The sources of capital and operational cost information (name, address, and phone)

- Evaluative data on the success of the project, including resident reactions.

When obtaining precedent information, look for cases of other sponsors who have made similar changes in your state or geographic region, then find examples from states with similar demographic, geographic, or other characteristics. If you provide a cross section of sponsors, you will demonstrate that the concept is not endemic to one type of facility or sponsoring group.

Other Important Documentation

Project Records.   It is valuable to keep written project records and notes. Assign someone to take formal minutes during the planning process. If the minutes are organized with a topic list, you can quickly find what was discussed. When minutes are checked, corrected, and circulated, they will stimulate useful responses before design funds are committed. It is a tragedy when groups go through the planning process and neglect to record their decisions. This often results in misunderstandings, needless repetition, and general frustration with the project.

"As Built" Drawings.   To adequately address many refurbishment, systems, and even interior design alterations, architects and designers require a set of "as built" drawings. For uncomplicated tasks, simple line drawings to scale (such as those used for fire evacuation plans) can be very helpful. For more complex jobs, the design team will need a detailed set of plans that shows existing spaces and their current uses. Sponsors must ensure that these drawings and related documents are available before the architects and designers can begin.

Cut Sheets.   Sponsors should develop a file for cut sheets (that is, manufacturer's product information) for all products brought into the facility. It is most important to keep identifying information for floor coverings, lighting, furnishings, and all appliances, but sponsors should also keep information about any product in which the institution invests. Having this information available, along with the names and addresses of all manufacturers, will aid in a variety of tasks, including repair, additional purchases, and maintenance.

COST ESTIMATION

When developing proposals for others to review, it is imperative to develop a cost projection. It should include these four parts:

1. Total project cost, including capital expenditure, interior alterations, equipment, contracts, fees, and interest
2. Operational analysis; that is, a comparison of the financial impacts of making and not making the proposed change. Some of the items

in this analysis might include the impact on occupancy, reimbursement rate, and labor costs.

3. Sources of funds for the project
4. The break-even point

The cost projection may also reflect other factors, such as the cost of bringing the building into full compliance or the relationship to normal capital improvements.

If you have made an analysis of the full facility, each project or step in the improvements can be assigned a cost, a priority, and a phase in relationship to the others. Although such an analysis may require input from cost-estimation experts, the result will be a valuable and realistic guide to what you can achieve. This is critical when you are considering renovation. Appendix D includes sample cost estimates for common refurbishment and renovation jobs.

10
Sources of Information

You may need information on the following:

- Current regulations
- Sources of funding
- Functional data on resident characteristics. You must obtain data that are relevant to your plans. For example, if you are developing a dementia care unit, you must think in terms of the degrees of impairment and numbers of people so inflicted. If these data are not aggregated, request them.
- Many different design solutions *and* research data on how they do and do not work (called post-occupancy evaluations). Newsletters and magazines published by the major membership organizations in long-term care frequently offer summaries of projects.
- Strategic information on planning or processing steps and schedules
- Cost data from similar projects
- Product and furnishing ideas
- Any concepts that seem to be of interest
- Names of people and agencies that might be of help

TIP. If you are unable to differentiate between descriptive project articles, such as public relations pieces, and more thoughtful empirical data that speak to the effectiveness of design, consider hiring a researcher to assist you. They can be found at graduate-level universities.

Other sources of information include:

Current magazines and journals on aging and health care, such as the following:

- *Gerontologist*, the major journal of aging, U.S.
- *Pride Institute Journal of Long-Term Health Care*
- *Journal of Health Care Finance Administration*

Membership organizations and their conferences, including exhibits

Alzheimer's Association
Suite 600, 70 East Lake Street,
Chicago, IL 60601
312-853-3060
*Publications, conferences related
to dementia*

**American Association of Homes for
the Aging**
Suite 400, 1120 20th Street NW,
Washington, DC 20036-3489
202-296-5960
*Publications, conferences, network
of innovators, legislative assistance, design exhibitions to nonprofit geriatric organizations and
individual members.*

American Foundation for the Blind
15 West 16th Street, New York
City, NY 10011
212-620-2000
*Publications, resource lists, films,
statistics, self-help materials, consumer information, technology and
product sources re: aging, environments for visually impaired and
blind persons and policy. Conferences.*

American Health Care Association
1201 L Street NW, Washington,
DC 20005
202-842-4444
*Publications, conferences, legisla-
tive assistance for for-profit geriatric organizations and individual
members.*

**American Hospital Association,
Committee on Aging**
840 North Lake Shore Drive, Chicago, IL 60611
312-280-6000
*Publications, conferences, telecon-
ference, media*

**American College of Health Care
Administrators**
820 Woodmont Ave. #200, Bethesda, MD 20814
301-652-8384
*Conferences, publications, mem-
ber forums, restraint reduction materials.*

American Optometric Association
142 East Ontario Street, Chicago,
IL 60611
312-280-5857
Publications, conferences

**American Physical Therapy Asso-
ciation**
1111 North Fairfax Street, Alexandria, VA 22314
703-684-2782
Publications, conferences

American Society on Aging
Suite 512, 833 Market Street, San
Francisco, CA 94103
415-543-2617
*Publications, conferences, network-
ing, technology information for
practitioners. Self-help, mutual assistance available.*

American Nurses Association
2420 Pershing Road, Kansas City,
MO 64108
816-474-5720
*Publications, conferences, network-
ing*

**American Occupational Therapy
Association, Inc.**
PO Box 1725, 1383 Picard Drive,
Rockville, MD 20850-4375
301-948-9626
*Publications, conferences, network-
ing*

Canadian Association on Gerontology
1080 167 Lombard Avenue, Winnipeg, Manitoba, Canada R3B 0T6
Publications, conferences, research, networking

Canadian Long Term Care Association
204-124 Bloor Street East, Toronto, Ontario, Canada M4W 1B8
Publications, conferences, legislation information

Gerontological Society of America
Suite 350, 1725 K Street NW, Washington, DC 20005-4006
202-842-1275
Publications, conferences

Health Care Financing Administration
200 Independence Avenue SW, Washington, DC 20201
202-245-6145
Nursing home reform information, costs/management data, research

Help for Incontinent People
PO Box 544, Union, SC 29379
803-579-7900
Information, product sources

Human Factors Society
PO Box 1369, Santa Monica, CA 90406
Publications, conferences, interest in technology, anthropometrics

Window on Technology
Program Technology Branch
Ministry of Community and Social Services
12th Floor, 5140 Yonge Street, Toronto, Ontario,
Canada M2N 6L7
416-730-6470
Publication and information on technology and products for older

people, including those with dementia.

National Institute on Aging
Public Information Office, Federal Building, Room 6C12,
900 Rockville Pike, Bethesda, MD 20892
301-496-1752
Research, resource directories

National Center for Health Services Research and Health Care Technology Assessment
Parklawn Building, Room 18-12, 5600 Fishers Lane
Rockville, MD 20857
301-443-4100
Data and statistics on aging, dementia, general technology for older people.

National Center for Health Statistics
3700 East-West Highway, Hyattsville, MD 20782
301-436-8500
Data and statistics on aging and long-term care.

National Citizens Coalition for Nursing Home Reform
Suite L2, 1424 16th Street NW, Washington, DC 20036
202-797-0657
Data on nursing home reform, practices, OBRA regulations

National Council on the Aging
West Wing 100, 60 Maryland Avenue SW, Washington, DC 20024
202-479-1200
Conferences, publications, media abstracts, computer access

National Geriatrics Society
212 West Wisconsin Avenue, Milwaukee, WI 53203
Three times per year publication on regulations

Self-Help for Hard of Hearing People
7800 Wisconsin Avenue, Bethesda, MD 20814
301-657-2247 (voice);
301-657-2249 (TDD)
References and products for people with hearing impairments

American Institute of Architects, Committees on Health Care, Housing for Elderly and Health Care Facilities Research Program of the AIA Association of Collegiate Schools of Architecture
1735 New York Avenue, NW, Washington, DC 20006
202-785-2324

Environmental Design Research Association
4977 Battery Lane #413, Bethesda, MD 20814
301-657-2657
Conference, research/practice on environmental design and theory. Network.

American Society of Interior Designers
1430 Broadway, New York City, NY 10018
212-944-9220
Publications, conferences

National Fire Protection Association
470 Atlantic Avenue, Boston, MA 02210
Publications, regulations, standards, research

State Associations
There are state and regional affiliates of most of these national organizations, particularly those in architecture, interior design, and long-term care (nursing homes).

Typically, the national directories have information on the local organizations.

Aging and You, CJRT-FM Open College
297 Victoria Street
Toronto, Ontario, Canada
M5B 1W1
416-595-0485
Radio course and taped course on aging with emphasis on environmental design and health care facility innovation; international roster of speakers. Coursebook and readings. Resource for distance education/self-study.

Epilogue

Improving the environment of nursing homes can be extraordinarily satisfying. Design professionals have the opportunity to attend conferences on quality of life and quality in design. We talk about the value of discussion groups and staff support, about creating centers of excellence and job enrichment.

Ironically, the frailer and more impaired the population, the less likely we have been to respond through a "designed" and thoughtfully created environment. The time has come to focus our efforts and realize a better later life by offering more options in our dwellings, particularly our health care facilities. With the required talent and knowledge in hand, we can now look forward to an era of informed design.

Appendix A
Population Profile Worksheet

Today's Date_____ Your Name_____ Phone Extension_____

This worksheet should be completed by someone who knows the residents well. From the responses for each unit, a combined total (frequencies and percentages) can be calculated for the building as a whole.

1. What units make up this building? Describe each unit by name, location, size, and general population.

Unit Name/Location	Average Size	Types of Residents
A		
B		
C		
D		
E		

2. Calculate or estimate the percentage of residents in each unit that match the descriptions below. The units refer to the description above. If you plan to add a new unit, make an additional column and estimate the profile of those residents.

UNIT

	A		B		C		D		E	
	No.	%	No.	%	No.	%	No.	%	No.	%
a. Ambulatory, no assistance										
Ambulatory, human assistance										
Ambulatory, cane or walker										
b. Wheelchair users										

185

UNIT

	A		B		C		D		E	
	No.	%	No.	%	No.	%	No.	%	No.	%

c. Geriatric wheelchair or recliner users

d. Bedridden for most of day

e. Restrained with body holder, vest, or similar device

3. Consider the descriptions of cognitive impairment that follow. Estimate the percentage of residents in each unit that are characterized by each description.

UNIT

	A		B		C		D		E	
	No.	%	No.	%	No.	%	No.	%	No.	%

a. No impairment; fully alert

b. Slow response time, typical of age; free of disease

c. Mild impairment: language; naming abstract information like dates, times, money, colors, directions

d. Moderate impairment: fact; emotion; social behavior

e. Complex impairment: physical needs eclipse other needs; flat affect; may not seem to participate

f. Complex impairment: behavior outbursts; belligerent; severe problems with socializing; severe agitation

g. Being evaluated or undergoing change

Total	100%	100%	100%	100%	100%

4. What percentage of the residents could be described as follows:

	UNIT				
	A	B	C	D	E
	No. %	No. %	No. %	No. %	No. %

  a. Need assistance in the toilet room
  • Are incontinent and would not be able to use a well-designed toilet room with assistance
  • Are incontinent and would be able to use a well-designed toilet room with assistance
  b. Need assistance in bathing
  c. Would prefer shower if designed well
  d. Would prefer tub if the room, bather, and lift were designed well and conveniently located and if appropriate assistance were available
  e. Could eat in a dining room on or near unit
  f. Could get outside if area were well designed
  g. Could attend a group program on the unit
  h. Could attend a group program off of the unit

5. Estimate or obtain information on the following:
  a. Average Age (Median) _____ _____ _____ _____ _____
  b. Average length of stay
    If days   _____ _____ _____ _____ _____
    If months _____ _____ _____ _____ _____
    If years _____ _____ _____ _____ _____
  c. Common Interests:
    Unit A: _____
    Unit B: _____
    Unit C: _____
    Unit D: _____
    Unit E: _____

Appendix B

Key to Interpreting the Environmental Design Inventory

IMAGE AND INTERIOR APPEARANCE

_____ **1.** The building looks nice, makes a good impression, and is the source of many compliments by residents and staff.

Great; go to 2.

_____ **2.** We painted, but it doesn't seem to be enough.

A good paint job touches only the surface; perhaps your needs are more than surface-deep. Or, perhaps the colors were not selected in relation to art and other objects in the environment. It is sometimes better to make walls the last thing you modify rather than the first.

_____ **3.** Our place looks like a hospital.

Start with this image, and then get more specific. What does _hospital_ mean? List the adjectives or descriptive phrases that convey this hospital image. Consider the visual, auditory, and tactile features of the environment as well as management policies and staffing. Check the surfaces. Are they shiny and smooth, unvaried by texture? Is the lighting intense and glare producing, or bleak and uneven? Visitors may sense the importance of order and regulations before they are oriented to the more comfortable, flexible, and relaxed qualities of the environment. Of course, the public areas may look like a hospital for appropriate reasons; perhaps the residential-use portions could be more personalized.

_____ **4.** We had a designer or a committee of people who helped us obtain art or who gave us some ideas, but it isn't enough yet.

Art, flowers, furnishings, and culturally or geographically interesting objects contribute to a lively facility image when appropriately chosen and located. Art should relate to the interests of those who make up the community of residents, staff, and sponsors. You may find that your art does not relate to those who reside or work in your facility. The work of outside consultants and participants can be very stimulating, but these efforts must be combined with staff and resident input.

Perhaps your art is not effectively placed. The location is sometimes as important as the pieces themselves. They should be clustered in different ways rather than positioned at exact intervals. Matching eye level is important, too. Plate racks (high shelves) or corner shelves facilitate display in dining and program rooms. A hutch or shelf is sometimes useful in the bedroom.

Note: Some libraries and historical societies will loan you items or set up your displays as long as the objects will be protected appropriately.

If the art is well chosen and well located yet not effective, you may be touching only the surface of the problem. The first acquisition of an art or design program sometimes reveals the extent of needs elsewhere.

_____   **5.** The building is old.

The age of the building is not necessarily the problem. Older buildings sometimes have familiar features and are well known to the community. They need not, however, appear outdated. Consider freshening the image with features that reinforce your contemporary approach to care: a lobby kiosk that displays your services, window boxes or awnings, or a covered entry that offers protection and gives a "cared for" look to the building.

_____   **6.** While our programs and activities are fairly varied, the place looks the same throughout.

Variations in decor may contribute to a positive image; sameness often supports an institutional image. Try to list the features that contribute to the feeling of sameness. Consider ways to accommodate variety in appearance and the desire to "tie the design" together. You may require the insights of a designer to select paints that are not all of the same tone or shade yet work well together.

Try to design options for personalization into the wall covering plan. For example, cover walls with a vertically fire-rated tackable wall surface (a wall covering you can put pins in), hang a picture molding (available from a lumber store), or designate an area on or next to the door that can be used for displays.

_____   **7.** The floors bring down the appearance of the building.

The floors will bring down your facility's appearance if they are dirty, tattered, or worn. However, they need not have fancy patterns or wild colors to improve the image. Patternless, medium-tone floors are best for walkways because the patterns may appear to residents to be objects. Floors do not have to shine to look good. In fact, nonglare floors are best. Glare makes it more difficult for the elderly to see and may contribute to disorientation and falls. New materials that look like carpet but wear more like sheet vinyl are increasingly available. Look into products such as Flotex™ or Powerbond™, for example. These materials can be used to update appearance, not only in hallways but also in bedrooms.

_____ **8.** The handrails do not seem to work; no one uses them.

Well-designed handrails do not detract from a facility's image. In fact, those who do not need to use the handrails may hardly notice them. Handrails are usually required by law. The regulations vary from state to state. Most codes prohibit rails that exceed 2″ in diameter and stipulate a distance of 1½″ from the wall. You may need to research applicable regulations.

If residents do not use the handrails, consider these questions:

- Are the handrails mounted at an appropriate height for the residents? Refer to your population profile (Appendix A) to understand the actual needs in different parts of the building. When residents are ambulatory, a height of 41″ from the finished floor is often best for a banister-style rail. In some cases, wheelchair-bound residents pull the handrail in order to speed their way along a corridor. In this case, lower rails of 31″ to 36″ work best, depending on the style and height of wheelchairs used. Some facilities have a dual handrail.
- Is the design appropriate? Many common handrail types are hard to use. Flat, board-style rails may look good, but often are too narrow and hard to grip. Round, pipe-style handrails can be hard to lean on. Some handrails are much too narrow (less than 1¾″ to 2½″); this is often true of outside rails. A bannister style handrail that is flat on top with rounded sides allows residents to grip the rail and permits them to glide along the rail, leaning on the forearm. Keeping the rail fairly close to the wall is necessary to reduce the possibility of inadvertently catching the arm behind the rail during a fall.
- Is the corridor lighting adequate? If the lighting fixtures are in the center of the hall, the area beside the handrail may be dark and perceived as less safe.
- Are the handrails free from obstruction? Check whether laundry or other items hang from the handrails or are stored on the floor in front of them.
- Are residents trained to use the handrails?

_____   **9.** Wheelchairs, carts, and other vehicles clutter the hall.

Cluttered corridors detract from a facility's image and make it more difficult for residents to maneuver themselves. Determine why equipment and devices are stored in the hall. It might be because there is no easily accessible storage, because staff are not trained to use the proper storage areas, or because the available storage areas are filled with items that should be elsewhere. Consider whether decentralized facilities could be developed for linen. Could other items be stored elsewhere? Make it your goal to return the corridors to the residents.

_____   **10.** Visitors only come to visit the people, never to admire the building.

The residents probably are (and certainly should be) the primary attraction for visitors. Your facility might simply provide a pleasant backdrop to their care, or it might offer some features that visitors can enjoy with residents. When a nursing home is particularly admirable, it can help attract people, provided the care is as noteworthy. If the facility is safe and functional, but lacks points of reference or local interest, consider what feature you might develop into a community landmark.

_____   **11.** People don't visit often, and they don't stay long when they come.

Many factors affect visitation, including the distance from the nursing home to other amenities. Check for odor problems, undressed or partly nude residents, parking or transportation inconveniences, unavailability of snacks, or rigid visiting rules that are inappropriate for local work patterns and lifestyles. Many visitors are themselves older people. Check to see that facilities are available for their comfort. Is there adequate seating, quiet area for conversation, and a place to get a meal or make a telephone call? Check on activities available to family members. Are there interesting places to visit in the building: places to share a private meal, areas for children to play or teens to enjoy? You might create a handout or poster to identify these places.

_____   **12.** We have a hard time balancing energy and cost savings with the lighting we'd like to provide.

Dim lighting can contribute to a shabby image, and it does not provide savings. Inadequate lighting sometimes contributes to instability or falls, and it may reduce self-care. Remember that older people require more light than younger ones. They need at least 50 foot-candles of light for everyday living spaces and 100 foot-candles for close work, such as reading or activities.

On the other hand, lighting that is too harsh may contribute to an institutional appearance. Make sure that all of your bulbs have lens covers, diffusers, or shades.

Check the types of fixtures your facility uses. Incandescent light bulbs are costly to purchase and maintain. Fluorescent lights may sometimes be used in the same fixtures; check with a lighting or hardware store. Make sure all products are appropriately rated by Underwriter's Laboratory for the watts you will use. Speak with a lighting expert at the local cooperative extension division or university regarding your specific lighting needs.

_____ **13.** The air seems stuffy or stale; bad aromas greet visitors as they enter certain areas of this home.

Fresh air is good for health and good for image. Stale air indicates the presence of a problem, and it may cause general fatigue among residents and staff. No one should have to live or work in a building with unsatisfactory air quality.

First, check the source of the problem and determine what might be done to manage it better. Would it help to air out space between users, such as when people are at lunch, empty containers more frequently, or use available fans? Then, check with the facility maintenance staff and engineer. Are all systems working as they should be? Must certain doors be kept open (or closed) for the system to work? Review the mechanical engineering expectations for the building. The amount of fresh make-up air often is reduced to save energy, resulting in stale air and odor retention. A good mechanical engineering evaluation sometimes suggests methods of correcting the problem of stale air. Consider eliminating indoor smoking. Or create designated smoking areas to improve air quality; make sure that these areas are well ventilated or aired out regularly.

RESIDENT POPULATION

Characteristics and Changes

_____ **1.** The building is flexible in that we can respond to changing needs and shifts in market demand. We are usually comfortably full with the type of residents we are licensed to serve and can respond to shifts in population profile.

_____ **2.** The resident population has changed over the past few years, and we have been unable to adapt to their needs and develop new programs.

Most facilities that have had no trouble meeting building inspections in the past now find frustration in the way that the population has changed (that is, it has become frailer, uses more mechanical devices, and appears more mentally confused). These new needs make an otherwise fine building seem less effective, which is why renovation is necessary.

_____ **3.** Our ideas seem superior to the building's capacity to support them.

Be sure not to lose those ideas. You may eventually find a way to implement them even in older facilities. Document your ideas. Develop a systematic corporate plan so that they can be implemented.

_____ **4.** We have a system of grouping people by abilities, but they keep spilling over into other areas.

Actually, that is quite common; after all, people do change. With continual admissions, deaths, and changes in resident populations, a grouping system needs flexibility in staffing and design to remain effective.

Tight systems of grouping people according to mobility, mental status, fragility of condition, or amiability may be nearly impossible to maintain. As an alternative, try less distinctive groupings. In a facility of 130 beds or more, for example, consider creating two areas for mentally impaired persons, each of which might expand or contract. In a smaller building of 40 beds, it might be better to offer special programs rather than special units. Design the assignment system from the beginning on the assumption that the demand may change. Some facilities try to create some "flex" areas or focus on programs that do not require perfect assignment of people to one area.

_____ **5.** We have trouble getting people of different abilities to mingle.

Separatism may grow from different sources: the expectations established through brochures or interviews on admissions policies, a fear of particular impairments, or the inequality of facilities for those impairments (fear of special units or floors).

To reduce the fear of people with different habits or potentially unpredictable behavior, try these techniques:

- Use role models to teach by example. Have staff who are comfortable interacting with different groups available at meals or programs to discuss techniques for effective interaction.
- Set up some shared amenities facilities. Develop some spaces or features for the enjoyment of all residents. Try an ice-cream cart that comes to an area where everyone can gather, for example, or a garden.
- Develop activities for small groups of people with different abilities. This is a way of introducing people and providing meaningful opportunities for exchange. These activities might be

simple teas, religious groups, or family sharing opportunities. Remember that people often mingle more successfully if mingling is not the primary activity in which they are engaged. That is, they should come together to share some experience: children's visits, religious observation, pet visits, or a picnic, for example.

When staff believe in strict separatism, families and residents quickly adopt this feeling. Unless all facilities within a setting have equally appealing programs, families may feel badly about an assignment to a particular area of the building.

Check for barriers in design that place one group at a disadvantage in participation. For example, vision-impaired people sometimes seek the front position for visually dependent activities. If they are in wheelchairs, their height may block the view of others. By planning one portion of a room for wheelchairs and the other for ambulatory people, based on your actual population, you may alleviate such communication tensions.

_____ **6.** We have a problem discharging people to their own homes or to a lesser level of care.

Do your facilities make residents appear less capable than they are? Make sure that you provide facilities that allow people to practice skills they will need in a less heavily staffed environment. Try to link the experiences, if not the appearances, of these settings.

_____ **7.** People under our care could look better.

Grooming problems sometimes indicate the following: inaccessible mirrors (particularly for short residents or those in wheelchairs); poor lighting near the mirrors; rushing through morning care; a lack of visitors, outsiders, or others to give an honest appraisal of appearance; problems of continence and frequent clothing change; insufficient clothing storage or access; or the distant location of dressing or grooming areas. When everyone looks the same, it indicates that uniforms are purchased or that hair is done in a standard way. Check the view from behind the wheelchair. Exposed buttocks are demeaning and call for a different garment closure or chair cover-up.

Quality of Life

_____ **1.** Next to their own homes, people tell us that this is one of the best places they have lived or that it's the place they would choose if they needed long-term care.

Great.

_____ **2.** People have choices, territory, access to privacy, control over their own belongings, freedom of schedule, or a sense of self-determination.

Super.

When these needs are not met, policy may be affecting how people use the available facilities. In that case, changing policy comes first.

_____ **3.** There are many ways of spending time; there are places and features to visit.

Terrific.

_____ **4.** Residents' rooms have a certain dignity and comfort; they match the cultures, backgrounds, or local customs of their occupants.

Wonderful. That's why no two buildings will be alike.

_____ **5.** We have a formal program of providing art or sculpture, designed gardens, or other visual amenities.

That's fortunate.

_____ **6.** There are touchable features available to 90% or more of the residents.

Great. Art objects, tapestry, gardens, pets, finger foods, and sculptural objects are all potentially valuable sources of tactile stimulation.

_____ **7.** Residents are roused quite early and go to bed quite early.

This suggests a lack of things to do, both self-directed (with low levels of staff involvement) and programmed (with staff or volunteer assistance). Consider the following questions:

• Do medications reinforce these patterns? Can they be changed in consultation with the physicians?
• What must you do to allow people to sleep later if they desired? Could you change the responsibilities of the night shift? Could you handle breakfast differently, with expanded hours or several shifts?
• Could the activities staff stay later a few nights a week to expand evening opportunities?

_____ **8.** Residents spend a lot of their time waiting.

Waiting is sometimes beneficial; watching is often a first step toward participation. Too much waiting, however, should be looked into.

Are residents unable to do much for themselves because of inaccessible fixtures, distances, inefficient scheduling, or location of programs? Perhaps more programs should be brought to the unit. Perhaps elevators should be operated during particular periods of the day. Perhaps programs should be brought to places where people must wait or perhaps waiting should occur in a recreation program room.

Check on the wait associated with mealtime. You may find a "herding" of residents to the dining area long before meals can be provided. Music, exercise, or some meaningful and interesting program could be offered to pass the time before meals arrive. Appetizers could be offered to curb the appetite if the food will be late.

_____ **9. Residents do not seem to know each other and often bicker.**

There may be inadequate opportunities for making the acquaintance of others. To compensate, staff can systematically offer introductions, especially for people with minor memory loss for names, or residents can do this through welcoming programs of their own design. Offering opportunities for residents to personalize their rooms may make it easier for staff and residents to get to know one another as individuals. Personal objects provide a topic of conversation.

Staff and elderly individuals may bicker over territory. This sometimes indicates crowding or unequal distribution of resources. If seating areas and aisles are too limited, arguments over territory may result. Residents and staff must work together to come up with ways to make space available to more people or to allow sharing of scarce resources.

People often become territorial about chairs or table positions because they have little specified territory in their rooms. They need a place to consider their own and to control. Try clearly identifying furnishings, secure storage, seating, and individual zones within bedrooms to reduce bickering and redirect staff time from refereeing conflicts to caregiving.

Note: Verbal abusiveness or cantankerousness may be habitual or a personality or cultural characteristic. Such behavior may also reflect emotional, health, or drug problems that are irritated by environmental design. Use a specialist to help determine the cause of individual behavior.

_____ **10. The environment is noisy; even the public address system seems penetrating.**

Noise contributes to agitation and stress, and it diminishes the quality of life. It should be viewed as a serious environmental problem that must be resolved prior to implementing other new programs. Noise abatement involves five steps: (1) identify the source or sources of noise, (2) change what can be changed, (3) relocate noise sources when feasible, (4) work out a schedule so that noisy tasks are performed when they will disturb residents least, and (5) become aware of the severe limitations on older people's hearing that noise imposes. Design interventions for reducing noise include the use of sound absorbing materials on ceilings and walls.

_____ **11.** There's no place for a person really to be alone—except maybe in the bathrooms, chapel, or outside.

Develop a plan to offer everyone actual and visual privacy despite their disabilities. This may involve arranging a few niches or places for retreat and having staff learn to respect individual needs for solitude.

_____ **12.** We tried personalization, but someone put paper cutouts and decals on the walls and now they look shoddy.

Ideas sometimes need to be tried again in new ways. Paper items, such as cutouts and decals, may signify personalization to some staff, but they usually have little personal meaning for residents. Personalization starts at move-in time, when family members and others are convinced of the importance of bringing in some items for the resident's room. Pictures, albums, and a safe and clean chair are items commonly used to personalize living areas.

_____ **13.** We have difficulty handling people's private possessions, including furniture and knickknacks.

Develop a policy regarding what may be brought to your facility and how it will be distributed following a move. Be sure the policy is well understood prior to admissions. Off-site storage facilities, billed to the family with their advance approval, are sometimes necessary.

_____ **14.** People complain of being lost, or they ask for directions.

If many people lose their way, it may indicate that the building is confusing or that it does not have enough nameable landmarks. People are the most credible and visible source of directions; prominently located nursing or housekeeping staff are likely to be asked for assistance. Landmarks, located at decision points in the building, should be used in providing verbal instruc- tions. Older residents may need actual "orienteering" training in how to find their way. Such training usually involves patient practice.

_____ **15.** People seldom get outside.

If residents are not going outside in good weather, consider the following. Is the door too difficult for residents or family members to open? Can trained volunteers help people get outside? Are outdoor paths level enough for ambulation or for wheelchairs? Are there shaded areas, sun hats, or wheelchair umbrellas available to protect sensitive skin? Is there a phone or call system outside? Where is the nearest bathroom, and is it accessible and clean?

RESIDENT-USE AREAS AND FEATURES

Bedrooms

_____ **1.** The bedrooms are well designed with good provision for privacy, territory, and personal possessions.

Great.

_____ **2.** The bedrooms are functional for wheelchair users; they can easily wheel up alongside the bed, get to and use the closets, and have space for visits in the room.

This will save staff time, especially in morning care.

_____ **3.** Bedroom windows are well designed for viewing, and residents have equal access to window space.

Good.

If this is *not* true of your facility, consider providing residents who do not have acceptable window views with dining room seating and lounge placements where they can see the outside. Make sure, though, that those views are protected from glare.

_____ **4.** Bedroom lighting is related to the activities that might occur there, including reading, visiting, and recognizing faces at the door.

Good.

If this is *not* true, analyze the activities in relation to lighting needs. Can task areas be rearranged to optimize the available lighting or to take advantage of floor lamps or portable lamps?

_____ **5.** Within the room, it is relatively quiet; one does not hear noises from people, the hall, or other sources.

This is good.

If this is *not* true, you may need to develop a combination of

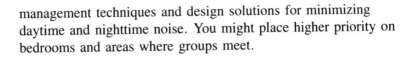

management techniques and design solutions for minimizing daytime and nighttime noise. You might place higher priority on bedrooms and areas where groups meet.

_____ **6.** Each person has places for his or her possessions, for securing valuables, and for displaying personal items.

Excellent.

_____ **7.** Each person has ready access to a mirror at the proper height for grooming.

Very fine.
For residents confined to a wheelchair, consider providing a wheelchair-height, nonbreakable (but conventional looking) mirror in the area where grooming takes place. For example, you might put it in the bedroom, on a side wall in the bathroom (provided there is no competition for bathroom use), inside a closet door, or in a grooming alcove in some other place on the unit.

_____ **8.** The bedrooms have little variety; they all look the same.

Variety is helpful for orientation, wayfinding, and creating a sense of home.

9. Each person's room is clearly labeled within eye level; and names appear on a legible, professional-looking identifying label or plaque next to the door.

Excellent.

_____ **10.** There are some three-bed rooms or wards here.

Some states have advised against three-bed rooms for most nursing homes. Problems generally develop in the form of compromised privacy and unequal distribution of the room's resources (for example, access, light, space, and seating). Since most residents are not bedridden, three-bed rooms rarely save staff time. At the very least, try to provide some visual privacy in three-bed rooms and offer some special consideration to the middle person. (See pages 60–61, 63 in Chapter 4.)

_____ **11.** We have quite a problem with residents wandering into other people's rooms and handling their things.

Rummaging can happen for a number of reasons, including the fact that rooms or furnishings look alike. The ability to distinguish one's own dresser from many similar dressers requires abstract reasoning abilities some residents no longer have.
Sometimes, out of sight *is* out of mind. Try closing bedroom

doors completely or part way, or consider creating a door band (a removable two-foot vinyl panel placed across the opening and attached with Velcro™). Encourage people to use their hands and manipulate appropriately designed objects. The more programs and interesting things available for people to do and touch, the less likely rummaging will occur. One of the first steps in resolving "problem" rummaging is to provide a rummaging room or niche, an area where people can explore, finger items, or experience objects in safety.

Rummaging may need to be discouraged when staff cannot supervise (even from a distance) or where corridors are hidden or lengthy. For specific cases of active rummaging, you may want to seek clinical consultation.

_____ **12.** Some rooms seem to get less attention or feel more remote than others.

When a few rooms are located in out-of-the-way areas, you must make every effort to compensate residents assigned to them. It is easy to unintentionally minimize the attention these residents receive.

Consider the following techniques:

- Fill the remote rooms with verbal and capable people rather than those who need more frequent attention.
- Set up a schedule of visits to these rooms.
- Make sure that all residents assigned to remote rooms are capable of using the call system.
- Ask staff for suggestions on how to optimize care in these rooms, using existing traffic or caregiving patterns.

_____ **13.** There isn't enough room for residents to move easily around their beds.

This is one of the more insidious, time-consuming problems in many facilities designed for older people. The space around the beds should be adequate for residents to wheel themselves. Sufficient elbow room and space for the wheelchair encourage independent access to the room and its furnishings.

There are ways of improving bedroom access. Check with your health department to determine whether beds may be placed against one wall rather than positioned perpendicularly. If the health department consents, explore more accessible room arrangements. Make sure that the head of the bed is at least 18″ from the edge of the window or that it meets appropriate code and comfort requirements. You might consider using smaller, shorter beds or removing the footboards, thus making beds shorter and the aisle wider. Note that not all beds work without footboards. Check with the manufacturer regarding the sturdiness of the bed before altering it. Some residents may be aided by a different style of wheelchair. It should be one designed for their particular physical and positioning needs, however.

Work with the occupational and physical therapists, nursing assistants, maintenance staff, and housekeepers to come up with ways to make rooms as accessible as possible. Get input from residents before and after reaching tentative decisions. Try solutions in a mockup or model space before implementing them throughout the facility. For controversial solutions, have the health department representatives or other officials help evaluate the mockup or films of the mockup.

Bathrooms

_____ **1.** Bathrooms are efficient for older people to use with or without wheelchairs and with or without assistance.

_____ **2.** Residents sometimes fall next to the bed or in the bathroom.

In the average nursing home, the greatest number of falls occur next to the bed, in the bathroom, and in entries. You may reduce the number of falls by improving safety features in these areas and increasing staff vigilance and willingness to assist with transfers.

Hazards near the bed include furniture that moves (dressers or beds on unlocked casters, for example), bedside rails that do not fully retract or hide, dark floor areas, full rather than partial grab rails, and beds that do not lower to 16″ from the finished floor.

Bathrooms have their own hazards. A common one is the lack of anything to hold onto when moving between toilet and chair. Many grab rails are poorly positioned for use when standing. Another hazard is the hard, potentially slick floors generally found in bathrooms. Solutions include sturdy, toilet-mounted or dual armrest hardware, such as Sheltering Arms™ or NOA™, and nonslip surfaces, such as sheet rubber, instead of ceramic tile.

To identify other potential hazards in your facility, ask staff members to cite other places, inside and outside, that appear risky. They may name certain ramps, steps, uneven flooring, "visual cliffs" (which give the appearance of steps), thresholds, and shower ledges. Older people sometimes fall for reasons that apparently have little to do with the environment. It is important, however, to reduce environmental hazards and to soften the effects of falls to minimize fractures.

_____ **3.** The bathroom is not as accessible as it could be; the door is difficult to use and people cannot use the available assistive devices.

Accessible bathrooms would likely boost the independence of residents, improve staff efficiency when help is needed, and increase the likelihood that people use the appropriate facilities for toileting, thus minimizing the problems associated with incontinence. In part, functionally accessible toilet rooms reduce the time between the "urge" and relief. This is very significant for older people who lose the muscle or cognitive capacity to wait while negotiating tight spaces or managing difficult doors.

_____ **4.** It takes staff members a long time to bathroom older people.

Older people often go to the bathroom more frequently than younger ones. Current literature on incontinence suggests that getting people upright and on the toilet is helpful in incontinence management. Toileting is usually preferable to diapering, although long-time staff members may have been taught otherwise in years past.

Many features in a bathroom can slow down staff work, including ineffective layout for wheelchair transfer, clumsy door design (doors that will not close or are difficult to close), and poorly located cleansing facilities.

Before making plans to renovate, ask the staff for input and review "Bathrooms" in Chapter 4.

_____ **5.** Use of commode chairs is widespread.

Commode chairs are less sanitary than flush toilets, they sometimes contribute to odor problems, and they are labor intensive (staff people must empty them). When commode chairs must be used, check that residents are not compromised in terms of visual or auditory privacy.

The widespread use of commode chairs may indicate a number of problems. First, there may be an insufficient number of bathrooms. Even a ratio of one toilet to every four residents may be insufficient when everyone is eating at about the same time and digesting at about the same rate. Second, existing toilet facilities may be inconveniently located. Consider adding accessible bathrooms near program areas (for example, in the shower room area or near dining and activities areas). Finally, the bathrooms may be poorly designed, making them inaccessible to many residents. The toilet seats may be too high or too low for the convenience of residents. For the latter problem, try seat extenders, which are available from many health care providers. Perhaps the doors could be reconfigured; switching from swing doors to sturdy accordion doors may improve access. Check with the architectural review division of your state health department. Some states prohibit the use of certain door types; others may want a full explanation of what you intend to do and why. Make sure that you mount the door with a sturdy track and gliding wheel. Consider using a magnet closer rather than a "hook and eye" to minimize reaching problems for wheelchair users.

_____ **6.** Privacy seems compromised in the bathrooms.

Take steps to minimize the problem. Privacy during toileting, even in shower rooms, is an entitlement. Solutions to compromised privacy include installing doors or curtains. If the stall is very narrow, try a track outside the cubicle, perhaps a curved track mounted on the ceiling (track sales representatives can help).

Odor and call system problems may contribute to compromised privacy. Doors are sometimes left open because of stale air, especially in shared-use toilet rooms, or because assistance is needed in transfer and the client cannot manage the call system.

SERVICES, STAFFING, AND RELATED SPACES

Nursing and Health Care

_____ **1.** There never seems to be enough staff where and when we want them.

Nursing units with a highly centralized design and/or management system often result in the feeling that calls are not answered quickly or that staff are not in the vicinity of residents. By decentralizing supplies and working out staff assignments based on where residents are located at different times of the day, it may be possible to stretch staff effectiveness.

_____ **2.** It takes the staff a long time to answer calls for assistance; residents or families complain that staff do not respond quickly enough.

Ask staff to work together to identify the source of this problem and to evaluate possible solutions. Suggestions aimed at improving the efficiency of toilet rooms will ultimately increase staff efficiency. The preceding questions on bathroom design may be helpful. Consider also the following:

- Are residents toileted on demand rather than on a schedule that anticipates their needs? Toileting on demand involves a lot of calling out that scheduled toileting would eliminate.
- Are the toilets too distant from the stations where nursing assistants congregate? Would it help if nursing assistants were relocated closer to the residents, especially for morning and evening care? The supplies the nursing assistants require must move with them, of course.
- What if residents were assigned to nursing assistants on a

primary-care basis, rather than by unit? Nursing assistants would have to plan for buddying up to participate in two-person transfers and to cover for one another during off-unit assignments and errands.

_____ **3.** Morning care is very chaotic here.

Analyze the full schedule of morning care tasks; consider ways to reschedule some of them. Breakfast scheduling often sets the stage for rushed care. See suggestions on Schedule Analysis. If you improve the efficiency of morning care, the entire day may run more smoothly and attendance at other activities may increase.

_____ **4.** It is difficult to handle two-person transfers.

Why are two-person transfers required? Note the reasons that apply to your facility:

- The person is very large.
- The person cannot balance or maintain his or her own weight, but to everyone's credit, the person is toileted upright.
- The available portable lifts are not used because the person is frightened of them, they do not work well, they do not fit in the toilet room, or they are not available when and where they are needed.
- The wheelchair does not fit in the bathroom or the space is otherwise poorly configured.

Now go back and consider where improvements might be made. Different lifts might reduce labor, door design might be improved, and centrally located, accessible toilets might help. Newer lifts require less space and do not involve swinging or slings. See, for example, Arjo™, Kebo-Parker™, Lumex™, NOA™, Century™, and Silcraft™ chair lifts.

_____ **5.** Nursing and activities staff have some difficulty deciding who's responsible for the activities, transportation, and grooming of some residents.

Transportation is a necessary part of the service provided by long-term care institutions. Responsibility for this task must be incorporated in the job descriptions of several departments. Transportation tasks usually fall on either nursing assistants or activities staff. These two groups should not be invisible to each other. As their informal communication is improved, special transport needs may be more easily worked out.

Inspect the devices used for transportation. Awkward wheelchairs sometimes slow the process and create wall and elevator damage. For off-unit programs, try using standard wheelchairs rather than bulkier recliners or geriatric wheelchairs, thus making space available on the elevator and contributing to seating comfort.

If population changes result in an increased number of residents who need assistance to get to remote locations, it might be time to change how and where you provide services. The objective is to provide for the residents' basic needs while optimizing staff time by reducing the time spent waiting for elevators or wheeling people to remote locations. Consider bringing programs—such as recreational activities, grooming, beauty shop care, and podiatry and other clinic services—to the residential unit. As an alternative, consider bringing meals to the unit to minimize the sense of "coming and going." Be careful not to overdo it, though. Residents should get off their floor at least once a day for some enjoyment. When people do go to remote areas, try to minimize the number of back-and-forth trips they make by providing necessary services there (for example, have medication, food, and toilet facilities available nearby).

_____ **6.** Staff members complain that there's no space for this or that activity; yet there seem to be unoccupied rooms or areas within rooms.

It may be time to make a schedule that includes all activities, structured and informal, and shows their locations. The schedule must include staff meetings and educational classes that take place in areas allocated for residents. Determine which activities, if any, must be reassigned. Refer to Behavior Mapping, pp. 30–31 for assistance in determining how rooms are used and whether they can be subdivided.

_____ **7.** There is much confusion around shift changes and dinner, bathing, and visiting times.

Confusion inherent in the facility, design, or activity itself often contributes to confusion among residents. Try to determine the cause of the confusion, and then look for solutions. If, for example, supplies are not conveniently located, consider reconfiguring aisle space and locating supplies where they will be used. Systematic Observation, described in pp. 29–30, may help you to determine what activities or services might be handled or scheduled differently. Try to separate service functions (deliveries, materials management, cleaning) from times residents are in a space or area. This may involve rescheduling and rerouting services or relocating residents' programs.

_____ **8.** Some parts of the facility get very dark at night, which causes concern for the staff.

Staff input may be helpful in determining which areas need improved lighting. You may find that by avoiding poorly lit areas, the staff inconvenience themselves or residents. For example, if staff break areas or dining facilities are dimly lit, members may choose to eat in resident areas, inadvertently waking residents with noise or food and beverage aromas.

_____ **9.** Many of the staff complain of headaches, which might be related to resident calling out.

To lower the incidence of psychosomatic symptoms among the staff, you must first determine the cause. Physical discomfort may result from many environmental factors, including poor air quality, foul odors (including cover-up smells), allergies (such as sensitivity to ammonia), eye strain or glare, poor seating, anxiety over competing client demands, and noise.

Resident verbalization (or calling out) may contribute to headaches among the staff. Verbalization (relentlessly repeated phrases, for example) warrants clinical evaluation to determine the cause. Positioning, aphasia, and pain, such as from glaucoma, have been associated with moaning. Calling out may be reduced when the underlying problem is resolved. Acoustically unsound environments increase the effects of verbalization. Hard surfaces that amplify noise or cause echoes may in fact encourage others to verbalize. Blaring televisions, annoying call buttons, and the excessive use of background music may also increase verbalization. (See "Noise Abatement" in Chapter 7.)

_____ **10.** Staff members balk at giving frequent showers or baths.

Check shower and bathing facilities to determine the source of the problem. Consider conducting a mock bath, if necessary, with a consenting resident or staff member wearing a swim suit. Among the problems you may uncover are these:

- Poor facility design and fixture location, which cause awkward and unsafe transfers or soak staff people
- The storage of soiled linen in the bathing room
- Unsatisfactory ventilation. In this case, define the problem, and work with engineering or maintenance staff, an informed mechanical engineer, or another consultant to reduce humidity and increase comfort.
- A lack of lifts or mechanical devices for transferring residents, which taxes safety and comfort
- An inflexible bathing scheduling that does not include evenings

_____ **11.** We do not have work space for physicians that comfortably accommodates charting, treatment, and communications.

The lack of adequate space for physicians or specialists makes efficient client contact and appropriate follow-up difficult. Attracting medical staff may involve providing them with access to efficient work areas, parking, and communications and treatment facilities.

_____ **12.** The staff station is not designed for efficient use by those who must do paperwork.

An efficient staff station meets the following criteria:

- It is quiet, or it has quiet areas.
- It is easy to find.
- Residents have easy access to it; they can communicate or conduct transactions at a comfortable conversational distance while making eye contact.
- There is good circulation in the staff station and no wasted space.
- There is ample space for charts; they can be moved as needed.
- If nursing assistants are expected to do paperwork (flow sheets and intake-output reports, for example), they have appropriate work space.
- Staff people have places to congregate on their breaks other than the staff station.
- Staff members have appropriate, private places to store their belongings.

_____ **13.** Residents often feel that too much time is spent waiting (for elevators, food trays, and staff to return from transport errands, for example).

A schedule analysis may help identify the factors that cause waiting (see Chapter 3). Ask staff to make suggestions on how waiting time could be reduced. Consider ways to use that time meaningfully.

If waiting results from food service problems, it might be time to study the efficiency of that department. Examine delivery and food service access to elevators and other needed resources. Perhaps the meal should be offered in parts, with juice, salad, or bread arriving first, so that people are not sitting without food.

Dining

_____ **1.** Mealtime is not a highlight for residents or staff members.

The idea is to focus on dining and eating. When mealtime is unpleasant for staff or residents, check out the food itself—its timely delivery, temperature, presentation—and the flow of people, food and meal completion. Mealtime tests the ability of dietary, nursing, and other staff to cooperate. Try meeting with all involved to develop a set of objectives and options for solutions.

_____ **2.** Too few people feed themselves; too many are "tube" fed.

Consult an occupational therapist for tips and staff training.

_____ **3.** The dining areas are not comfortable; there is too much noise and glare.

Noise and glare are deterrents to concentration. Noise abatement and glare control, often through the use of soft materials for window covering and art work, help absorb noise.

_____ **4.** The dining area lacks adequate space at the tables and in the aisles.

Time spent in the dining rooms involves serving and traffic as well as eating and conversation; the design of these areas must reflect this. Can a few tables be removed or smaller ones be used?

_____ **5.** There are no convenient toilets near the dining area; residents must be taken all the way back to their rooms during meals.

Toilets located near the dining area save staff time and give residents security. They may even reduce behaviorally based incontinence.

_____ **6.** The chairs do not fit well under the tables, preventing residents from getting tucked closely under the table.

If the chairs fit better, people would feel more comfortable, and there would be more food that gets into the individual. Try leaving wheelchairs for some at the entry and transferring to well-suited dining chairs. This will also increase aisle space.

_____ **7.** People are lined up along long tables for meals.

Tables that fit four, one on each side, are best. Four is a good conversational group and this arrangement allows each person to contact the others and pass things. Tables of this size can be arranged efficiently if they are placed like diamonds on a playing card, at an angle to the walls to make greater use of aisle space.

_____ **8.** Tables have sharp edges.

Tables with rounded edges are more comfortable for residents and the staff people who serve them, and they often show less wear than tables with sharp edges.

_____ **9.** The dining room is not set up for efficient staff assistance; serving beverages and feeding are difficult.

Substations and beverage stands might be helpful. Place the equipment or food to meet residents' requests in handy locations.

_____ **10.** Some residents prefer to eat alone in their rooms rather than with others in the dining area.

If the dining room is crowded and noisy, residents may prefer their bedrooms. Also, noise and glare problems often deter residents from dining areas. Try to solve these problems to make the dining room more pleasant for everyone, rather than allow increasing numbers of people to eat alone. Perhaps residents should dine in shifts or on a staggered schedule to reduce crowding and noise.

Poor attendance may also indicate that the dining room is too far from the unit, that the staff is not making an effort to get residents there, or that better alternatives exist on the unit or floor. With more people in wheelchairs than in the past, it is often an ordeal to get residents to central dining areas. Many facilities make the effort, though, as part of their commitment to social programs.

_____ **11.** We use feeding tables in our facility.

Half-circlular feeding tables may seem like a good idea at first, but consider these issues:

• They take up more room per person than do square tables with rounded edges. Do you have the space?
• They often require more staff than most facilities can assign to such a small group of diners (1:3 or 1:4). Do you have the staff?
• The seating arrangement is not traditional; a staff member feeds residents from across the table rather than next to the person. Can you accomplish this with dignity and without spilling?
• The tables set the tone and character in a dining area. Is this the image that you want to convey? Staff people may be able to work just as efficiently sitting between two tables when those tables are arranged at angles, like diamonds on a playing card.

_____ **12.** Many people here are fed using feeding tubes or nasogastric feeding techniques.

Are feeding tubes (devices that look like giant hypodermic needles or caulking guns used to squeeze presoftened food into the mouth) and nasogastric feeding the only options available? Consider carefully before adopting feeding tubes. Work with physicians and specialists in eating, such as occupational therapists and speech specialists (who are experts on swallowing) to develop alternatives.

Activities

_____ **1.** Nearly everyone in our facility is involved in some aspect of the activities program.

Terrific. This means programs have been developed to respond to the needs of diverse residents, especially those with cognitive impairment. Your facility is probably an interesting place to visit!

_____ **2.** There is great variety in the type of activities offered here, including space to accommodate nearly all of our residents.

Good. Such activities often include exercise, music, baking or partial aspects of meal preparation, and/or gardening.

_____ **3.** Activities staff have moved many of their programs to where residents are: onto the unit and to the bedrooms, and are offering them in smaller groups.

This is also good. Although getting off the unit is valuable for residents, when transportation becomes a problem it may help to mobilize the staff and bring the programs to the unit. Smaller groups are often more effective than larger ones, and decentralization may lead to more meaningful programs.

_____ **4.** We have nighttime activities and can offer them without disturbing those who prefer not to attend.

This is a nice feature and often results from using creative scheduling rather than traditional 9–5 efforts.

_____ **5.** It is difficult to get people to go to activities.

Why? Evaluate both the programs and the settings. Are the activities related to the residents' previous interests and lifestyles? What is the activities area like? Check for noise, crowding, glare, and poor seating arrangements. Is there a bathroom nearby?

_____ **6.** Activities focus on programs, entertainment, games, and crafts in the hobby shop or activities room.

This has traditionally been viewed as a good program, but does it meet the needs of all of today's nursing home clients? Often, only a handful of people can take advantage of these hobbies. Many more would benefit from some facilitated social activity or memory development program. To be successful, programs must sometimes be extended onto the units and beyond the boundaries of the original program area.

_____ **7.** Activities focus on games, holidays and birthdays, large group events, and making items for sale.

This is common, but is it enough? Today's activities must be more than parties. Let volunteers handle the parties, and use professionals to carry out the more challenging programs, like memory development, sensory stimulation, music, exercise, and outdoor events. Use part-time specialists for music, cultural and religious events, and reminiscence groups when these require skills outside those of full-time staff.

_____ **8.** Fewer people get to programs or participate in crafts than once did.

Look for the underlying cause. If fewer people are able to make the distance, it may say something about changing mobility requirements and needs for assistance. If fewer people are receiving activities or recreation staff members' attention, that suggests programs may need to come to where people can be more easily gathered.

_____ **9.** Fewer people participate in crafts or activities than once did.

Fewer older people in nursing homes have the full attention span and physical dexterity necessary to be artisans. What other programs can you offer?

_____ **10.** The activities room looks cluttered.

Consider combining storage and display facilities. Look at some of the newer books on storage, and find an organizing system that does not minimize the motivation derived from viewing work-in-progress as well as finished projects, and yet does help the appearance of order within the space.

_____ **11.** The activities room lacks storage.

Many activities rooms were "designed" as four walls with tables and chairs and perhaps some windows and a sink. Little thought was given to the quantity of objects, large and small, that would be stored and displayed. An activities room usually needs several types of organizing and storage facilities: a store room, cupboards, areas for display, and somewhere to keep half-finished projects. To free up space within the room, try moving holiday decorations and seldom used items to fire-rated storage locations elsewhere.

Socializing and Lounges

_____ **1.** Lounges work really well; residents and families alike seem to get a great deal of enjoyment out of these spaces.

Hats off to you.

_____ **2.** Social areas work well for our alerter and more ambulatory older people, but they seem less successful for our frailer, more confused, and multiple-impaired residents.

All residents need access to some social area outside of their bedrooms. Examine the existing area and its furnishings. Perhaps there is too much furniture in your present social area, or perhaps the furnishings are not appropriate to the programs offered there. For example, couches, coffee tables, and easy chairs compromise exercise groups, which require more upright seating. Can you develop special social areas with touchable objects and appropriate furnishings for the frailer and more confused people?

_____ **3.** There doesn't seem to be sufficient space in our social area for residents, especially those in wheelchairs.

The usual method for estimating space requirements is to allow 25 square feet for each person confined to a standard wheelchair. Ambulatory older people require somewhat less space; those in geriatric wheelchairs need more. See Appendix D for the formula. Using your profile of residents, calculate your needs by unit. Perhaps the space _is_ too small. Consider possible solutions. Can other space be found, developed, or scheduled? Is all the furniture in the existing area really needed? Can you replace low end tables, coffee tables, and excess chairs with more space-efficient furnishings? Can residents sit in conventional chairs and use their wheelchair just for transportation?

_____ **4.** Residents line up around the walls.

This somewhat uncomfortable conversational position gives the facility an institutional appearance (to say nothing of the feelings of individuals). Look for alternatives. How could an appropriate room, with plenty of activity, be developed as a substitute?

_____ **5.** The lounges go unused; people gather in the halls or in front of the nursing station.

This situation suggests that more action and conversation occur in these areas than in the lounges. Interesting events (like activities) and people might help attract residents to the lounges. Consider, also, the environmental and social factors that affect lounge use. Are there toilets nearby? Is there a call system available? Is glare, noise, or odor a problem? Do staff members visit the lounges often enough so that residents feel they are able to attract their attention?

_____ **6.** It's difficult to run programs and serve meals in the same room.

Dining requires setup and extensive cleanup. Successful multiuse of dining rooms for activities may work on special occasions, but for daily programs to reach the majority of residents and for effective work in small groups, separate program rooms are preferred.

_____ **7.** Residents here do not join in social activities.

This occasionally reflects a preferred former lifestyle. More often, however, the activities or their location are to blame. Activities must be culturally or socially relevant, sufficiently mature, and varied to attract participants. Problems with the location or its distance may keep residents away.

_____ **8.** Lounges or dayrooms look cluttered, barren, or unused. If lounges vary, describe each:

		Description
a. Location _____	1.	_____
b. Location _____	2.	_____
c. Location _____	3.	_____

Too much stimulation is as problematic as too little. Try to work on lounges one at a time to minimize clutter and to give them texture, views of interesting activity such as animals or entries, art work, or focal points. Avoid the other extreme: a perfectly arranged room. Try and strike a balance of interest without confusion and informal without being haphazard.

_____ **9.** Our residents sit around a lot, and they don't seem to do much; the television is on, but they don't seem to be watching.

Could activities (such as music, exercise, or even visiting pets) come to the floor to offer some stimulation? Residents, unless avid followers of a particular television program, would benefit from more lively contact.

Lobbies

_____ **1.** The first things people see when they enter our facility are _____ _____. These give the impression that we are _____ (homelike? comfortable? security conscious? financially oriented? focused on rules and regulations? a grand hotel?).

Think carefully about the first impression your facility makes on visitors. What do you want it to be?

_____ **2.** The lobby is a popular gathering place for residents; some staff or visitors object to this.

The lobby might attract residents because it holds the promise of interesting visitors and presents a change from other spaces. If other spaces were more active and interesting and looked better, would residents find them more appealing? If residents continue to congregate in the lobby, they might give a better impression seated at tables rather than hunched over or sleeping in chairs. Visitors may need to understand that this is a home as well as a "village" and people like to know what's going on.

_____ **3.** If someone is hurt, dies, or is newly admitted, he or she is taken through a well-used and occupied area.

Is there any alternative? If not, work out an explanation that respects the dignity of all involved.

GERONTOLOGICALLY MEANINGFUL PROGRAMS

Care of Mentally Impaired People

_____ **1.** The facility's location, equipment, furnishings, and design pose no evident hazards, risks, or problems for mentally impaired people.

This is a good start. A safe environment fulfills one obligation of an institution, protection of those with impaired judgment. Today's long-term care facility strives for more, including programs and interventions to address the residual capacities of mentally impaired persons. Those abilities may include physical motion, attention for short-term groups, sensory responsiveness, and ability to respond to over-learned routines or information acquired throughout one's life.

_____ **2.** We do not offer enough services for people who are mentally impaired.

A full-service program affords referral or direct services for assessment and interventions for each type of mentally impaired resident, from mild to severe.

Recognizing that there are different degrees of needs and different requirements for intervention is an important part of providing a meaningful service.

Services that are more satisfying may embrace nursing, dietary, social services, clergy, activities, volunteers, and even housekeeping and administration.

_____ **3.** We have a unit for mentally impaired people.

Units are merely areas of a facility; they do not ensure that a program is in place. A program is a set of services that includes nursing, activities, and food service and responds to a variety of individual and group needs. Protective environments are only one aspect of a program.

_____ **4.** We are uncertain how to respond to mentally impaired people.

Effective facilities respond to the needs of the mentally impaired by

- Reducing noxious stimuli, such as noise, glare, and objectionable odors
- Offering options for free movement within a secure but interesting range
- Creating an indoor area with objects, features, seating, and amenities that are safe for individual use
- Providing a safe but restraint-free or "least restrictive" environment

_____ **5.** Mentally impaired people do not look well cared for or carefully groomed; they do not have healthy-looking skin.

Can they get their hair done? Perhaps on-unit facilities are called for. Do they get outside in temperate weather, even for short periods of time? Are they dressed in nice clothing and appealing colors and patterns that show off their features to advantage? Is the lighting warm and pink rather than harsh white or dim yellow? Are they nourished? Is the humidity appropriate, and are lotions used to keep skin supple?

_____ **6.** Mentally impaired people rarely get outside or have access to fresh air.

Check that there is easily accessible, supervisable outside access and fresh air near the unit. Sometimes, mentally impaired persons need a protected area and devices that signal staff that they are attempting to leave. Staff or volunteer supervision is generally essential. Check that doors are easy to use and that the surface is safe.

_____ **7.** We have problems with people who seem to lack judgment and who elope from the facility.

Perimeter security and protection from hazards (such as highways) are two important ways of responding to potential runaways. Perimeter security includes locked doors that release under emergency conditions and work in conjunction with fire alarms. Security may also involve decorative hedges or fences and wearable telemetric systems that signal staff if an individual leaves a specified area. There is, however, no substitute for vigilance.

Physical restraints do not necessarily prevent elopement, and their use raises a number of questions about rights. As part of your self-assessment, consider different forms of intervention. *Guidelines for Wandering* by L. Demotrack and A. Tourigney (Washington, D.C.: American College of Health Care Administrators, 1989) may be helpful.

_____ **8.** We have a wandering garden.

A wandering garden can be beneficial when part of a full-service program for mentally impaired people. The garden alone does not fulfill the daily program needs of the mentally impaired, particularly in cold climates. Can features from the garden be brought indoors?

_____ **9.** We have a wandering loop or protected area inside the building for people who wish to explore.

Although better than tying people to chairs, the loop itself is not a program. Consider creating an interesting area for exploration. This may be a specially allocated room with space and features that satisfy the need to move about freely and to explore.

Allied Health and Education

_____ **1.** Residents get training in gait, balance, manual dexterity and coordination skills, both in appropriate therapy spaces and on their living units.

The combination sounds especially appealing.

_____ **2.** The therapy rooms seem to be a jungle of equipment.

Perhaps it is time to develop storage facilities in the room or elsewhere, even off-site. Therapy rooms should be designed to encourage the easy and efficient use of equipment and to motivate people. Exercises are often repetitious, and they should be done in an interesting place that reinforces images of fitness or progress.

_____ **3.** There are good facilities and spaces for podiatry and dental care and the staging or waiting involved.

Excellent. In most facilities, people wait in long, dehumanizing lines.

_____ **4.** The admissions area has no space for effective family meetings.

A space that is open, comfortable for communications, and easy to find can alleviate the anxieties and feelings of confinement that may be experienced during initial discussions about nursing home admissions. Windows, friendly furnishings, a "round-table" rather than office layout may all contribute to more relaxed discussions. The admissions office should preview the image and philosophy of care one will see when touring a resident unit.

_____ **5.** We have no facilities and little equipment for the ongoing education of staff.

Easy access to new publications in all relevant fields (not just nursing) and rooms that are easy to set up for formal classroom

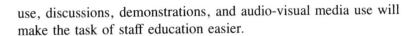

use, discussions, demonstrations, and audio-visual media use will make the task of staff education easier.

_____ **6.** There is a hair care salon with good facilities.

A well-designed and well-equipped salon contributes to a positive self-image for men and women. It is important that such a service be extended to all older people. This space warrants a little character: color, pattern, meaningful pictures, and features reminiscent of the best shops in town are all assets to the service and the image of the space.

FURNISHING AND EQUIPMENT

_____ **1.** Every person has a chair that has been selected in relation to his or her personal preferences, bodily needs, or seating comfort; that is, chairs fit the people.

This will provide long-term benefit to the individual in terms of comfort, upper body strength, digestion, and normal breathing. Ideally, a chair is fitted to the individual like a pair of shoes. It is selected because it fits the body and allows the individual to sit upright with feet touching the floor.

_____ **2.** Chairs are not uniform or standardized.

Chairs should be varied, but within the general range of sizes of the residents. The objective is comfortable seating fitted to each resident and matched to each activity. As a result, chairs will be of different styles.

_____ **3.** There are some chairs that are gliders or that swivel, providing exercise.

As long as chairs are well balanced and will not inadvertently tip, motion can be great for many people. Check with the resident's physician if there is any question.

_____ **4.** Some people's feet do not touch the floor. Five percent or more of the residents slump in their chairs (that is, they lean to one side or lean forward, sliding out of the chair).

The feet should make solid contact with the floor. This improves posture and balance, keeps the midriff area erect (improving digestion and sensitivity to the need to eliminate), and minimizes the potential for circulatory problems and foot dropsy. If the chair cannot be changed immediately, try footstools.

In some facilities, physical therapists fit chairs and wheelchairs. In others, nurses provide this service.

Leaning to one side often indicates a poor person to chair fit. The chair may be too wide and the materials too slippery, or the individual may not be able to support him or herself. Rolled bolsters, on either side of the sitter, will make the chair narrower. There is a host of materials available for chairs that may be more suitable and less slippery than traditional vinyl. Supporting the seated person's feet may also minimize the tendency to slide around in the chair.

_____ **5.** Most chairs lack armrests or have loose or spindly ones.

Armrests are an important feature that help people get out of chairs. They must be wide enough to support the forearm comfortably. Narrow tubular metal or spindly wood armrests may actually bruise the older person. Armrests can sometimes be padded, greatly added to their comfort.

_____ **6.** Chairs are low and soft.

Low, soft chairs are hazardous and difficult to get out of because the sitter's center of gravity is too low. The cushions can sometimes be replaced with firmer foam, making the chair sturdier and the seat higher. Try redoing one. Make sure that the new covering is stain and fire resistant, that any foam or cushioning meets flammability standards, and that foam is enclosed in a fire-protective case such as Nomex™, available from many catalog retailers.

_____ **7.** Many chairs go unused.

It might be that people in wheelchairs are not being repositioned in conventional chairs for some periods of the day. Alternatively, you may have too many chairs for your population's needs, especially if the chairs were purchased without an understanding of today's clientele. You should have enough chairs to accommodate residents and visitors without limiting the space required by those in wheelchairs.

_____ **8.** Chairs tip easily.

Chair balance is important to stability. A person should be able to lean on the front edge or on one armrest without rocking or dislodging the chair. Remove unstable chairs.

_____ **9.** Pressure sores are a problem.

Work with physicians on individual cases. Pressure sores generally are a function of poor nutrition and pressure resulting from excessive weight on one portion of the body or lack of air, moisture, or motion. It is important to encourage people to exercise and sit in different chairs. Also, consider chairs that rock gently, and remember to move frequently people who are prone to pressure sores.

_____ **10.** Odor is a problem.

Work to find and eliminate the source. Geriatric centers remain free of odor not by using cover-ups, but by managing incontinence, smoking, food, and soiled laundry effectively. They remove trash and soiled laundry frequently, store it in sealed containers in ventilated holding areas, and keep areas clean.

Check for odor that comes from placing incontinent people on foam cushions to minimize pressure sores. Either the cushion or the incontinence must be managed differently. One alternative is to place an incontinence pad designed for absorbency on a gel-filled cushion. Another is to manage the incontinence. Clinics now emerging in geriatric evaluation centers can help match incontinence treatments with the total needs of the client.

_____ **11.** There are people who do not have a chair.

Each person should have access to a chair. If the bedroom chair is not truly accessible in its present location, consider moving it elsewhere.

_____ **12.** We use geriatric wheelchairs or tray/table chairs in our facility.

Why? There are better alternatives, including elongated supportive wheelchairs that have trays, large wheels, and a smaller overall dimension or "footprint." (See post-1990 Lumex™ line of posture and supportive seating.)

_____ **13.** We use recliners in some areas.

Are the recliners really needed? Are they the sole form of seating for those who use them? Recliners often place an inordinate amount of pressure on the lower back or buttocks, and they become a bad habit. Some nursing homes choose not to use them except in extraordinary cases of severe contractures, thereby improving the upper-body strength and digestion of residents. Work with physical therapists to determine whether some people would be better served in other seating or by being more mobile. Consider the development of a program to phase out recliners. Reducing the number of geriatric chairs will make the space roomier and often improves the facility's image.

_____ **14.** More than 5% of the older people are in bed at 11 A.M., and more than 20% spend over 20 hours per day in bed.

It is time to determine whether bedridden status is truly required for these residents or if it has become a management pattern. While it is difficult to change patterns of care, certain ones warrant careful follow-up. Lying prone may add to an individual's ailments. A medical or nursing consultant may help you to formulate suggestions for getting individual residents out of bed and into some form of stimulation. This is not to say that bed care is inappropriate for every resident; it is, however, inappropriate for the majority of long-term care clients. Better seating and time spent in more interesting places may be beneficial.

Use experienced medical and nursing staff, social services, and activities professionals to consider three types of plans:

1. For newly admitted residents: to keep them from becoming unnecessarily bedridden
2. For those who are currently bedridden: include options for appropriate fresh air, supportive seating, and rotation
3. For those who are terminal or must spend long periods in bed: bedroom improvements to emphasize comfortable bedding, interesting focal points, and touchable surfaces

QUESTIONS TO HELP GUIDE PLANNING

_____ **1.** Staff members seem eager to see some changes and have started a core group to discuss quality of life, staffing, and environmental implications.

This is a good way to begin. Support the interest, assure adequate representation, link activities to initiatives such as (in the United States) the Nursing Home Reform Act, and keep good records of the topics.

_____ **2.** Everyone complains that "things aren't like they were."

In health care for older people, things _aren't_ like they were even ten years ago. People's needs are more complex, and we know more about what can be done for them. There are new products and technologies, and consumers ask for more. We are no longer satisfied to "take old age to bed." All of this places tremendous pressure on environments designed in the seventies, sixties, or earlier.

This complaint often suggests that different people must be consulted in the planning process than in previous years and that changes seem to take longer. Perhaps you can come up with ways to make changes in reasonable lengths of time.

_____ **3.** We would like to have a more functional environment, but we have so many other priorities.

Nursing, medication, food, finances, and religious services all have their own professional and community advocates. These are people charged with responsibility for these areas, who make them their priority concern. Who is responsible for your facility's environment? Appoint a group of advocates for the environment, and make advocacy a central part of their scheduled activities. Until some person or group takes responsibility, it is difficult to take the first steps toward better environmental design. Maintaining the environment is not nearly as hard as getting it to the point where maintenance is possible. This extra effort sometimes requires special assignment, or other responsibilities will prevail. Eventually you may discover that functional environments ease other priorities.

_____ **4.** There's not much we can do with what we have.

Rethink this. If it is really true, then move ahead and start on things that are portable or can be used in the new environment.

_____ **5.** The staff is exhausted from, bored by, or embittered about more changes.

This sometimes indicates that previous environmental or other changes did not actively incorporate staff views or added to their inconvenience. Changes should make things better; when changes add to stress, change itself is resented. Good, stable leadership may reduce bad feelings. Can you start with something that everyone agrees to and thus develop a track record of success? Staff people often feel threatened by changes in which they are not involved. Can they be more fully informed about the plans? You might try rehearsing the change so that they can help each other, the residents, and their families to adapt. Finally, consider the timing carefully. When will a change be most effective and least inconvenient? Sometimes, the time to plan is *now,* but the time to start making changes is a bit later.

_____ **6.** Our management, staff, and families establish most of the patterns for activity, which then dictate design. If they would do more _____ and less _____, our environment would not be so problematic.

One individual, department, or cluster of people cannot be expected to effectively plan a full-service environment. Equalize the balance by including some outsiders to offset the influence of more domineering members. The outsiders must be well respected for their knowledge or have good communication and group skills. While a smaller group may be effective at implementation, making the right decisions involves a cross section of individuals who must live and work in the space.

_____ **7. We have communications problems.**

Try resolving some of these problems before launching a full-scale environmental design or renovation project. The facility may be changing, growing, or experiencing staff changes. If staff people have had to give up meeting areas for resident use, develop a plan for creating additional spaces for them, perhaps by locating some storage or other amenities elsewhere. Also, recheck the quality and utility of internal communications systems: phones, pocket pagers, computers, paper flow, mail, charting, and resident-initiated discussions.

_____ **8. We don't spend money on the facility environment because we can't obtain the funds.**

There are innovative ways of obtaining money for the smallest and largest of ideas. Consider, for example, community or corporate partnerships and grants. Don't neglect conventional financing, though. All are possible sources of funds. A plan is the essential first step toward obtaining money, whatever the source. You must convey your ideas about the use of the money in a proposal or business plan. Should these suggestions fail, remember that not all changes require money. What can you accomplish without spending anything?

_____ **9. We know what we want to do, but the regulations are too stiff to allow for any innovation.**

Join with others in architectural, long-term care, nursing or gerontological organizations before submitting specific plans; work on mutually beneficial suggestions. Try to clarify your ideas in operational terms. What will your idea cost? How much will it save? What references can you offer? If the idea involves a one-time (capital) investment, how long will it be before it pays off (perhaps through labor savings)?

Consider health department personnel as collaborators rather than adversaries. Always provide the required documentation and try to work within the system. Sponsors often fail to make a good case for their ideas, thus making it difficult for states to approve. If the idea is new to the state, it will need appropriate documentation to reach a decision. Look for precedents in other states or nearby communities to support your plan.

_____ **10.** After we make changes, we never evaluate what we have done from the point of view of all those affected.

Ongoing evaluation is essential. Each change may need fine tuning. How does the change affect people from various departments, visitors, night versus daytime workers, longer-stay versus newly admitted residents?

Appendix C
Planning Social Spaces and Dining Rooms

TECHNIQUE

1. Estimate the number of people who use the area for different purposes. Include residents, staff members, visitors, and volunteers.
2. Assess their mobility levels.
3. Calculate the required space, referring to the following chart:

Activity or Program	Number of Users	Mobility Allowance			Total (sq. ft.)
1. Dining					
Older people	_____	Mobile	×	18 sq. ft.	= _____
	_____	Wheelchair	×	25 sq. ft.	= _____
	_____	Geriatric Chair	×	28 sq. ft.	= _____
Staff	_____	Mobile	×	15 sq. ft.	= _____
Visitors	_____	Mobile	×	15 sq. ft.	= _____
2. Area needed for special furniture:					
Piano and stool					_____
Other:					_____
Subtotal Area for Dining					_____
3. Programs					
4. Visiting					
5. Other:					
a.					
b.					
c.					

4. Measure the available space; use a floor plan drawn to scale, if possible. Subtract space used for door swing, columns, aisles, and other features not related to resident use. Also subtract the space blocked by ill-fitting furniture.
5. Develop a plan for room arrangement that uses the best mix of furniture, based on the mobility of residents.

Appendix D

Estimating the Cost of Common Refurbishments*

Whether renovating an entire facility or just making a minor change, sponsors need an estimate of the costs involved before they begin work on a project. This appendix looks first at the refurbishment costs associated with a major facility renovation; then it examines common refurbishment projects individually.

MAJOR FACILITY OVERHAUL

What would it cost to refurbish an entire facility? Let's take as an example a 100-bed facility with a total of 500 square feet per bed to be refurbished. The desired changes are listed below:

> Walls: improvements and refinishing
> Floors: installation of carpeting or vinyl covering
> Ceilings: some changes in type; improvement of acoustics
> Lighting: major improvements
> Acoustics: installation of noise-abatement materials
> Lavatories: modest improvements in access grab bars and doors
> Doors: refinishing; occasional replacement
> Furniture: replacement of chairs and dining tables; no bed replacement
> Layout: slight modifications in terms of space swapping; related cabinetry or sign improvements
> Equipment: replacement of assistive devices for residents

Table D–1 shows the estimated costs for each of these refurbishments. Note that the costs are shown as ranges. The low end represents cosmetic improvements. With these changes, the building will look better, but the effectiveness of the environment will not be altered significantly. The high end of the range

---

*I am indebted to Zachary Rosenfield, AIA, of NBBJ Rosenfield, Inc., New York, New York, for preparing the following information.

Table D-1   Sample Refurbishment and Renovation Costs

Item	Cost Per Square Foot	Total Cost
Walls	$1.00-2.00	$ 50,000-100,000
Floors	1.50-6.00	75,000-300,000
Ceilings	1.00-4.00	50,000-200,000
Lighting	4.00-6.00	200,000-300,000
Acoustics	1.00-3.00	50,000-150,000
Lavatories	1.00-2.00	50,000-100,000
Doors	.50-1.50	25,000- 75,000
Furniture	3.00-6.00	150,000-300,000
Layout	5.00-8.00	250,000-400,000
Equipment	1.00-2.00	50,000-100,000
TOTAL		**$950,000-1,875,000**

represents more therapeutic renovations; that is, changes in the environment to make it work better for older people and their caregivers.

COMMON REFURBISHMENTS*

Common refurbishment projects are described below, and the estimated costs are given in 1990 prices to help you begin the budgetary process. Note that the numbers given are relative. Verify the products, quantities, and costs for your area. This model assumes a 100-bed facility of mostly double-occupancy rooms.

1. Improve bathroom safety and independence
   a. Add appropriate grab bars:
      Wall-mounted fixtures required by the state (which do not work for most older people since they cannot reach them)
      $150/bathroom
      Sturdy, armrest-style fixtures, like Shelter Arms™ or NOA™ $75-100/toilet
   b. Replace sink with accessible vanity, add easy-use wrist-blade-style faucets, and full wall mirror or tilt mirror
      $750/bathroom
   c. Replace bathroom doors: remove swing-style, solid doors; increase width of opening; replace molding; and install wood-look, slatted folding door $750-900/bathroom
2. Install handrails in hallway
   Install bannister-style handrails with flat top, oval section and rounded edges on either side of hall; block and secure at 41″ from finished floor, unless state regulations require otherwise.† $10-20/lineal ft. × 240 lineal ft. of hallway $2,400-4,800

---

*I am indebted to Keith Anderson, AIA, of Engberg Anderson, Milwaukee, Wisconsin, who assisted in pricing many of these options.
†Try to obtain approval for a handrail height that will allow ambulatory people of normal height to slide along on their forearms. Wheelchair users who pull themselves along will be able to use a rail at this height.

3. Improve a medium-sized nursing station
   a. Use fire-rated, soft wall materials along back wall and front of counter and provide acoustical ceiling $3,200
   b. Develop signs at the station, including a fire-rated awning; lower desk and replace top with nonglare counter. Demolition may be higher depending on existing station $6,000
4. Replace and upgrade chairs
   a. Replace chairs with unsafe cushions, or chairs that are too low, long, or slippery; devise a program of fitting chairs to people. Meet fire regulations for seating materials.
      40 lounge chairs of several sizes, $180–500/chair $7,200–20,000
      30 chairs with arms for use at tables, $90–200/chair $2,700–6,000
   b. Develop a program of safe rocking and moving chairs.
      20 rocking chairs, $400–850/chair $8,000–17,000
5. Personalize bedrooms with tackable wall surfaces and individualized drapes or bedspreads
   a. 100 sq. ft. of acoustical/tackable material per room × 50 rooms, $100–300/room $5,000–15,000
   b. Window covering at $3.00–9.00/sq. ft; 50 rooms × $150–450 $7,500–22,500
   c. Urge individual purchase of bedspreads; purchase remainder, 50 flame-retardant spreads washable in institutional temperatures, $50–120/spread $2,500–6,000
   d. Privacy curtains (existing track) with fire-retardant finish and mesh top: 35 lineal ft. × $6.00/ft., 100 curtains × $210 per curtain $21,000
6. Replace flooring with nonslip material in high-risk areas
   Note: An appropriately licensed professional should help study floor conditions such as evenness of base floor and implications in terms of asbestos or other material handling prior to making these changes. Professional fees are not included for this analysis.
   a. Replace flooring in resident toilet rooms and shower or tub rooms with a product such as Noraplan™ Solid 1144, 100% synthetic rubber, Class I fire-rated (according to Radiant Panel Test); $5.00 per sq. ft., installed.
      42 sq. ft./toilet and sink room $210/toilet room
      350 sq. ft./shower or tub room $1,750
   b. Seal concrete slab with materials like silicate liquid before finishing: $.15/sq. ft. for 1 coat, $.22/sq. ft. for 2 coats.
      25 toilet rooms × $6.00–9.00 per toilet room $150–225
   c. Replace curb with curbless shower: demolish curbs, remove ceramic tile, seal floor, replace floors with sheet rubber or trowelled-on monolithic composition flooring; $5.00–8.00/sq. ft. or $1,750–2,800 per bathing room × 4 bathing rooms $7,000–11,200

7. Remove and replace carpeting
   a. Remove existing carpeting; prepare flooring (see 6b, above) for new carpet or carpet-look materials; labor and materials, $3.00/sq. yd.

      120 ft. hallway, 8 ft. wide $960
      400 sq. ft. dayroom $400

   b. Install new carpet, direct "glue-down" application, including shipping, mark-up, sales tax (assume competitive bidding). Purchase 10% to 15% extra for repairs.
      $15.00/sq. yd. nylon or Olefin fiber, level loop pile construction.
      $30.00/sq. yd. combined cut pile and level loop construction with stain resistance and soil release finish; solution dyed.
      $35.00/sq. yd. for new carpet-look vinyl products like Powerbond™

      120 ft. hallway, 8 ft. wide $1,600–3,200
      400 sq. ft. dayroom $667–1,333

   c. Change baseboard coving.
      Remove existing (vinyl) cove base, $.25/ft. × 240 lineal ft. $60
      Purchase and install 4″ vinyl or rubber cove base, $1.00–1.25/ft. × 240 lineal ft. $240–300
      Purchase and install 4″ wood base coving, $2.00/ft. × 240 lineal ft. $480

8. Painting
   A 20′ × 8′ wall is about 160 sq. ft.; one gallon of paint covers about 350 sq. ft.
   a. Paint cleaned and prepared wallboard (materials and labor), $.25/sq. ft./coat × 2 coats. Hallway, 120 sq. ft., both sides (minus some doorways) $60
   b. Door or window frames, $.50/lineal ft./coat × 2 coats = $18–20 per doorway × 8 doors $144–160
   c. Paint ceiling, $.25/sq. ft./coat × 2 coats for dayroom of 400 sq. ft. $200
   d. Paint 300 sq. ft. bedroom area, including door frame, window, and ceiling, 2 coats, $620 × 50 bedrooms $31,000

9. Replace vinyl wall covering with new vinyl
   a. Remove existing covering, prepare walls for new covering, $.70/sq. ft. × 1,600 sq. ft. corridor wall area (120 ft. corridor, 2 sides) $1,120
   b. Purchase solid vinyl wall covering with Class A flammability rating (not vinylized or coated), preferably strippable for easier future refurbishments.
      27″ width rolls, retail price $.25–.50/sq. ft.

54″ width rolls, retail price $.60–1.50/sq. ft.

For 300 sq. ft. of wall (2-person bedroom) — $75–450

   c. Install 27″ wide rolls, $.50/sq. ft.

Install 54″ wide rolls, $.45/sq. ft.

For 300 sq. ft. of wall (2-person bedroom) — $135–150

Purchase and installation × 50 bedrooms — $10,500–30,000

10. Transform cinder block walls, improve acoustics and appearance

   a. Purchase acoustical underliner that allows cinder block to be covered with vinyl; 30 sq. ft. rolls @ $.70/sq. ft. For 2000 sq. ft. of hallway area, 67 rolls — $1,407

   b. Install underliner @ $.75/sq. ft. × 2000 sq. ft. of hallway area — $1,500

11. Replace soiled or broken acoustical ceiling tiles

   a. 2′ × 4′ ceiling tile, $2.00/sq. ft. Materials and labor, $16.00/tile. Assume 30 replacements — $480

Install detailing features for walls and trim

   a. Crown molding or chair rail, including materials (retail), labor, painting two coats,$2.25–3.50/lineal ft.

Two walls, each 2-person bedroom $45–70 × 50 bedrooms — $2,250–3,500

Four walls, 2,000 sq. ft. dining room or 180 lineal ft. — $8,100–12,600

   b. Corner guards of vinyl (materials only, assume staff installation), $10–15 each

For four major intersections, 16 corners — $160–240

For additional cost information, refer to R.S. Means Co., *Building Construction Cost Data and Interior Cost Data: Partitions/Ceilings/Finishes/Floors/ Furnishings.* Available in many libraries and architecture or construction offices or directly from the publisher, R.S. Means Co, Inc., 100 Construction Plaza, PO Box 800, Kingston, MA 02364.

Appendix E
Sources

REFERENCE MAGAZINES, NEWSLETTERS, AND CATALOGS

Catalogs

1. Sweet's Catalog's
2. Sear's Roebuck Health Catalog
3. Ways and Means
4. Comfortably Yours
5. Sharper Image

Newsletters

1. Housing the Elderly
2. Untie the Elderly
3. Provider

Magazines

Note: None of these have articles every month on environmental design. Some have special issues annually on designing for older people.

Architecture (formerly AIA Journal)
Generations
Gerontologist
Journal of Geriatric Nursing
Provider
Journal of Gerontological Nursing
Housing the Elderly Report (for sponsors and managers of housing and long-term care facilities)
Pride Institute Journal of Long-Term Home Health Care
Construction Specifier
Architectural Record
Interiors
Progressive Architecture
Journal of Alzheimer's Disease and Related Disorders

Annotated Bibliography

Alvermann, M.M. 1979. Toward improving geriatric care with environmental intervention emphasizing a homelike atmosphere: An environmental experience. *Journal of Gerontological Nursing* 5(3): 13–14.
Empirical and contextual evidence on the advantages of residential features in orientation.

Andreasen, M.E.K. 1980. Color vision defects in the elderly. *Journal of Gerontological Nursing* 6(7): 383–384.
Explanation of lens yellowing and its impact on color discrimination. Advantages of color contrast.

Andreasen, M.E.K. 1985. Make a safe environment by design. *Journal of Gerontological Nursing* 11(6): 18–22.
Focus on visual factors and reduction of falls.

Barton, E.M., Baltes, M.M., Orzech, M.J. 1980. Etiology of dependence in older nursing home residents during morning care: The role of staff behavior. *Journal of Personality and Social Psychology* 38(3): 423–431.
Significance of morning care in the overall efficiency of the day. Methods of evoking and cueing independence and participation with empirical data.

Beck, C. 1981. Dining experiences of the institutionalized aged. *Journal of Gerontological Nursing* 7(2): 104–107.
Optimizing self-feeding and social behavior through appropriate arrangement and utensils.

Beck, M.A., Callahan, D.K. 1980. Impact of institutionalization on the posture of chronic schizophrenic patients. *American Journal of Occupational Therapy* 34(5): 332–335.
Inappropriate seating contributes to poor posture and results in diminished mobility, poor balance, and poor coordination, which have an impact on mobility.

Berkowitz, M., et al. 1979. *The role of health care institutions in satisfying the reading needs of residents with print limitations.* Vol. 3 of *Reading with print limitations.* New York: American Foundation for the Blind.
Study of visual behavior included visits to more than 50 nursing homes. Implications for reading and social behavior on a facility-by-facility basis.

Burnside, I.M. 1980. Wandering. In: I.M. Burnside, ed. *Psychosocial nursing care of the aged,* 2nd ed. New York: McGraw Hill, 298–309.
Confusion over wandering results in unnecessary restraint.

Butler, R.N. 1978. Exercise: The neglected therapy. *Journal of Aging and Human Development* 8: 193–195.
Seminal plea for motion even for nursing home clients.

Carroll, K. 1978. *Mealgroups,* 3rd ed. Minneapolis: Ebenezer Center on Aging and Human Development.
Techniques for optimizing self-feeding and mental function using mealtime. Emphasis on small groups.

Carroll, K., et al. 1978. *Therapeutic activities programming with the elderly*. Minneapolis: Ebenezer Center for Aging and Human Development.
Explanations of programming for the confused elderly, with an emphasis on the use of cues and objects, for groups of various sizes.

Carter, R.M. 1986. Strategic planning: A design lifeline. *Provider for Long-Term Care Professionals* 12(4): 6–9.
Support for territoriality through biaxial bedroom design.

Coen, P., Milford, B. 1988. *Closets: Designing and organizing the personalized closet*. New York: Friedman.
A practical paperback on closets and storage planning with applications for nursing homes. Well illustrated.

Demitrack, L., Tourigny, A. 1989. *Wandering behavior and long-term care: An action guide*. Alexandria, VA: Foundation of American College of Health Care Administrators.
Detailed guidelines for policy and practice on wandering, restraint reduction, and risk management.

Duffy, L.M. 1987. Managing urinary incontinence in persons with Alzheimer's disease. *American Journal of Alzheimer's Care and Related Disorders and Research* 2(5): 13–19.
Demonstrates the value of working with mentally impaired people in appropriately designed programs for managing urinary incontinence.

Fahland, B. 1976. *Wheelchair selection: More than choosing a chair with wheels*. Publication 713. Minneapolis: American Rehabilitation/Sister Kenny Institute.
Characteristics and measurements of wheelchairs.

Faletti, M. 1984. Human factors research and functional environments for the aged. In: I. Altman, M.P. Lawton, J.F. Wohwill, eds. *Elderly people and their environment*. New York: Plenum, 191–238.
Focus on considerations in manual dexterity.

Fehr, L.A., Fishbein, H.D. 1976. The effects of an explicit landmark on judgments. In: P. Suedfeld, J.A. Russell, eds. *Proceedings of the Environmental Design Research Association*. Washington, D.C.: Environmental Design Research Association.
The value of landmarks and practice in wayfinding.

Firestone, I.J., Lichtman, C.M., Evans, J.R. 1980. Privacy and solidarity: Effects of nursing home accommodation on environmental perception and sociability preferences. *International Journal of Aging and Human Development* 11(3): 229–241.
Some advantages of private accommodations.

Fozard, J.L. 1981. Person-environment relationships in adulthood: Implications for human factors engineering. *Human Factors* 23(1): 7–28.
Overview and summary of empirical data illustrating how better lighting, acoustics, and sensory properties of environments can optimize the behavior of frail older people.

Fozard, J.L., Popkin, S.J. 1976. Optimizing adult development: Ends and means of an applied psychology of aging. *American Psychologist* 33: 975–989.
The cognition of older people may be improved by responding to features of the environment that maximize attention span.

Grey, K., Carroll, K. 1981. Memory development: An approach to the mentally impaired elderly in the long-term care setting. *International Journal of Aging and Human Development* 13: 15–35.
A formal approach for optimizing attention span and cuing behavior that requires group work and appropriately organized stimuli.

Groom, J.N., Harkness, S. 1976. *Building without barriers for disabled*. New York: Whitney Library of Design/Watson-Guptill Publications.
Methods for designing to wheelchair specifications.

Hanley, I. 1981. The use of sign posts and active training to modify ward disorientation in elderly patients. *Journal of Behavior Therapy and Experimental Psychiatry* 12(3): 241–247.
Evidence that behavior can be modified by appropriate use of identifiable cues to help wayfinding.

Hartigan, J.D. 1982. The dangerous wheelchair. *Journal of the American Geriatrics Society* 30(9): 592–593.
Poor positioning contributes to problems in manual dexterity; suggests need to fit wheelchairs to people.

Herman, J.F., Bruce, P.R. 1981. Spatial knowledge of ambulatory and wheelchair confined nursing home residents. *Experimental Aging Research* 7(4): 491–496.
To improve orientation, increase the experience of people with their surroundings.

Hiatt, L.G. 1978. Architecture for the aged: Design for living. *Inland Architect* 23: 6–17.
What is special about the design of facilities for older people? Discussion of mobility, visual, and other features and commentary on the difference between meeting codes and meeting needs.

Hiatt, L.G. 1980. Color and care: The selection and use of colors in environments for older people. *Nursing Homes* 30(3): 18–22.
The selection of wall and feature color based on the yellowing of older persons' lenses and the need to consider what should stand out.

Hiatt, L.G. 1980. Designing therapeutic dining. *Nursing Homes* 30(2): 33–39.
Techniques for improving self-feeding and staffing effectiveness.

Hiatt, L.G. 1980. Disorientation is more than a state of mind. *Nursing Homes* 29(4): 30–36.
Methods for improving wayfinding, with a worksheet for the environment.

Hiatt, L.G. 1980. The happy wanderer. *Nursing Homes* 29(3): 34–39.
A plan based on empirical data for dealing with nonthreatening wanderers who pace within buildings.

Hiatt, L.G. 1980. Moving outdoors. *Nursing Homes*. 29(2): 42–46.
Why some outdoor spaces are not effectively used and how to increase the value of these spaces for nursing home clients.

Hiatt, L.G. 1980. A self-administered checklist: Renovation for innovation. *Nursing Homes* 30(1): 33–39.
Self-assessment of existing facility, with suggestions for establishing priorities.

Hiatt, L.G. 1981. Touchy about touching. *Nursing Homes* 29(6): 42–46.
The value of texture in the environment and a recognition that humans differ in their approaches to human contact, with alternatives.

Hiatt, L.G. 1982. The environment as a participant in health care. *Journal of Long-Term Care Administration* 10(1): 1–17.
The function of the environment and the role of planning.

Hiatt, L.G. 1982. The importance of the physical environment. *Nursing Homes* 31(4): 2–10.
Examples of why the environment is not merely cosmetic in long-term care.

Hiatt, L.G. 1983. Effective design for informal conversation. *American Health Care Association Journal* 9(2): 43–46.
Social arrangements that appear to improve the effectiveness of lounge and dayroom design. Emphasis on interior space planning.

Hiatt, L.G. 1983. The significance of environmental design to personalized care of older people. In: C. Nicholson, J. Nicholson, eds. *The personalized care model for the elderly*. New York: Department of Mental Hygiene, 59–90.
Fully referenced review of the literature and theoretical presentation of the role of the environment in the care of older people.

Hiatt, L.G. 1984. Creating the substance of images. *Contemporary Administrator for Long-Term Care* 7(4): 17, 18, 20, 22, 55.
Distinguishing between superficial design features and those that are meaningful to older people. Emphasis on noise abatement.

Hiatt, L.G. 1985. Understanding the physical environment. *Pride Institute Journal of Long-Term Home Health Care* 4(2): 12–22.
Overview of the characteristics of older people, with environmental design implications and sources of information.

Hiatt, L.G. 1985. Wandering behavior of older people in nursing homes: A study of hyperactivity, disorientation and the spatial environment. Ph.D. diss., Graduate Center, City University of New York. *Dissertation Abstracts International* 46(86-01): 653.
Study of 167 nursing homes and their practices in design, restraint, and intervention for nursing home clients who are mentally impaired or wander.

Hiatt, L.G. 1986. Effective trends in interior design. *Provider* 12(4): 28–30.
Use of features to optimize the behavior of older people. Differentiation among spurious approaches to interiors and more empirically based decisions. Request to go beyond visual "look."

Hiatt, L.G. 1986. Innovation in overall services for older people and the vision care specialist. In: A.A. Rosenbloom, M.W. Morgan, eds. *Vision and aging: General and clinical perspectives*. New York: Professional Capital Cities, 363–372.
Suggestions for activities, interventions, and training for visually impaired older people and those who work with them. Emphasis on environment.

Hiatt, L.G. 1986. The vision care professional and institutional settings. In: A.A. Rosenbloom, M.W. Morgan, eds. *Vision and aging: General and clinical perspectives*. New York: Professional Capital Cities, 231–242.
Methods for relating vision evaluation to care plan and interventions for the visual environment of nursing homes.

Hiatt, L.G. 1987. Designing for the vision and hearing impairments of the elderly. In: V. Regnier, J. Pynoos, eds. *Housing the aged: Design directives and policy considerations*. New York: Elsevier, 341–372.
Systematic suggestions for policy and design for vision and hearing impaired older people.

Hiatt, L.G. 1987. Environmental design and mentally impaired older people. In: H. Altman, ed. *Alzheimer's disease: Problems, prospects and perspectives*. New York: Plenum, 309–320.
Common approaches to designing for mentally impaired people, with alternatives to special units and a discussion of the least restrictive alternatives.

Hiatt, L.G. 1987. The environment's role in the total well-being of the older person. In: G.G. Magin, E.L. Haught, eds. *Well-being and the elderly: An holistic view*. Washington, D.C.: American Association of Homes for the Aging, 23–38.
How sponsors work to balance medical and psychosocial considerations and staff and resident values.

Hiatt, L.G. 1987. Supportive design for people with memory impairments. In: A. Kalicki, ed. *Confronting Alzheimer's disease*. Owings Mills, MD: National Health Publishing/American Association of Homes for the Aging, 138–164.
Step-by-step suggestions for designing for the mentally impaired, based on data on cog-

nitive function and how it operates in old age. Emphasis on reducing noxious stimuli, improving appropriate cues, small groups, and "energy outlet."

Hiatt, L.G. 1988. Environmental design and memory impaired older people. In: *A Guidebook for Long-Term Care Providers Alzheimer's Disease Patient Care: Techniques for Long-Term Care Providers.* Proceedings, First Annual Long-Term Care Providers' Workshop, October 1987. Phoenix: Greater Phoenix Chapter, Alzheimer's Design and Related Disorders Association, 1–14.
Suggestions for caring for older people using simple design interventions.

Hiatt, L.G. 1988. Mobility and independence in long-term care: Implications for technology and environmental design. In: G. Lesnoff-Caravaglia, ed. *Aging in a technological society.* New York: Human Sciences Press, 58–64.
Typical design approaches minimize independence and do not meet the objective of getting people to walk or wheel independently. Need to consider elbow room in wheelchair planning.

Hiatt, L.G. 1988. Does innovative design exist? *Provider* 14(9), 12–14.
Discussion of designing from the inside out, including approaches for staff efficiency (cluster design) and features that optimize access and sensory function and improve flexibility.

Hiatt, L.G., Merlino, N., Ronch, J., eds. 1987. *Proceedings: Innovations in care of the memory impaired elderly, June 11–13, 1986.* New York: New York State Department of Health/Hunter College.
Presentations of dementia care programs in progress—what worked and what needed to be done. Introduction emphasizes the need to relate programs to a better understanding of mental function and staffing effectiveness, implying that older people with dementia appear more sensitive to problem features of the environment.

Hussian, R.A. 1981. *Geriatric psychology.* New York: Van Nostrand.
Emphasis on environmental techniques for working with institutionalized older people and reducing agitated behavior.

Jirovec, M.M. 1987. Urine control in patients with chronic degenerative disease. In: H. Altman, ed. *Alzheimer's disease: Problems, prospects and perspectives.* New York: Plenum, 235–247.
Argument for working with cognitively impaired and frail older people on incontinence; support for toileting.

Kauffman, T. 1987. Posture and age. *Topics in Geriatric Rehabilitation* 2(4): 13–28.
Factors in posture affecting mobility; implications for maintaining self-reliant mobility patterns and good positioning.

Koncelik, J.A. 1976. *Designing the open nursing home.* Stroudsburg, PA: Dowden, Hutchins, Ross.
Classic book on considerations in nursing home design, illustrating how spaces are used and how they could better be used.

Koncelik, J.A. 1979. Human factors and environmental design for the aging: Physiological change and sensory loss as design criteria. In: T.O. Byerts, S.C. Howell, L.A. Pastalan, eds. *Environmental context of aging.* New York: Garland, 107–118.
Literature review emphasizing sensory function and environmental design.

Lane, A., Steward, K. 1980. Typical chairs: 1949–1968: An analysis of style and evolution. *Home Economics Journal* 9(1): 36–44.
Explanation of chairs; useful when choosing styles for health facility design.

Lawton, M.P. 1981. Sensory deprivation and the effects of the environment on management of the senile dementia patient. In: N.E. Miller, G.D. Cohen, eds.

Clinical aspects of Alzheimer's disease and senile dementia. New York: Raven, 227–252.
Significance of appropriate levels of stimulation; suggestion that overstimulation is likely a result of inappropriate and conflicting stimuli. Understimulation is not advised as the solution.

Lawton, M.P. 1985. An introduction and overview to environment. *Pride Institute Journal of Long-Term Home Health Care* 4(2): 1–11.
Presentation of the theory behind utilizing the environment more aggressively in therapy and design to evoke competency.

Leib, R.K. 1982. How to buy chairs. *American Health Care Association Journal* 8(7): 21–24.
Consideration of human factors, with an emphasis on how people get out of chairs.

MacDonald, M.L., Butler, A.K. 1974. Reversal of helplessness: Producing walking behavior in nursing home wheelchair residents using behavior modification procedures. *Journal of Gerontology* 29(1): 97–101.
Methods for improving self-propulsion.

Marsh, G.R. 1980. Perceptual changes with aging. In: E.W. Busse, D.G. Blazer, eds. *Handbook of the psychology of aging.* New York: Van Nostrand, 147–168.
Medical overview of changing visual, auditory, and tactile sensitivity and related functions, with implications for compensation, including design.

National Center for Health Statistics. 1979. The national nursing home survey: 1977 summary for the United States. *Vital and health statistics.* Series 13, No. 43. Hyattsville, MD: National Center for Health Statistics, Government Printing Office.
Data on populations and facilities.

National Center for Health Statistics. 1985. An overview of the 1982 National Master Facility Inventory Survey of Nursing and Related Care Homes. *Advance data from vital and health statistics.* No. 111, DHHS Pub. No. (PHS) 85-1250. Public Health Service. Hyattsville, MD: National Center for Health Statistics.
Especially interesting data on population changes.

National Center for Health Statistics. 1986. Nursing and related care homes as reported from the 1982 National Master Facility Inventory Survey. *Vital and health statistics.* Series 14, No. 32. DHHS Pub. No. (PHS) 86-1827. Public Health Service. Washington, D.C.: Government Printing Office.

National Center for Health Statistics. 1987. Aging in the eighties. Functional limitations of individuals age 65 and over. *Advance data from vital and health statistics.* Series 133. DHHS Pub. No. (PHS) 87-1250. Public Health Service. Hyattsville, MD: Government Printing Office.

National Center for Health Statistics. 1989. The national nursing home survey: 1985 summary for the United States. *Vital and health statistics.* Series 13, No. 97. DHHS Pub. No. (PHS) 89-1758. Public Health Service. Washington, D.C.: Government Printing Office.
Contains data on people, staff, lifestyle, and building features, especially useful in understanding the norms for facilities built from 1950–1975.

Ouslander, J.G., Kane, R.L. 1985. *Technologies for managing urinary incontinence.* Case study 33. Washington, D.C.: Office of Technology Assessment.
Costs of incontinence and the value of aggressive interventions on each level.

Ouslander, J.G., Kane, R.L., Abrass, I.B. 1982. Urinary incontinence in elderly nursing home patients. *Journal of the American Medical Association* 248: 1194–1198.
Characteristics and costs of incontinence.

Parsons, H.M. 1981. Residential design for the aging: For example, the bedroom. *Human Factors* 23(1): 39–58.
Summarizes the use of bedrooms and the general criteria for design.

Pastalan, L. 1986. Six principles for a caring environment. *Provider for Long-Term Care Professionals* 12(4): 4–5.
Social areas must respond to varying group sizes. Privacy is part of the continuum of social function.

Pendergast, D.R. et al. 1987. Muscle rehabilitation in nursing home residents with cognitive impairment: A pilot study. *American Journal of Alzheimer's Care and Related Disorders and Research* 2(4): 20–25.
Empirical data support the conclusion that severe cognitive impairment does not prevent significant improvement in response to an intense, inexpensive muscle rehabilitation program. Interpretations suggest design implications.

Perlmutter, L.C., Tenny, Y., Smith, P. 1980. *The evaluation and remediation of memory problems in the aged.* Boston: Memory and Learning Clinic, Veterans Administration Hospital.
Advantages of techniques for reducing some aspects of memory loss.

Philips, R.H., Salmen, J.P.S. 1983. Building for accessibility: Design and product specification. *The Construction Specifier* (Feb): 20–34.
Approaches and manufacturers for building details that optimize efficiency, from hinges to materials.

Poppleton, L.A., Cox, M. 1985. Environmental influences that affect nursing home staff. In: National League for Nursing. *Strategies for Long-Term Care.* New York: National League for Nursing, 123–132.
Argument for using management functions to guide efficient design for older people, including workload distribution, laundry, team communications, and motivation.

Pyrek, J., et al. 1978. *Human development assessment and care planning.* Minneapolis: Ebenezer Center on Aging and Human Development.
Technique for making assessments that convert directly to care planning.

Quattrochi, T.S., Jason, L.A. 1980. Enhancing social interactions and activity among the elderly through stimulus control. *Journal of Applied Behavioral Analysis* 13(1): 159–163.
Use of objects to stimulate social behavior. With empirical data.

Raschko, B.A. 1984. *Housing interiors for the disabled and elderly.* New York: Van Nostrand.
Criteria for bedroom design. Estimating the size of dining rooms using furnishings.

Robb, S., Monsour, M. 1982. Wandering behavior in old age: A psychosocial exploration. *Social Work* 27(5): 411–416.
Empirical data illustrating that previous lifestyle and history may predict the style of wandering behavior.

Snyder, L. Hiatt. 1974. An exploratory study of patterns of social interaction, organization and facility design in three nursing homes. *International Journal of Aging and Human Development* 4(4): 319–333.
Empirical data on factors that improve social interaction, such as the placement of furnishings and the use of conversational props.

Snyder, L. Hiatt. 1974. Self-reliance and design for the elderly. *HUD Challenge* 4(5): 10–12.
Commentary with examples on how some nursing home regulations do not fully respond to the characteristics of older people.

Snyder, L. Hiatt. 1976. Geriatric wheelchairs, older persons and living environments. *Journal of Gerontological Nursing* 2(1): 17–20.
Characteristics of chairs that impose undue suffering.

Snyder, L. Hiatt. 1978. Environmental changes for socialization. *Journal of Nursing Administration* 18(1): 44–55.
Improving options for social interaction and conversation through better arrangement of social spaces.

Snyder, L. Hiatt. 1982. Environmental considerations in understanding and designing for mentally impaired elderly people. In: H. McBride, ed. *Mentally impaired aging: Bridging the gap,* rev. ed. Washington, D.C.: American Association of Homes for the Aging. 22–34.
Explanation of wayfinding.

Snyder, L. Hiatt, Ostrander, E.R. 1974. *Research basis for behavioral program: New York State Veterans Home, Oxford, NY.* Ithaca, NY: New York State College of Human Ecology, Cornell University Department of Design and Environmental Analysis.
Empirical study of the characteristics of older people, with implications for nursing home design; emphasis on bedrooms.

Snyder, L. Hiatt, Ostrander, E.R., Koncelik, J.A. eds. 1972. *The new nursing home: A response to the behavior and lifestyle of the aging.* Proceedings of a Conference for Nursing Home Administrators. Ithaca, NY: New York State College of Human Ecology, Cornell University.
Critique of the functioning of five nursing homes.

Snyder, L. Hiatt, Pyrek, J.D., Smith, K.C. 1976. Vision and mental function. *Gerontologist* 16(3): 491–495.
Empirical evidence that undetected vision problems may be interpreted as diminished mental function. Data illustrate the underserved vision care of older people in nursing homes.

Snyder, L. Hiatt, Rupprecht, P., Pyrek, J., Smith, K. Carroll. 1978. Wandering. *Gerontologist* 18(3): 273–280.
Empirical study of eight matched pairs of wanderers and nonwanderers, with recommendations for dealing with risky wandering behavior.

Sowell, V.A., et al. 1987. A cost comparison of five methods of managing urinary incontinence. *Quarterly Review Bulletin Journal of Quality Insurance* 13(12): 393–414.
Comparison of four padding methods and a toileting procedure. Toileting emphasized as the preferred method for dealing with incontinence.

Stotsky, B. 1968. *The elderly patient.* New York: Grune and Stratton.
Psychiatrist's seminal description of resident behavior in nursing homes, with special insights on nursing station socializing.

Tate, J.W. 1980. The need for personal space in institutions for the elderly. *Journal of Gerontological Nursing* 6(8): 439–449.
Nursing analysis emphasizing the value of privacy and territoriality in reducing confusion and behavioral problems.

United States Comptroller General. 1979. *Entering a nursing home: Costly implications for Medicaid and the elderly.* Washington, D.C.: General Accounting Office.
Contribution of factors like incontinence to the expense of care.

Waller, J. 1978. Falls among the elderly—Human environmental factors. *Accident Analysis and Prevention* 10: 21–33.
Contrasting features, insecure handrails, and poor lighting are among the factors contributing to falls.

Weber, R.J., Brown, L.T. 1978. Cognitive maps of environmental knowledge and

preference in nursing home patients. *Experimental Aging Research* 4(3): 157–174.
An attempt to understand why older people are disoriented and how more explicit cues may assist in the identification of particular spaces.

Weisman, G. 1987. Improving way-finding and architectural legibility in housing for the elderly. In: V. Regnier, J. Pynoos, eds. *Housing the aged: Design directives and policy considerations.* New York: Elsevier, 441–464.
Practical issues in improved wayfinding.

Weiss, J.D. 1969. *Better building for the aged.* New York: Hopkinson & Blake.
Illustrated volume of case studies showing architecture for older people that was new and innovative in the sixties in terms of types of spaces, funding, and materials.

Wells, T.J., Brink, C.A. 1981. Urinary incontinence: Assessment and management. In: I.M. Burnside, ed. *Nursing and the aged.* New York: McGraw-Hill, 520–547.
Techniques to minimize the difficulties of incontinence, including toileting.

Windley, P., Scheidt, R. 1980. Person-environment dialectics: Implications for competent functioning in old age. In: L. Poon, ed. *Aging in the eighties.* New York: Plenum, 407–423.
Theoretical approaches are offered suggesting the significance of providing options and dealing with the paradoxes raised in planning environments for older people rather than focusing on directives and feature specifications.

Zarit, S., Zarit, J., Reever, K. 1982. Memory training for severe memory loss. *Gerontologist* 22(4): 373–377.
Options for teaching people to prevent mental deterioration.

Index